# TWICE ROUND
# ON THE HOBBY HORSE

For Mary —
nobody really needs
a gall-bladder!
Best wishes,

Anita Robinson

Derry born of County Down parents, ANITA ROBINSON was brought up on the east bank Waterside area of the city (which is a different place entirely), and went to a rural primary school. Her character was later moulded by the Mercy nuns and "finished" by the Dominicans. A teaching career followed happily, dedicated to the education of the mixed infants of the Creggan and Carnhill parishes of a troubled city. Abiding interests in drama, public speaking, debate, writing and broadcasting developed along the way. Today she writes a weekly column in both *The Irish News* and *Derry News*, has a regular slot on BBC Radio Foyle, contributes frequently to Radio Ulster and keeps in touch with her inner child through story, poetry and creative-writing workshops in schools. She lives contentedly with the Loving Spouse and Daughter Dear, both of whom have developed immunity to embarrassment.

# TWICE ROUND
# ON THE HOBBY HORSE

Anita Robinson

THE BREHON PRESS
BELFAST

First published 2007 by The Brehon Press Ltd
1A Bryson Street, Belfast BT5 4ES, Northern Ireland

*Dedicated to
the Loving Spouse and Daughter Dear
and my father Jack Armstrong
(who ought to have written a book but never got round to it)*

ISBN: 978 1905474 13 4

Design: December Publications
Printed and bound by JH Haynes and Co Ltd, Sparkford

# ACKNOWLEDGEMENTS

This is the bit of a book nobody bothers to read unless they're looking for their own name. It is, however, the Oscar speech of the writer.

Heartfelt thanks then…

to Aunty Geely Matthews of BBC Northern Ireland's *Children's Hour*, who gave me, aged ten, a voice on radio and big ideas thereafter:

to Ian Kennedy, Station Manager BBC Radio Foyle, who re-discovered me twenty-five years later;

to the Colmcille Debating Society who, in the interval, taught me the value of expressing oneself succinctly;

to the Pushkin Trust who transformed my approach to language, written and spoken;

to *The Irish News* and *Derry News* for the on-going opportunity to indulge my opinions weekly;

to a succession of generous BBC radio producers across the network who have always found a niche for my work;

to Melanie Bradley, whose speed, accuracy and capacity to decipher my handwriting bring scripts to your eye or ear.

And lastly – to all the people, known and unknown, I've observed and eavesdropped on – thanks for the material. I couldn't have done it without you.

*Anita Robinson*
*July '07*

# FOREWORD

GENEALOGICAL INTEREST HAS already a high and healthy profile in this part of the world – what with returned Yanks anxious to excavate their roots and an increasing number of us locals taking to stumbling about in graveyards, poring over parish registers and writing pleas for information to obscure second-cousins three times removed in Calgary or Coatbridge. Like an itch that needs scratching, once begun the search, one feels compelled to continue. Why do we do it? What purpose does it serve apart from satisfying our pathological nosiness? I think in a fast-paced, rootless and transient society it gives us a marker to put down, a context for where we fit in the great scheme of things. We place ourselves on history's time-line and become reasoners of family riddles, solvers of family puzzles, completers of family jigsaws, part of the great wheeling cycle of human society.

But oh! I wish I'd started earlier! Born a "wee late one" with both sets of grandparents already deceased and a garrulous gossip of elderly aunts to whom, I'm ashamed to say, I never bothered to listen, I'm hungry now for the feast of family lore and anecdote I once let go without tasting. I've inherited an archive of sorts. An old uncle, a fanatical photographer from the age of sixteen till he died, past eighty, snapped anything that moved. I have drawerfuls of his pictures, sepia-tinted, curling slightly at the edges. But who are these smiling girls in swagger coats and young men in high-waisted, flapping-legged flannels, my father cutting a dash among them in plus-fours and James Joyce spectacles? There's nobody left to ask. They stroll arm-in-arm on country roads with nothing to identify them but the set of an eye, the shape of a nose, the line of a jaw that says we are kin.

Here too are the formal studio portraits of severe-looking grandparents – his Dundreary whiskers and her Edwardian pompadour accurately marking them out as the gimlet-eyed master and mistress of the village school. Look at the flapper dresses and cloche hats of strapping country girls striving to be fashionably smart. Further in the past, there's a photograph of my paternal grandmother as a young married woman taken about 1897. She already had four children (there were to be another eight) and the youngest, staring out of the picture in calico pinafore and button boots, is identical in every sulky feature to my own daughter, born in 1981. These are affinities we seek, to be links in the chain – my grandmother photographed with my mother; my mother with me; me with my daughter – all bound by the spiralling interlocking strands of DNA that ensure the triumph of the family nose down four generations.

I have images galore, but few of the stories. The jerky old eight-millimetre cine-films show people younger than I remember them, self-conscious in front of the cine-camera, grimacing at picnics in the rain or clowning in their best clothes at weddings. But where's the sound-track? It's through people's stories that their spirit stays alive.

We have no forum for family story now. We gravitate each to our separate space in our houses like drones in a hive, coming together briefly to eat, with our eyes fixed on the flickering screen in the corner that tells us instead the stories of strangers. Shared memory and remembrance of things past is fading. Maybe this genealogical craze is what we need to galvanise us into digging up a few ancestors. Some of us may have to cast the net wide. Others find what they're looking for on their doorsteps. It's an interesting but not entirely comfortable experience to walk through a country churchyard and find your mother's people buried down one side, your father's down the other and your own inherited name already amongst them.

Not all the information we turn up may be pleasant. Previous generations were as renowned for rogues, scoundrels and ne'er-do-wells as our own and there's nobody's closet without a few colourful skeletons to rattle their respectability. I'm immensely proud of an ancestor of mine who was a Northumberland border reiver – a cattle raider – celebrated in verse.

Johnny Armstrong –
"Five times outlawed had he been
By Scotland's king and England's queen."
A roaring boy indeed!

It's rather nice to have a bit of a rebel in the family – at a safe historical distance, of course.

I WAS A "WEE LATE ONE". Born fourteen-and-a-half years after the rest of the family, I caused a minor sensation. In fact my mother thought I was the menopause. "Sit down, Mrs Armstrong," said Dr Dan Kelly, "I have something to tell you." On being apprised of the happy news of my impending arrival, my mortified forty-six-year-old mother-to-be immediately donned an all-enveloping swagger coat and went nowhere for the next six months, lending a literal interpretation to the term "confinement". Like an infectious illness it was thought necessary only close relatives be informed of the happy event. These excluded my teenage siblings who must've won trophies for lack of observation in the subsequent six months. Thus it was I burst upon the world relatively unannounced to the astonishment of all, a bit like a fairy in a pantomime. Squeaks of disbelief were followed by sincere expressions of maternal congratulation, but few exhalations of envy at the prospect of starting the relentless business of child-rearing all over again just when she'd got the rest of them relatively independent.

Post-war babies were born round and dimpled with hamster-pouch cheeks, thighs like turkey drumsticks and bracelets of fat at wrist and ankle. My baby photos bear a glowering resemblance to Winston Churchill. The terms "bonny" and "bouncing" were synonymous with a pneumatic plumpness interpreted as "thriving" and the picture of the Cow & Gate baby on the formula-feed tin could've passed for a suckling pig. As I lay in my shiny new pram, wheeled by a succession of honorary aunties, there came to lodge in my ear the notes of a refrain that would echo throughout my life, "Is this the Wee Late One?" I'm absolutely sure I suffered early bone malformation from being held up by the shoulders like a jumper for inspection. To this day I come across the occasional insistent eighty-year-old who denies my existence despite hefty visual evidence to the contrary. "I knew Jack and Sally well," they declare emphatically, "and they only had four of a family." There is nothing more pathetic in middle age than having to repeat doggedly, "But I'm the wee late one."

Are there any advantages to being born late and last? Not many. Big brothers teach you to play football, kill bluebottles with a piece of elastic and all the lyrics of "The Big Rock Candy Mountain". Big sisters buy you dresses, tell you stories and paint your nails but they'll only humour you for a little while, then go off and do their own thing. As a wee late one you're the "trophy baby", treated for the most part with indulgent forbearance, but separated by almost a generation from your brothers and sister, you'll always be "the baby" no matter how old you grow. Nothing much makes up for being regarded as a kind of curio and along with the label comes a set of preconceived ideas.

Despite our sophisticated insight into the uniqueness of the individual we still lump members of families together as if they're only squares off the same bar of toffee. A wee late one is invariably measured by the severest benchmarks of all: the looks, brains, talents and aptitudes of the siblings who went before. With a magnificent disregard for whatever innate potential the little scrap is born with, ill-informed strangers plot its future with glib certainty. "I'm sure this is another clever wee mathematician. Yes indeed, and a gifted artist and a talented musician." Wearing these expectations like a set of matching millstones and carrying the broken mirror of its identity, the poor child lurches forth to make its way in the world and confound all expectations by being absolutely average out of pure spite. Wee late ones do occasionally get to twinkle in their own firmament, but only when the elder stars are dimmed or they have the strength of character to clamber out from under the family bushel.

My mother was a formidable little lady from a small village outside Banbridge, County Down, who devoted all her considerable energies to the rearing of her children and the efficient running of a house. She spent herself selflessly on our behalf in years of duty and sacrifice – a fact we signally failed to appreciate until it was too late to thank her. She and my father had been at school together, she from the top of the hill, he from the foot of it. His parents were schoolmaster and mistress. Of their courting days she never spoke, but we knew by heart the saga of how she'd exchanged the gently rolling drumlins of Down for the harsher contours of the Sperrins.

In the last year of her life, at her request, we drove out of Derry through the prosperous Faughan valley with its undulating tracts of tidy Protestant ploughing. The hedges thickened with new green and the early April sun caught the glistening crest of each furrow where industrious crows found rich pickings. Cows turned their backs to the wind and the windows glinted in the four-square farmhouses. As we took to minor roads, the landscape changed imperceptibly, scored with ditches and dykes and the black-faced slabs of peat-cuttings. Outcrops of mottled rock shouldered through thin soil, fastened by a wiry net of heather. In the waterlogged fields, new lambs sheltered in the lee of their mothers, lipping the rusty bracken, and over all frowned the bare brown dome of Mullaghash Mountain. "It's here," she said suddenly, "just stop here." "Here" was a triangular crossroads in the middle of nowhere. In the tongue of the triangle stood a derelict stone-built edifice, its windows boarded, its stout door barred. Incised above it in the stonework was the legend "Fincairn National School".

We looked at it, a lone sentinel in a lonelier landscape, standing in a quarter acre of tussocky grass, combed flat by the wind off the mountain. "That was the garden," she said. I'd been reared on stories of this place – how she'd come all those years ago, sitting bolt upright in the hired car, elegant in her fox-collared coat and cloche hat. Over another hill and another, up and down again. In the brown distance a single dwelling interrupted the bleak horizon. Its mean windows squinted in the weak sunshine and a dismal thread of smoke issued from the chimney. "They have the fire on for ye anyway," said the driver cheerfully.

It had seemed, on the face of it, such a good opportunity for Jack. "Principal required for two-teacher school. Residence attached." He'd gone alone to view his new domain. She realised he'd underplayed the "dwelling house attached". It had lain empty these many years. Hasty and inexpert renovations had been carried out to make it habitable for the new master. Patches of raw plaster indicated the installation of electric light and a new brass tap dripped peaty water into a stained stone jaw-box in one corner of the flagged and gloomy kitchen. She stood heartsick before the rusted range. Seething with sudden resentment she marched up the rickety stairs to unpack, noticing with some irony that the weeping walls of the bedroom were already rejecting their new coat of cheap distemper. Dampness mapped the bulging ceiling. Abandoning all thoughts of making a start, she sat down upon the iron bedstead and wept too. Choked with tears and rage she remembered what she'd left behind, her beautiful little house in County Down. They'd furnished it throughout for £104.17.6. She hadn't dared tell her mother, with Jack on only £16 a month. With its Chinese-patterned wallpaper and its piano in the parlour, it was the talk of two parishes. What was she to do, marooned here for the foreseeable future with four small children and a weekly bus the only tenuous link with civilisation?

Eventually she got down to the business of establishing order and some degree of comfort. Out went the rusty range and, roped securely to an ancient lorry, came an American stove of the latest design from town. With it came a large wireless in a walnut veneer cabinet. Word had it the new master's wife had fancy ideas.

Each morning she unlocked the schoolroom, inhaling its dusty compounds of chalk and country children. She straightened the rows of wooden forms, wiped the gritty slates and swept the floor. It was the start of a day of unrelenting toil interrupted by neighbours calling on the slimmest of pretexts and sometimes none at all. Though she never received anything but courtesy from them, she felt uneasy. Under their straight gaze she became uncomfortably aware of her unsuitable shoes, smart townie frocks and different accent.

They had a great word on the master. He fished, he shot, he slotted easily into card-playing and ceili-ing company and unfailingly could be relied upon for a story or a song in his rich bass voice. Oh yes, there were always two eggs and a glass of whiskey for the master whenever he visited, and frequent bags of turf or potatoes found their way to the schoolhouse door. His casual enquiry about a gun-dog produced three pups – a Labrador, a pointer and a greyhound – all of which had to be kept, sooner than cause offence.

The four children were in their element; the littlest crawled into the schoolroom and was taught along with the rest. The others ran wild in dungarees, riding horses, picking potatoes, turning hay, threshing corn and the youngest one with the cloud of red curls and the fierce expression tramped the furrows after the plough until he cried with the pain in his four-year-old legs. A bachelor farmer in the area took to him so greatly that he offered to buy him. When his generous terms were turned down, he contented himself with keeping the child out until all hours, driving erratically round the country on a ramshackle tractor stopping at every pub.

Meanwhile she drudged at sink and stove, looking out the window at the indifferent back of Mullaghash, but once a week she donned the black fitted coat, the hat with the silly little veil and took the bus to civilisation, shopping and the pictures.

The school garden had been his idea really. In the immediate vicinity of the house was an irregular triangle of land, about a quarter of an acre. Within weeks he was supervising the barrowing of stones, levelling the ground and instructing squads of raw country boys in the finer points of horticulture. He'd grown things they'd never heard of in this part of the world and were persuaded would never "do" in that soil. It was looked on as one of the master's wee vagaries and sure it was an interest for his missus. Cows trampled it, goats invaded it, the wind soughed down off the mountain and flattened it – she herself in the dark had mistakenly snipped the tops off the infant cabbage plants under the impression they were watercress – but it flourished and throve. Once established, the care of the garden fell more and more to her. She sublimated her misery in a fierce taming of the soil until every inch was quilted and stitched like a Victorian sampler, a jewel-box of colour in the brown landscape. He didn't tell her until quite late that he'd entered the garden for the Northern Ireland Schools' Horticulture Cup. Redoubling her efforts towards perfection, she spent hours weeding in the bitter breeze or working until bedtime in the damp dusk. On the day he was photographed for the local paper proudly holding the trophy, she was upstairs with viral pneumonia, the doctor in attendance and the priest sent for.

Change came when least looked for. Chance informed him of a larger school and the possibility of a suitable house in the city. A terraced house in a busy cobbled street, with stone pillars framing the door and a big front window. There was no garden.

She got out of the car and advanced a few paces. "There's nothing left," she said, walking towards where the garden had been. "No, don't come with me." We hung around shivering, watching her disappear behind the house. Minutes passed. "She'll catch her death in this wind or break her ankle," I said. We followed and found her crouching in the overgrown ditch, scrabbling in the earth with her good leather gloves. "Look," she said. There, all but smothered by briars and nettles, was a grey-green sprig of something. "I planted this," she said, "forty years ago. Snow-in-summer we called it. This bank was white with it." And carefully uprooting it, she carried it back to the car.

> "THE ACCENT OF ONE'S BIRTHPLACE LINGERS IN THE MIND
> AND IN THE HEART AS IT DOES IN ONE'S SPEECH"
> *Duc de la Rochefoucauld*

AND SO OUR FAMILY BECAME DERRY by adoption and I, by dint of being born in the city, the only member who could claim true citizenship. Mind you, we did take up residence in the Waterside, which some say is a different place altogether! This is a situation grudgingly recognised by Citysiders who dimly perceive that the Waterside ones are somehow just a shade superior. And what irks the Citysiders is that they can't quite put their finger on what it is that makes Waterside people so.

You see, Waterside people are great observers of bye-laws. They are the kind of people who take notice of notices. They are a prudent people. They do not put their heads out of train windows, nor pull the communication cord for a laugh, nor flush the toilet while the train is standing in the station. They do not stick bills where bill stickers are liable to be prosecuted. They are a responsible people. They rinse out their milk-bottles and fill in their census forms on the right day and do not have the enumerating officer calling back three times. They are an ethical people. They don't put things back in the wrong places on supermarket shelves nor feed foreign coins into the supermarket trolley system. They are civic-minded people. They neither uproot litter bins nor the council wallflowers in suburban flowerbeds out the Limavady Road. They do not walk on the grass nor (with certain exceptions) write on walls but when they do, one can be sure that the graffiti is accurately spelt and there is evidence of the correct use of the apostrophe. Standards, you see, it all boils down to standards.

Keeping up appearances is important to Waterside people – shining brasses, swept steps, barbered lawns, hardy annuals that bloom in strict rotation so there's a bit of a show all year round. I tell you, sometimes it can be a very great strain, since, of course, none of it can be done on a Sunday. Sunday is for church – high attendance – all denominations – in good suits. The young Waterside matron wears a pantie-girdle, keeps receipts, sends away guarantees and owns at least one hat (bought in Coleraine). Her children wear proper shoes, not trainers to church. Her husband may stretch Sunday observance to visiting a DIY store where he'll purchase primer, undercoat and enough for two applications of satin finish, with a view to applying same on Monday after tea. The Citysider, to whom the letters DIY often mean Don't Involve Yourself, will slap on a single coat of magnolia on Sunday afternoon and sit down to watch the snooker. This feckless attitude is anathema to the soul of the Waterside citizen whose industrious life is based on the Reformation ethic of the washing out on Mondays, the swings all closed on Sundays and the bills all paid on time.

You can witness it as you drive up Rossdowney Road on refuse collection day. By unspoken agreement the residents have positioned their wheelie bins an exact 53 centimetres from the edge of the kerb. There they stand, grey sentinels, scrubbed within and without, rubbish hygienically bagged before stowing, fit for inspection anytime.

It is adherence to the same principles that allows Waterside people to leave their blinds up in the dusk of a summer evening, secure in the knowledge that (a) nobody passing is ill-bred enough to stare in the windows, (b) they're not doing anything to be socially ashamed of and (c) the lounge is always tidy anyway and the scatter cushions plumped. So, the average Waterside citizen doesn't dread the chance caller. There is always a home-made Victoria sandwich in the freezer and the downstairs toilet in pristine condition with the good quality toilet paper ready to roll. Often it's only taken advantage of once a year on the Twelfth by the occasional weak-bladdered Orangeman. A shame really. Come over sometime and see how the other half lives. But don't move here please. You have to be bred up to it to be really happy.

Meanwhile, Derry city, cradled in the valley of the Foyle, snug as a bosom in a brassiere, is growing. Like June, it is bustin' out all over. Even without reckoning the phantom thousands of citizens unaccounted for in census returns, Derry is overflowing and needs to go up at least a cup size. Yet from the top of any hill you can still see the whole city and a brisk fifty-minute constitutional will take you from one boundary to the other. The thing is, Derry people will not walk the length of themselves. They'd take a bus to a place within sight of their own door. With the exception of a masochistic minority who regularly make the five-mile circuit of the two bridges – a penitential rite engaged in by weight-watchers, coronary candidates and half-marathon freaks – the rest of the population are sofa-surfers to a man, whose take-away pizzas are delivered by taxi.

The expansion of the city and commensurate increase in road traffic has forced people in the northwest to revise their thinking. In an historic city which was not so much planned as let happen, one can hardly blame our ancestors for current traffic congestion. The ancient architects of the city walls never foresaw the siege of the city by armies of articulated lorries. The Georgians didn't reckon on accommodating an unending procession of accountants' Audis crawling up Clarendon Street. And the Victorians, who were into pagoda-style public toilets with curly ironwork, could hardly conceive of the difficulty of reversing 500 gross of frozen burgers into Wellworth's entry. Then, as now, forward planning was never our forte.

But I believe our equivocal attitude to the automobile dates from the 1970s and 80s when Derry was detonated into one huge free car park. The recent building boom brought about by pseudo-peace has proved to be a mixed blessing. We rejoice of course in the resurgence of the city centre, but recoil at the price of progress. Secretly we believe that paying for parking is legitimised piracy.

This idiosyncratic mindset extends to many other aspects of etiquette governing driver and pedestrian alike. Unlike his Belfast or Dublin counterpart, the Derry driver will rarely run over anyone. A sullen truce exists between him and the peripatetic punter, a grudging respect for the innate decency one recognises in the other. This is manifest daily in a city of many slopes. Witness the pedestrian's implicit faith in a driver's ability to hang on the handbrake, revving furiously upon a steep and greasy gradient without slipping backwards and wiping out an entire sub-species of Doherty or McLaughlin who have chosen that moment to ramble leisurely across behind the vehicle.

Regrettably the City Council's extensive programme of pedestrianisation has been a signal failure. Derry people, they say, will march for anything, but walk for nobody. The traditional Saturday afternoon "passeggiata" of the young is conducted now in the semi-tropical conditions of the shopping mall. Surprisingly, you are at a statistically higher risk in this city of being knocked down by a car in a so-called "traffic-free zone". Blithely indifferent to bye-laws, the Derry driver thinks they apply to everybody except him and he'll just chance it this once through the ornamental bollards onto the fancy paving. "Sure it's only me," he reassures himself, scattering shoppers like sheep and fetching up bumper to bumper with an irate Mr Softie abusing him roundly to the accompaniment of "Edelweiss" on the chimes of his ice-cream van.

As the pace of life grows ever more hectic, I must draw your attention to a unique traffic-calming measure evolved here at no cost whatsoever to the taxpayer. It is both cheap and effective, utilising as it does two of the city's most plentiful resources – mothers and pushchairs. Like all revolutionary ideas, its genius lies in its simplicity.

Picture if you will, the Derry mother, preparing to cross a busy road. She positions herself safely on the edge of the kerb. Then, with great deliberation, she propels the pushchair containing the latest of her numerous brood over the edge of the pavement down into the gutter where it stands, front wheels rampant, projecting well into the road. The oncoming driver, finding himself nose-to-nose with a goggle-eyed infant in a woolly hat, mouth plugged with an enormous dummy, naturally screeches to a halt. The mother, chatting animatedly to her friend, strolls casually across the thoroughfare, an untidy straggle of other siblings in her wake and the bug-eyed baby in the buggy waving its mittened fists in triumph. The apoplectic driver, meanwhile, is beating his head off the steering wheel in sublimated rage, before remembering the danger of triggering the air bag.

This is a technique I have never seen fail. With very little training, no doubt other mothers in the province could perform it equally effectively and prove a cost-free boon to Education and Library Boards no longer able to afford school-crossing patrols.

"THE OBJECT OF TEACHING A CHILD IS TO ENABLE IT
TO GET ALONG WITHOUT A TEACHER"
*Elbert Hubbard*


MY OWN EDUCATION BEGAN EARLY. For somebody who spent her
whole life in school, in fact never left it, my first day was not
auspicious. I hated the whole of the first year. I was three-and-a-half
and despatched against my will to Sister Laurence's kindergarten class
in Artillery Street, premises now occupied by the Playhouse Theatre.
Every time I go to see a play there I find the smell and dark stairs are
the same and I'm catapulted back to the misery of it all.

Each morning I got on the bus with my big sister, and for the
princely sum of a halfpenny (and a buff-coloured bus ticket) was
conveyed safely across Craigavon Bridge.

I liked that bit. It was at Ferryquay Gate I rusted and had to be
hauled screaming up Artillery Street, being prised off every lamp-
post, appealing piteously to shocked passers-by, while my sister, who
was a very newly-qualified teacher, died of embarrassment. This was
my "what's to be done with that child?" phase. I even tore my long
stockings to shreds in temper. They were brown lisle, held up by great
metal suspenders that dangled off the end of my liberty bodice. But
no matter, every journey ended in being dragged through the gloomy
archway and put struggling into the arms of Sister Laurence while my
sister, on the brink of tears, ran upstairs to teach the "big girls" class.

Everything in that place was brown, brown and shiny with
precipitous stairs, lethal linoleum and polished parquet floors, totally

unsuitable for very small children. The health and safety people, had there been any, would've had a blue fit. In the brown-painted classroom were high windows you couldn't look out of and building blocks and coloured wooden spills with splinters in them and sludge-coloured Plasticene with small greasy boards to roll it out on. The Plasticene stank to high heaven – so much so I never allowed it in my own infant classes.

Dear Sister Laurence! She believed cold milk chilled the stomach dangerously, so as a treat, she'd wedge the milk crate under the massive claw-footed radiator until it was well warmed through. I cannot describe the daily ordeal of removing the waxed cardboard bottle-top, smelling the viscous yellowish cream and inserting the thick waxy straw which had a taste all of its own. My stomach churns now just thinking about it. Should I die of the drouth for want of it, I have never been able to drink so much as a sip of milk since.

At kindergarten I learned not to pick my nose, nor to scratch around knicker-level and never to sit with knees apart. These accomplishments, combined with a regular supply of American dresses from a kind relation who had heard about "the wee late one", confirmed that I must be a girl; but, unlike Edna O'Brien, Fay Weldon or Clare Boylan, it didn't impinge enough on my consciousness to make a living out of in later life.

AT THE AGE OF FOUR-AND-A-BIT, me and my ladylike ways were suddenly transplanted to a very rural primary school where the salient features were newly-erected flush toilets – religiously examined by the parish priest on each visit – and boys. Fine, strapping country boys, who smelt of clay and damp sacking and stayed at school till they were fourteen, except for a fortnight off for the potato picking. That my father was principal turned out to be a mixed blessing. They used to shout after me in school, "Ginger snap, penny a bap, two for tuppence ha'penny!" which struck me even then as seriously unsound economics. Half the hassle of being a redhead is the cosmetic disadvantage that goes with it: pale skin, freckles, thready white limbs like celery sticks reared under a jam-jar and a reputation for a fiery temper. The chief drawback about being ginger is that it's hard to escape unnoticed. My father used to tell a celebrated tale of how, when he was a boy, the local Church of Ireland school's Sports Day would be held in Laurencetown demesne, County Down. Highlight of the athletic events was the 100 yards dash. At a given signal, the entire field of runners pursued their way to the finish line, where stood the Church of Ireland minister, an immensely tall man, holding aloft the prize, a large bag of sweets.

Suddenly, out of the halfway hedge, dodged a boy. Running like the wind and outstripping the field, he leapt like a cat to snatch the bag of sweets and ran on towards the horizon till he was out of sight and sharing the Protestant sweeties with his brothers.

Alas, his roaring red hair lit his flight like a beacon and he was instantly identified as Jack Armstrong, the Catholic schoolmaster's son. Retribution swiftly followed.

My trials began early. As a city bred child at a country school I was, to put it vulgarly, on a hiding to nothing. That school was a nursery for one of the finest cricket teams in the northwest, every senior boy a budding Flintoff. I was the one with the youngest, shortest and most cowardly legs, which buckled regularly as the scarlet blur of a lethal yorker whistled past at ear-level. Banished to Master Mullan's field to retrieve yet another of Cyril Ward's sixers, I stood miserably among the nettles, freckles erupting audibly in the savage sun. I resolved then, as soon as I'd be old enough, to spend my days lying on a sofa with a lace hankie and never run after anything again in my life – not even a man – though I revised the latter part of the resolution in adolescence.

Not till I reached grammar school did I realise there was such a subject as "Physical Education". We all played rounders, then graduated to cricket about the age of nine. A Ministry of Education inspector called one summer morning to find the whole school sitting on the walls surrounding the playground, watching a needle match played out against threatening thunder-clouds building up on the horizon. Somehow he found himself postponing his inspection and keeping score instead. My father, a law unto himself, had that effect on people

His astringent attitude towards parents manifested itself on the day three new pupils came to enrol. Round-eyed with astonishment we saw them arrive in a car accompanied by their parents. The first was a novelty, the second a thing unheard of. New pupils were traditionally brought into school by an older sibling or a neighbour's child. These were doctor's children with upmarket accents; the elder two girls – aged ten and eight, I suppose – looked pale and apprehensive. The youngest, a boy of six, clung to his mother and whinged. When the parents attempted to leave, he kicked his mother in the shins and took refuge in the car, screaming and thrashing about. We were aghast at this exhibition that would've earned any of the rest of us a hammering. "Tell you what," said my father, turning on his heel, "send him back with his sisters when he's learned to behave himself." It's a tactic that might be worth reintroducing in schools.

I happened to observe recently in the course of a public talk what a pity it was that we're the last generation ever to learn anything by heart – be it catechism, tables or poetry. A ripple of rueful nostalgia ran through the audience as each of us conjured up in our mind's eye the dust motes dancing in a beam of slanting sun under the big oilcloth map of the British Empire and heard again in the mind's ear the singsong classroom chant of children. "Twelve elevens are a hundred and thirty-two, twelve twelves are a hundred and forty-four." "Is there anybody there?" said the traveller, knocking on the moonlit door." "The curfew tolls the knell of parting day. The lowing herd winds slowly o'er the lea. The ploughman homeward plods his weary way, And leaves the world to darkness and to me." Learning by rote was a fixed part of every day's timetable. "Sixteen ounces, one pound; fourteen pounds, one stone; eight stone, one hundredweight." And very useful it was too. You could reach into the recesses of memory and pull out the formula or the quote for the occasion. Understanding was not considered strictly necessary. That might or might not come later with maturity. Till then we were advised to take advantage of the quick, efficient trick. Now, alas, learning through discovery means the wheel has to be re-invented every day and it all takes any inordinate amount of time.

The modern education system flatters itself on its broadly based and varied curriculum, with the value-added element of extra activities at the individual school's discretion. In my father's school we read Dickens, Buchan, Twain and Conan Doyle and the sagas of the Four Provinces; there was algebra and geometry; we were taught tonic sol-fa so every child could sight-read music. Round the four walls of the classroom ran a Wild West wagon-train mural with Indians in full war paint in hot pursuit, driving a stampede of cattle before them, painted with the leftovers of the doing-up of the parish hall by a couple of talented senior boys who couldn't find paper large enough but had an inspiring teacher. There was nothing unique about the school I went to. Schools in those days were presided over by tyrants, eccentrics or visionaries who performed miracles in near-autonomous fiefdom to a distant and largely indifferent government department. Modern school principals are so busy minding their Ps and Qs and doing paperwork for the Department that they haven't, with the exception of the toughest, time to be memorable.

And what did that style of education give us? It gave us breadth of vocabulary and dimension of ideas; it filled the rooms of our imagination with the colour and texture and music of the spoken and written word; it introduced us to truth, beauty and the distilled purity of genius; it enhanced our quality of life. It strikes me by comparison today that the spaces of young minds, like intellectual loft conversions, are sparsely furnished with the bare basics. This is the significant difference between the generations. The young only have to know where to find the knowledge – we actually had to know it! There is no longer need for the mind to be cluttered or summoned up at electronic will and formulae; reference material and texts may be freely taken into examinations. Where we parroted received wisdom, they are encouraged to spew forth immature opinions devoid of either originality or imagination, based on the questionable values of popular culture. One student I knew submitted for "O" Level a critique of Shakespeare's *Much Ado About Nothing* based entirely on Kenneth Branagh's film version, since she'd never read the play.

We thirsted for learning while they have access to excess of it. The danger of a surfeit, as Shakespeare knew, is "the appetite may sicken and so die". Like their eating habits, the young graze upon education rather than feed upon it. The result? They may not be dumber, just intellectually anorexic.

EVERY FEMALE SCHOOLCHILD (and some boys too) learned to knit properly about the age of eight. "In the wee rabbit hole, round the wee tree…" we'd recite inwardly, our tongues protruding in concentration the same way they did when we tackled joined-up writing. We'd all done French knitting of course – the hollow reel with four nails hammered in the top, which extruded spaghetti coils of grubby yarn wound painstakingly into tablemats, but that was kids' stuff. We started simply with thick wool, chunky needles and plain stitch. The object? A scarf. I'm always amazed when people say they find knitting relaxing. How they can focus on television and conversation, their needles automatically clacking away without a glance? I found that impossible.

My neck and shoulders set like concrete, my arms and wrists ached after five rows of stocking stitch. My difficulty was tension, not just the physical sort, but the tendency of my stitches to get tighter and tighter till I could no longer get them off the needle. My scarf wavered in width from eight to four inches and "rip it out" was a phrase I became very familiar with. I was also the world's slowest knitter, since I never developed the knack of flicking the wool niftily round the needle with one finger, but had to loop it round with my whole hand every time. Consider my misery then as we graduated swiftly to mittens in two colours with ribbed wristband and integrated thumb. Mine were a dreary mix of burgundy and fawn and the tightness of the thumb cut off the blood supply, but mittens were a logistical doddle compared to socks, which involved four needles and the dreaded exercise of "turning the heel". And we were still only ten years old!

Of course your mammy and your granny knitted and all your aunties. I never had a school cardigan or winter socks out of a shop till I was in my teens. Women's fingers were always busy with bootees, matinee coats and christening shawls spun from cobwebs for their own, their relations' and neighbours' families. Granny Millar knitted grey knee socks for every school-age child in our street. Most homes had a well-thumbed stock of knitting patterns. They featured smooth-looking young men with brilliantined hair and either a pipe in their mouths or a hand on one hip. Inside was a strange kind of shorthand, a mystery to the uninitiated. Many women, my mother included, prided themselves on never using a pattern and produced traditional Aran sweaters rich with cable and blackberry stitch, entirely out of their heads. And the speed! A left sleeve took a matter of hours. In the true spirit of domestic economy, outgrown woollens were unpicked and knitted up again in a different guise. Did we children appreciate their skill and industry? Did we heck! All we yearned for was a smart "bought" sweater with a scratchy label at the back of the neck. Oh the boredom of standing stock-still, holding taut a skein of wool outstretched hands, while mother wound it swiftly into a neat and perfect sphere, hard as a tennis ball. Leftover wool was carefully hoarded in the knitting bag for darning – an art, alas, now stone dead. Show a modern child a darning mushroom and they'd be baffled. My mother's darns were well-nigh invisible.

There was always something "on the needles". If it wasn't knitting, it was crochet they were at. Countless doyleys, runners and place-mats in cotton and silk were churned out for the gracious style of living none of us enjoyed. They were doomed to circulate in perpetuity round Sales of Work where the best-selling item was the knitted cotton dishcloth, a permanent sinkside accessory, steeped daily in bleachy water in the best regulated households, left in a slimy heap on the draining board by the less house-proud.

Suddenly in the mid-Sixties, cottage industry caught up with fashion and the crocheted mini-dress (as modelled by Twiggy) became, briefly, all the rage. Suppliant daughters badgered mothers and grannies into Herculean labours with the crochet hook and battles royal ensued over the length of the finished garment. "She's away out in thon thing and it no longer on her than a simmet!" sniffed one disgusted grandparent. And indeed, country dancehalls were full of saucy big girls whose spare tyres and hefty thighs strained through the crochet like semolina escaping from a string bag, but they'd sooner be out of the world than out of the fashion.

School was a mixture of treats and traumas. Readers of a certain vintage will recall the school medical. Today, it would be a whole siege, with parents notified in advance, but then it was just a bald announcement the day before that "the doctor is coming and be sure to come to school well-washed, in clean socks and underwear".

We turn up next morning unnaturally pink, nails trimmed, their half-moons of permanent grime excavated by a penknife. Class by class we line up outside a vacated room. In vest and pants, friends look vulnerable and strange with so much flesh on goose-pimpled display. We shiver with cold and apprehension. No strangers to dread, the school dentist has already instilled in us equal consternation. He engages your head in a half-nelson, inserts a mirror and a crochet hook in your mouth and hokes his way down decaying avenues of milk-teeth, droning out a litany of putrefaction to his assistant.

Most of us have been photographed for First Communion with tight-lipped Mona Lisa smiles. We've endured already the agony of gumboils and the benison of oil of cloves for a raging toothache, but only wild horses or a mother at her sleepless tether's end would drag us to a dentist. Predictably, all of us get a letter informing our parents of the urgent need for treatment. No shame in that, but a letter from the Nit Nurse is stigma indeed.

We present our frowsty, unwashed heads to her searching hands and gimlet eye. Crown, nape, behind the ears, there is no hiding-place for anything that creeps or crawls. The girl who sits in front of me has thick hair, glossy as a crow's wing. When she tosses it back, strings of tiny, shiny seed pearls clinging to the hair shafts catch the light. My mother has the head scoured off me with a fine-comb and a bottle of yellow sulphurous stuff on standby for the inevitable infestation.

We're a scrofulous bunch waiting here to see the doctor with rashes, ringworm, chesty coughs, bad throats, festering cuts, deep gashes that ought to have been stitched, and everybody has warts. Most of us bear the purple and yellow badges of bravery of gentian violet and iodine. Batch by batch, we're admitted to a heavy smell of disinfectant and the teacher's familiar table made alien with kidney dishes, cotton-wool swabs, tongue depressors and a battery of syringes, big as Halloween rockets, each sporting the sinister glint of a long, long needle, fine as a hair. Panic sweeps backwards along the queue. Are we getting a jag? In our sock soles we stand, heels down, against the height gauge. The starchy nurse, who is distantly kind, brings the measuring arm down on top of our heads. We step on the scales, while with narrowed eyes, she fiddles with sliding weights.

The doctor's crisp shirt-cuffs protrude from the sleeves of his white coat with a brief glitter of gold links and wristwatch. He smells professional and prosperous. The stethoscope's cold, the spatula dries the tongue, the alcohol swab icily brief, the needle swift and bright as lightning – a sharp point of pain at the centre of spreading numbness and a dull ache. Some of us are stamped with six little needles in the tenderest part of the inner forearm, leaving a circular multiple puncture wound. If it swells and stings, they say, you escape the big jag in the upper arm. Shocked and sore we look hopefully towards a saucer of sugar-lumps – surely a reward for our stoicism? Indeed, we each get one, only to discover it tainted with some vile-tasting substance. Fully-clothed, we settle down to multiplication and long-division.

The government plans to re-introduce school medicals as a means of monitoring child health. In our day they were testing for rickets, T.B. and the malnutrition of want. Today, it's obesity, diabetes and the malnutrition of excess. Already, people are bleating about "the Nanny state" and "an incursion on their rights". The fact is, there are as many neglectful and ignorant parents today as there were years ago. So much for progress – but then, as Edmund Burke put it, "the march of the human mind is slow". We've made a great progress in the last fifty years, but all I notice we're doing better is eating.

MORE THAN FIFTY YEARS AGO, when such things were rarer, my father instituted an annual school bus run to Culdaff. Had it been to the moon we couldn't have been more excited. Squashed three to a seat, the hard dusty plush of the seats scourged the backs of our bare legs, while the old green and white U.T.A bus coughed its way through Donegal as we noisily hanged people in strict rotation from the sour apple tree, interspersed with rousing choruses of "Valderi, Valdera". I have never forgotten it, or the cheer that went up when we arrived at the beach, and a bevy of country children cascaded out of the bus and, with one accord, ran into the sea fully clothed. What a day we had of it. So long ago that only fragments float back – dipping in rock pools with your skirt tucked into your knickers; tin buckets and razor edged spades; the transparent wonder of jellyfish; the 1,000 shells you must bring home; coconut buns and Cantrell and Cochrane's brown lemonade spilt and hissing into the brown sand like acid.

A new generation will carry their own images of visits to magical places where they ground grain, made candles, carded wool and handled the possessions of their own ancestors and, perhaps for the first time, gained a dim realisation of their place in the great march of history. To accompany children on occasions like this is to realise afresh why you became a teacher – their spontaneity, their wide-eyed astonishment as they stand in the blacksmith's forge, watching him work a red-hot horseshoe or laughingly create firework effects to please them by throwing metal dust on the fire. As we turn another corner and they recognise another piece of history, "It's just like the picture in the book, isn't it, teacher?" they say. "Didn't I tell you?" I say and they look at me half accusingly as if I'd no right to prior knowledge.

Children fix on insignificant details, often missing the bigger picture by a mile. In a Neolithic hut our guide is at pains to point out the reed thatch, the double thickness wattle-and-daub construction of the walls, stuffed with straw in an early form of cavity wall insulation. But the children's attention is solely on a lone brown hen long-stepping it about the clay floor pecking at scattered grain. I suppose city children don't often see a hen close up. Anyway, in the big write-up when we get back to school every darn one of them mentions the hen!

What a pity they hadn't the experience I had, of the day my father sent out to the house nearest the school for the loan of a hen, laid it on its side and drew a long chalk line from its eye along the classroom floor. The hen sat completely still, eye transfixed, utterly hypnotised, so long as nobody crossed the line – when it went berserk. I don't know what scientific concept the experiment was supposed to consolidate, but it was a memorable experience.

Of course I told the story to the children in my class and, naturally, the request went up: "Can we do it?" I pointed out that (mercifully) hens are scarce as hen's teeth on a city housing estate. There's hands-on education and hands-on education but I draw the line at a hen!

MAGIC OF A DIFFERENT KIND sets memories in motion. I was driving along a country road in Fermanagh when a fellow on a big old-fashioned motorbike passed me and I suddenly thought of Fernie. You must remember Fernie, the magician who came round primary schools in the spring and early summer years ago? You could've set clocks by him. As soon as the first primroses showed their pale faces under the hawthorn hedge in Ardmore, you'd look out of the big window of the Master's classroom and there he'd be, propping up the old motorbike on its twin forks, shaking the rain off his long oilskin coat and smacking his wet black beret against the school wall before pulling it on again. The big boys would be sent out to help bring in his stuff – a couple of battered wooden boxes painted with faded cabalistic signs and a bundle rolled up like a hearthrug in waterproof sheeting.

Fernie supervised the carrying and placing of these items as if they were the crown jewels. Meanwhile, with a great scraping and rumbling, we'd pull back the heavy iron-framed desks, leaving a generous expanse of dusty floorboards in the middle of the room as performance space. We were allowed to sit on top of the desks with our feet on the seats. The mixed infants filed in and took their places cross-legged on the floor round the edge like a flower border. We were ready.

Without preamble Fernie began. Ping-pong balls were swallowed only to crop up in his pocket; coloured string gushed from his mouth; items disappeared under silk scarves; a boxful of tinsel stars was suddenly empty. We ooohed and aaahed on cue. Then came the murmured request for the help of a reliable, honest and truthful boy to assist with the magic. Half-crowns were plucked from behind Eddie's ears, reddened with embarrassment at being singled out; playing cards changed suit and colour in the twinkling of an eye, and three shining and unbroken hoops of steel miraculously passed through one another to the palpable and speechless astonishment of Eddie and loud applause from the rest of us. Through it all Fernie's face remained impassive. He probably didn't even like children. Performance finished, a privileged few were allowed to help him pack and load the motorcycle. Then, with a single salute of his gauntleted hand, he was off. To where? We never knew. Nor where he came from, if he had a home, a family.

Fernie was already past it by the time he came to us. His motorbike was ramshackle, his performance tuxedo green and greasy with age. His gentle David Nixon banter and simple conjuring tricks with interlocking rings, coloured handkerchiefs and rather flattened and mangy artificial rabbit were already passé for a generation who went home to the sophistication of winning a cabbage on *Crackerjack!* No matter. Along with marbles and tadpoles and skipping ropes, Fernie was a harbinger of spring.

NO EVOCATION OF A DERRY UPBRINGING would be complete without mention of religion.

It permeated our lives in a way today's more secular society could barely credit. A recent item about church incense possibly putting altar-servers at carcinogenic risk gave me momentary cause for concern. Incense is barely used now in churches except at High Mass and funerals. The Catholic childhoods of my generation were saturated with it. Its acrid, peppery, sneeze-inducing scent impregnated the air of every church. And we spent a lot of time in church. Routine attendance (non-negotiable) at October devotions, May devotions, the Stations in Lent, the Easter ceremonies, the Retreat, First Fridays and the Holy Hour guaranteed us Chernobyl magnitude exposure.

Do you remember the Forty Hours? The banks of flowers, the pyramids of candles, the many-branched votive lamps burning ruby-red around the golden sunburst of the monstrance and the hypnotic swing of the thurible, the regular silvery clink-clink of its metal chains and the blue fume that ascended heavenward, then rolled down the church to the anticipatory noses of the congregation. We're far more likely to be killing ourselves today with perfumed candles, joss sticks and essential-oil burners, synthetic air fresheners, deodorisers and neutralisers. Nobody's house smells of dinner or polish or people any more. Even people don't smell of people.

Question: "Who are excused from fasting?" Answer: "Sick people, labourers, women with child, old people and persons of languishing constitution." Like Pavlov's dogs, a conditioned response. Any page, any question and back comes the answer pat – the legacy of bitter winter mornings stood out around the classroom answering in turn, the only prospect of warm hands being the two slaps you got for missing the question. Suffer little children, indeed!

In the old days, the litmus test of a good teacher was that he or she would "put the fear of God into ye". Many of them proved adept at this, their only tools being a sixpenny copy of the *Derry Catechism* and a stick. Many of us of a certain vintage recall the confused misery engendered by imperfect understanding of intellectual concepts far beyond our grasp. What did our eight-, nine-, ten-year-old minds make of it all as we nightly conned our well-thumbed and often tear-stained catechisms in preparation for the grilling on the morrow? The Divine Aspirations – a spiritual steeplechase with fallers at every fence – their demise marked by the dry thwack of the descending stick; the Commandments of the Church chanted in mantra-like monotone, encouraging us to pay our dues to the "awful plasters" of the church, a role fulfilled by many an unctuous young curate who hadn't the least idea how to talk to children; the exhaustive explanation of all the Ten Commandments, save the sixth and ninth which were not explained at all, but dimly associated in our uninformed minds with not hanging upside down from the hawthorn tree in the playground, showing our knickers. If "ye must become as little children to enter the kingdom of heaven" was the text, the inference was that we sinful wretches were not the little children the Lord was referring to.

Years later I came upon the famous plea of St Augustine – that prayer of all procrastinators – "Lord make me virtuous, but not yet." I recognised it for what it was at once, a postponing of penance, presumption on God's mercy, one of the sins against the Holy Ghost. I'll tell you what, St Augustine would have got short shrift in fifth class with Master Heaney!

TO HEAR THE ROSARY DESCRIBED on the World Service news bulletin as "a meditation exercise with mantra-like prayers recited by millions of Roman Catholics world-wide" sounds oddly alien to those of us reared with it as an intrinsic part of the day. Or if not every day, then certainly the months of May, October and the weeks directly following the Parish Retreat, where backsliders and the spiritually lukewarm were encouraged in stentorian tones by the missioner to "Prrrrray the Rrrrrrosarrrrry!" and obediently did so.

The increase in religious fervour that accompanied the Marian Year saw us as school children inoculated with the Rosary needle and become stalwart upholders of Mary's banner and the daily post-teatime recitation of the prayer, lisping out the responses, our bare knees aching and our noses buried in the dusty upholstery of the living-room armchairs. Alas, concentration soon drifted to the loose thread in the cushion that unravelled satisfactorily stitch by stitch, Hail Mary by Hail Mary, in the course of the Sorrowful Mysteries.

Religious zeal rekindled with a remarkable degree of alacrity about the age of twelve or thirteen, when the October devotions became the only legitimate midweek social life countenanced by Catholic parents. We set off in the lilac dusk of an autumn evening to whisper with our classmates in the dimly-lit church and speculate on which altar boy will come out to light the tall candles with a taper. Will it be the cute one, or the lanky boy with the acne? At 7.30 precisely a solemn procession of six altar boys precedes the priest to the foot of the altar, their heads bowed, their black soutanes and white surplices investing each of them with a borrowed innocence that'll be quickly doffed in the vestry as soon as Benediction is over.

The altar boys shift uneasily from knee to knee, conscious of one hundred pre-pubescent female eyes boring into the backs of their heads. Should the priest choose to deliver a sermon, they will have to sit facing forward, meeting the direct gaze of their fans. The girls are longing for a sermon. It is, assuredly, the only stage of their lives they'll be described as "gospel-greedy". But now the priest intones, "Thou O Lord wilt open my lips…" and the familiar invocations begin. We fall to our knees and fumble in our little leather horseshoe purses. The Rosary beads run silkily through our fingers like smooth grains of polished rice. Voices rise and fall, regular and monotonous, as the ebb and flow of a quiet tide. The "Hail, Holy Queen" and prayer to St Joseph are a coda in a different rhythm and a minor key.

If you scrunch your eyes up, everything goes misty and beautiful and out of focus and the candle flames become individual starbursts of light. To a hypnotic soundtrack we are spiritually lulled, safe and warm in the bosom of the church, with no presentiment that forty years on, at deathbeds, at wakes, at gravesides, our middle-aged lips spontaneously shape the familiar phrases still. Meanwhile, orisons complete, we dally round the church gate, our breath making clouds in the sharp autumn air, waiting for the altar boys to come scuttling out the vestry door, making a beeline for home.

IN THE RAINBOW-COLOURED DAYS of remembered childhood, Lent was relentlessly grey. Forty days of unremitting gloom punctuated by one of gloriously green self-indulgence from which the countdown to the egg-yolk yellow of Easter could be longingly begun. Poor St Patrick! Try as I might to associate his day with the advent of Christianity, the banishment of snakes, or the strange predilection of some people to parade in horizontal rain to the accompaniment of an accordion band, my most vivid memories are of being green at the gills from a surfeit of sweets.

The concept of self-denial was inculcated early. Any negative, bad or unpleasant thing like the cancellation of a treat, vile-tasting medicine or getting your hair put in curl papers on a Saturday night for ringlets on Sunday, was to be offered up uncomplainingly for the Holy Souls. The Holy Souls, our imperfect understanding led us to believe, were an unfortunate set of spirits whose transgressions when alive had earned them the punishment of being lightly grilled both sides in Purgatory when they died. Apparently our earthly disappointment, remorse and sacrifice, if willingly offered up, was enough to release them. In a long and scrupulously sacrificial childhood I must have offered up sufficient to clear the place entirely.

The idea that mortification of the flesh was good for the soul was endemic. In the absence of our volunteering to give up things for Lent, our parents did it for us and informed us of our sacrifice. Oddly enough, for the other 46 weeks of the year, our infant hearts were rent and withers wrung with vivid accounts of starving, skeletal children in the Third World. We were encouraged to eat up or there'd inevitably come a day when we'd "follow the crows for it" as they had in famine times. Now, for this six weeks, we were commanded to rein ourselves in.

Though not to suffer the daily exigencies of "one meal and two collations", we understood that we were entering a treat-free phase. Cake, biscuits and jam disappeared, as did sugar on porridge or in tea. Fruit, being expensive, was a rare substitute and I certainly never remember getting a whole apple or orange to myself. My brother, with a well-developed sense of retrospective injustice, used to say he was reared on half-cups of tea and half-bananas, but he grew to six foot two inches, so it obviously did him no lasting damage. A tall screw-topped sweetie jar was begged from the shop at the bottom of the street and into this we put, under supervision, all the sweets we were given between Ash Wednesday and Holy Saturday. Worse still, as generous relatives donated Easter eggs, a kind of shrine evolved behind the cruets and sauce-bottles in the dark of the dining-room sideboard. As the eggs accumulated, the daily chore of setting the dinner table became an exquisitely refined form of psychological torture. When you reached into its dim recesses for the salt and pepper, the salad cream or pickles, your eye was caught by the oval-shaped glimmer of coloured foils, flanking like sentinels the stained glass grail of the sweetie jar, its sides mosaic-ed with dolly mixtures, glowing with the rubies of clove rock, the amber of brandy balls, the crinkled sheen of cellophane-wrapped toffees, the luminosity of lollipops, the sticky jewels of fruit drops, all congealing happily together in the cedar-smelling warmth of the sideboard – all as inaccessible, as unassailable as Fort Knox.

Lenten days seemed permeated by the wet-knickers smell of fish. The herring man called in the street more frequently than usual and the cloying glar of parsley sauce tainted everything on the dinner plate it came in contact with. I had an almost superstitious terror of swallowing small hair-like fish bones which, I believed, wedged themselves horizontally across your gullet like a grating and choked you to death, or else punctured your windpipe so you expired in gurgling agonies. Whence these myths arose I know not, but I remember the taste and feel of fish revolving in my mouth like chewed newspaper with pins in it and I couldn't have swallowed it to save my life.

The highlight, or perhaps more appropriately, the black spot of Ash Wednesday, was getting your ashes. A big square County Tyrone priest with a big square thumb splayed by turf-cutting, plastered a great plus sign on your brow that left you marked as indelibly as a tree to be felled, whilst intoning the words, "Remember man that thou art dust and unto dust thou must return." This sudden revelation of our own mortality had a salutary effect upon our young minds and the teasing of older siblings, who rolled their eyes and chanted, "The worms creep in, the worms creep out, they go in thin and they come out stout", ensured we remained in a state of healthy terror for the whole six weeks.

The finer points of Christian doctrine impinged upon us not at all. We read in Bible History of Christ's fasting in the desert, and being tempted, but relished more the accompanying picture of the Devil, complete with horns, tail and toasting fork and bearing an uncanny resemblance to the actor Simon Callow. Temptation we empathised with all too well. Looking back through the telescope of time, it amazes me how self-centred all that self-denial was. It was negative rather than positive, "don't" rather than "do", a sense of sin rather than grace. How little it benefited society in general or the deprived bits of it in particular. And the guilt!

The sideboard door swings open. As the eight-year-old Judas hand hesitates towards the sweetie jar, the reproachful brown eyes of the Lord Jesus cloud in pain. You'd betray him for a liquorice lace or a sherbet dab would you? I know people who're too frightened and ashamed to go back to organisations like Weight Watchers or Unislim because they've fallen from grace to greed. Tell you what, it's nothing like as bad as burgling a sweetie-jar on a Good Friday evening while the others are out at church!

THOSE OF US REARED IN THE FAITH remember the Saturday evening shove-up in the church pews as we waited our turn in the dark foetid-smelling broom-cupboard of the confessional, our well-rehearsed laundry list of wrongdoings on the tip of our tongue. If it was on the light side you added a few for interest. A dry screak of a shutter and a patch of lighter dark was the cue to rattle it off. Then, the act of contrition taken at a run and the terror of forgetting your designated penance prayer, which would mean a "bad confession". As you rose from your knees, relieved and shriven, God's grace ran through your veins like golden gravy. What a pity you couldn't resist the temptation to play knick-knock all the way home!

But that was in the era of "thou shalt not", "grave matter" and "eternal damnation". Galvanised by fear we toed the moral line. As a young teacher, I recall shepherding trembling seven-year-olds into the dark and seeing, more than once, a little puddle appear from under the door. At seven it was presumed children had reached the age of reason and were therefore capable of sin.

Today all is light and love and reconciliation with God and each other, but a church gravely damaged from within neither exerts the same authority nor exacts the same respect as it once did. It's dealing anyway with a secularised society, pick-and-mix Christianity, where religious conviction is often shallow-rooted. Funny how people are willing to reveal their murkiest personal secrets in front of a baying audience on zoo television but balk at the notion of doing it one-to-one in an atmosphere of reverent meditation.

BEING A CHILD OF ELDERLY PARENTS, death was not unfamiliar to me. They both came from large families and at least twice a year (or so it seemed) we'd all have to traipse off to County Down to assist at somebody's obsequies. My abiding memory is the strangely surreal effect of mirrors and pictures blinded with cloths, and a child's intuitive understanding of the emptiness vacated by a human soul.

From downstairs comes the pervasive aroma of boiling ham and the polite tinkle of aunties in clean crossover pinnies serving tea to decent men in collar studs and shiny boots. Upstairs, through the wooden slats of the foot of the bed, I'm looking at Great-Uncle James, yellow as candle-wax, his nose sculpted like a bird's beak. Somebody's knuckle is in my back, urging me to kneel and say a prayer. I stare very hard at the knotted fringe of the white bedspread. Two years later, the same hand-worked linen counterpane lies over Aunt Nita, her beautifully manicured hands interlaced, the half-moons of her nails already blue. Dead of tuberculosis at forty-two.

But then, these were old people. Old people died and you dreamed about it a couple of times and got on with the business of growing up. Until, that is, Terry Hargan died. Terry Hargan was eight years old and in my class. He was a thin boy with transparent skin and bony knees. Terry developed leukaemia, the first time I'd ever heard of the disease, and we, his classmates, followed his small coffin in the rain to the country chapel and formed a guard of honour in the graveyard. Later in the playground, I gouged a marley-hole with the heel of my shoe in the beaten yellow clay and thought of the compacted earth lying in tons upon his wasted little body and from that day I was afraid.

That day I realised the inevitability of death, the random selection procedure that said "you and you and you" and against which there was no appeal. I've been afraid ever since.

I think death is feared more by my generation than any other. We products of the post-war baby boom, whose characters were forged in the rock 'n' roll years, we're the "me" generation, and we've such a highly developed opinion of ourselves that we wonder how the world will manage without us. We are the movers and the shakers. We believe ourselves still to be the invincible golden young who substituted healthy scepticism for religious certainty. We will not go gentle into that good night.

> "THE EXPERIENCE OF CHILDHOOD IS IRRETRIEVABLE.
> ALL THAT REMAINS IS A HEEDFUL OF BRILLIANT FROZEN
> MOMENTS ALREADY DANGEROUSLY DISTORTED BY THE
> WISDOMS OF MATURITY"
> *Penelope Lively*

CHILDHOOD IS A MAGIC KINGDOM ruled by the child himself. He must learn to make independent decisions, calculate risk and cope with success and failure. As surely as his parent goes out to work each day, so ought the child go to his job – which is play – and to a large extent be let enjoy it, without undue interference from adults with their hearts in their mouths prophesying incipient disaster.

I have a theory. Half the trouble with today's children is they are never alone. They're always under someone's eye, or within calling distance, constantly supervised, however loosely. A child may be unaccompanied in his or her room, but a room so packed with electronic gizmos that he can't be said to be isolated. I remember when a bedroom was a sparsely-furnished place for sleeping in and you never spent a single waking minute in it, except as punishment.

In earlier, safer summers, no matter what the weather, we were hunted out of the house as soon as we'd had breakfast and weren't expected to darken the door again except for meals. The Angelus bell and the factory hooter quartered our days and it was perfectly safe to ask passing male strangers, "Hi mister! Have ye the time on ye?"

Left to our own devices in an environment almost totally devoid of facilities, we gave rein to our imagination. Some people had mothers who didn't object to an invasion of their back yards by a rabble of playmates and were frequently generous in the distribution of Marie biscuits and diluted orange. They were equally sanguine about allowing the use of clotheshorses and counterpanes for the construction of tents and dens, but drew the line at the good cushions off the parlour settee. Less salubrious experiences of a similar nature were enacted on patches of waste ground among the rubble of derelict buildings where the catalogue of dangers included dog-dirt, rats, broken glass, rusty iron railings to get stuck between or impaled upon, and the likelihood of being burned, scalded or poisoned, and probably all three, as a result of lighting fires, boiling spuds in an empty paint tin and eating them half-raw.

When it was wet, we hunkered impatiently in somebody's vestibule waiting for the rain to stop. Frequently we ignored the downpour to float lolly-sticks down the swirling gutters. There is no sensation to compare with deliberately letting the rainwater rise over the uppers of your Clarks sandals to trickle coldly through their triangular cut-outs and watch it turn your white ankle-socks irretrievably grey.

"Drinking the rain" was another favourite activity – twirling slowly like windmills with arms outstretched, mouths gaping like nestlings to the sky. We weren't even afraid of thunder, for didn't everybody know St Columba had promised that nobody in Derry would ever be struck by lightning. My mother, who actually was struck while living in Fincairn near Dungiven, used to observe somewhat bitterly it was obvious that neither St Columba's promise nor his power extended as far as the county! As you ran home for tea inhaling the smell of wet wool cardigan, you hoped your mother wouldn't reach out and touch you and discover you were saturated to the skin.

As children we were seriously over-clothed. I remember a woollen vest and a liberty bodice of some flannelette-feeling stuff, good thick navy knickers and hand-knit knee-socks held up with knotted elastic garters that created a lump behind each knee like an incipient varicose vein. Over all of this went a warm pleated skirt, a home-knitted jumper and a cardigan – and that was just indoor wear. We pled for ankle-socks, sandals and summer frocks from Easter onwards, but it was fully the month of May before the spectre of catching a cold in your kidneys was dispelled by warmer weather. Mothers were mortally suspicious of heat and always insisted you "take a wee cardigan" in case the treacherous temperature dropped like a stone and you'd get pneumonia. They were always buttoning us up, happing us in pixie hoods, mufflers tied at the neck and mittens with tight thumbs till we could hardly move.

My early life was blighted by ugly, practical footwear chosen by my mother, best described by that foul and fell term, "serviceable" – the annual brown Clarks sandals for spring, the Kiltie two-bar shoes for Sunday and years of big, black clootery lace-ups for school. Slip-ons were forbidden – "not enough support; you'd be walking out of them in weeks" – and your feet would be put to wiggle in the X-ray machine that showed your bones and generous growing room in the toes of the hateful black lace-ups.

NO ASPECT OF OUR UPBRINGING WAS OVERLOOKED. Mothers were obsessed with toileting. A rich lore grew up about regularity and frequency. Sitting on cold stone steps or damp grass was a sure means of damaging the kidneys and copious daily draughts of California Syrup of Figs were fed to us as stern reminders to Mother Nature to move things along – for constipation was the precursor of all childhood ills.

And that wasn't the worst. Along with spitting on a hankie to wipe your face clean with scented saliva, security-minded mothers yanked your knickers viciously up under your arms, which necessitated you running around on tiptoe until the elastic gradually migrated southwards towards your middle and comfort was restored.

Economy decreed wringing the last ounce of wear out of knickers. When their exhausted elastic eventually let you down (usually in humiliating public circumstances) it was replaced with agonisingly tight new elastic, inserted in the waistband channel by the cunning means of a closed safety pin. The purple weals about your midriff attested there were months of wear left in those knickers yet.

The horrors of public toilets were dinned into us. Their foetid air, alive with germs; their suspect surfaces rife with disease. We were warned to touch nothing, sit on nothing, walk on our heels to prevent contagion of the sole and preferably not breathe at all if we could possibly help it. The heavily-contaminated chain was to be pulled by a hand firmly wrapped in a protective mitten of toilet paper. To this day a friend of mine operates the cistern handle with her elbow – in her own home.

The ultimate ordeal for the fastidious was the dry toilet down the country with the worm-eaten seat, where your doings disappeared into an inky, stinking void and squares of *Thompson's Weekly* hung on a rusty nail from a stout loop of hairy twine. A strong and chilly breeze fanned your nether regions and your feet were perfectly visible to passers-by under the rickety ill-fitting door. Sybaritic it was not.

CHILDHOOD MEMORIES OF DERRY ARE LEGION, well-documented and two a penny. It always struck me that it is so much easier to write graphically about childhood if your circumstances were (a) poverty-stricken, (b) blighted by unemployment, (c) overcrowded, or (d) peopled with feckless but colourful wastrels. It's a hard life trying to write when you come from a respectable law-abiding, circumspect, hardworking, professional family with no debts and a piano.

Squalor is so much more picturesque in literary terms. Phil Coulter may have had a gas yard wall to play by. We had Hobby Square, a huge (to our eyes) area of waste ground at the bottom of Bonds Hill which gave access to Simpson's Brae via a steep and pitted slope like the north face of the Eiger, just right for scootering down at kamikaze speed in an early form of motocross. It got its name, I suppose, from when a funfair would come with its grubby red and white canvas booths, hobby horses and swing-boats, but mostly it was deserted, the scummy puddles magic with petrol rainbows.

For an empty space it offered infinite leisure options. The hill offered nettles and dockens to sting and soothe in equal measure and sulucks to set your teeth on edge. The ground by the wall was just soft enough to dig your heel in to make a hole for marbles. The sun winked on the broken yellow and green of smashed bottles as you squatted and aimed your marley, inhaling the heady odours emanating from the bonded warehouse next door. Adventurous afternoons were spent climbing up the back of the billboards onto the electricity substation roof with Mrs Curtis and Mrs Cheshire out at their doors in Simpson's Brae shouting, "Get down or we'll tell the police." Being nice children from good homes we believed them and did what we were told. Only the really bold would risk banging on the side door of the Midland Cinema in the middle of the matinee performance.

Derry had five cinemas then. We, in the Waterside (the "crème de la crème") patronised the Midland, whose square canopy of tinted glass proclaimed in large dimpled letters, "Continuous performance from 2.30." The routine never varied. Part one was buying sweets in Bridie's – clamouring five deep at the counter and Bridie's mouth a tight line of disapproval, "Yahoos, all of yez!" Oh the choosing! Clove rock? Aniseed balls? Jap dessert? Watching with bated breath the silvery arrow of the Avery scale tremble on the two-ounce marker while Bridie's eyes narrowed and her hand hovered to withdraw the one sweet upon which depended her profit or the poor-house. Never in my life did I see her add one. We jumped with impatience as she twirled the paper bag and slowly took change from the worn wooden drawer.

The queue must be nearly round the corner into Hobby Square by now! It was. A seething mass of juvenile humanity being barked into order by a pockmarked commissionaire, irreverently referred to by regular patrons as "Dartboard". Dartboard patrolled the queue, cuffing the unruly into position and yanking out by the scruff those banned for previous unsocial behaviour. These miscreants, cast out of Eden as it were, immediately took themselves round the back where they scaled the flat roof over the emergency exit and sat there, drumming their indefatigable heels against the wooden panels of the door throughout the advertisements, *Movietone News*, two trailers, a travelogue and the big picture.

The ticket kiosk enshrined a gently lady of deathly pale complexion – naturally she was known as "Daisy". At two o'clock on the dot, the doors opened to a vociferous cheer. Daisy's ticket dispenser burped and rattled like a machine gun and we charged into semi-darkness. The stalls smelt of oranges and pee, the balcony of oranges and tobacco.

The prickly red seats scoured the backs of our bare legs and sprang up with a loud slap – a favourite ploy indulged in by the rowdies during a particularly tense or tender scene on screen. Dartboard strode about wrathfully in the gloom, beaming his torch on those climbing over the rows or with feet up on the seats. A period of relative quiet would be punctuated by a scrape, a flare, a smell of phosphorescence and down the aisle he'd pound to ask the obvious – "Are you smoking?" "Ah am not mister!" lied the culprit indignantly, the glowing butt searing one cupped hand thrust well down between the seats, the tell-tale whorls of blue smoke plainly visible in the projectionist's beam.

The magic words THE END unleashed a concerted stampede for the exit and we went streaming and screaming up the street, the empty sleeves of our coats like banners behind us, running over people's doorsteps knick-knocking as we went home to Ronald Rosser's *Northern Ireland Sports Report* on the radio and our tea.

THE WATERSIDE'S ONLY PASTORAL LEISURE AMENITY was St Columb's park. Now, the park enjoyed a curious dual reputation. On one hand it was the sole aim and objective of the Sunday afternoon family walk, mother, father and all the wee ones (not all that many wee ones, for the Waterside people practised moderation in all things) in their Sunday best. For the rest of the week it was classed as an area of moral danger and you never let on you were going. Every bush, shrub and tree was reputed to harbour shoals of sailors from Sea Eagle or worse, American bigamists from the Naval Communications Station, known as the "Yankee Biss", who'd been specially drafted in by their governments to corrupt and despoil the flower of Waterside womanhood. Far more dangerous were the big boys, all of twelve or thirteen, who would push you into the stream, twist the chains of your swing or walk up the banana slide with muddy shoes after you'd spent an age polishing it to a high gloss with the waxed paper wrapper of a Stevenson's sliced plain. Of the agents of the devil we saw nothing, though we often expounded innocent theories on the origins of the strange patches of flattened grass we found in remote spots overlooking the railway line where we went to wave to the trains. Perhaps they were early corn circles?

BROOKE PARK IN ITS HEYDAY, in all its closely-barbered splendour, complete with lily pond, goldfish, geometric flowerbeds and crunchy pebble walks, was a cut above St Columb's. Abandoning my Waterside origins, I took two buses and a string bag of books to spend the summer days there, playing and visiting the big brown linoleum-smelling library with its lion-paw radiators and gothic-lettered "Silence" signs.

Up at the Rosemount end it took weeks to pluck up the courage to tackle the banana slide. So many times you climbed the dizzy iron steps only to chicken out at the top when you saw the brassy glitter of the narrow chute hurtling to the concrete far below. Your stomach came up to your throat as you coasted over the bump, progress much facilitated by the waxed bread-wrapper and you shot off the bottom of the slide, your knickers black as the ace of spades.

Second in terror was the maypole, each pendant chain ending in a stout stirrup-shaped handle, where the big boys hurtled horizontally through the air, their heels in imminent danger of knocking the teeth out of an envious circle of younger bystanders.

The polite part of the park had grass like Axminster because, of course, nobody was allowed to walk on it. The flowerbeds were a regimental riot of blooms all standing to attention and all exactly the same height, their feet cool in little cushions of white alyssum and blue lobelia. Guardian of this Eden was the "parkie" who roamed his domain with a whistle and a stick.

Bigger and bolder children romped yelling through the shrubbery or deliberately hurled their jumpers onto the grass, making darting shortcuts across the forbidden sward to retrieve them. This was known as "tantin' the parkie". One demented "peep!" of his whistle and every child within earshot, guilty or not, ran for his life. All paths led eventually to the pond where waxen lilies floated, exotic to us as lotus blossoms and the dim green water flickered with fish. There was neither litter nor vandalism, nor danger from strange solitary men. It was a charmed spot.

EVERY MORNING OF MY CHILDHOOD I looked from my bedroom window in the Waterside across Craigavon Bridge to the great terracotta-coloured façade with its large white letters spelling out TILLIE & HENDERSON LTD. Its factory hooter regulated my days better than the Midland Station clock, which was either fast or slow or stopped.

Walking across town on a sunny afternoon, the prosperous thrum and clack of machinery emanated from the many-storied ranks of windows half-open in the summer heat and at tea time the factory girls, threads clinging to their overalls, came cascading down the iron outer staircase four or five abreast. Chattering like starlings they linked each other up Abercorn Road, Wapping Lane or Carlisle Road, down John Street, Foyle Road or across the bridge, wisecracking, laughing and full of what they'd wear that night to Borderland or the Embassy.

Large as ocean-going liners, the shirt factories were the biggest things we had – bulwarks against want. They were cathedrals of commerce, guaranteeing employment for five female generations of side-seamers, buttonholers, cuffers and banders. We couldn't conceive of them failing.

All industries have a shelf life and there is no point in attempting to prolong it beyond its expiry date. The Belfast shipyard will never again resound to the rhythmic clangour of a riveter's gun. The glory days are gone, the gantries shrunken shadows of themselves, victims of the seismic shift in world markets.

A simple ruthless rule rules the marketplace. "If nobody's buying it, reduce the price. If they're still not buying it, stop making it." Each of us underpins it in every retail transaction we make. If we want it at all, we want it cheap. Who in Derry, for example, ever bought a shirt in a shop?

The camaraderie of the factory floor was legendary; the good-natured taunting of the supervisors, the elaborate practical jokes, the tying to the lamp-post of the newest bride-to-be. Mothers, sisters, daughters, aunts, an entire community represented in the long lines of female heads bent obediently to the task of creating with mathematical accuracy and impossible speed. Sleeve-piecers and collarers, each proud of her singular skill, earning a ticket per dozen and machining her quota of tickets firmly together, lest the wages clerk miscalculate her due.

In the week you left school somebody "spoke for you". You got a start and were mothered and teased in equal measure till you found your feet. The factory was a family in every sense of the word, interdependent and utterly relying on the paternal benevolence of the employer who beamed upon you like old Mr Grace and told you, "You're doing very well!"

It wasn't like that at all though, was it? There was nothing romantic about it. It was boring, repetitive, hard graft for little money. Piece rates – work like the wind to make a living wage; no rights, little chance of promotion, a prey to petty tyranny and arbitrary treatment. It was women's work. Their nimble fingers cost considerably less to employ than a man's in conditions not warm enough to qualify as a sweatshop.

Well it's over now and the factory hooter is sounding somewhere else far, very far away.

CERTAIN PHRASES AND TURNS OF SPEECH were endemic to the Waterside. You notice for example I say *the* Waterside. Only outsiders who know no better call it "Waterside". Crossing the river was "going over the town" and you went over the town and back in a green and white snub-nosed bus with a proper conductor in a peaked cap, a greasy satchel and a pinging machine which punched a hole in your halfpenny buff, penny white or tuppeny pink ticket. His duties also included pulling the leather cord connected to the driver's cab and shouting out the stops. "Enna-the-bridge! Enna-the-bridge! Fer Gawd's sake missus, ENNA-THE-BRIDGE!"

ENNATHEBRIDGE BROUGHT YOU INTO DUKE STREET. Kennedy's for quality shoes, Cassoni's Italian ice-cream and Quigley's the butcher where Patsy would ask if you wanted the meat delivered. "Thank you, I have my own transport," responded the eight-year-old me, indicating with regal gesture the scooter parked outside with string bag dangling from the handlebars. Scootering on a sunny Saturday morning down the street past Cochrane's Row with its doll-sized houses, you had to put your heel on the brake to stop at Harper's the Bootmaker's window – a source of abiding wonder. Boots and shoes were displayed upside down, their soles and heels inlaid in sky-blue and scarlet and yellow leathers with butterfly and flower patterns picked out in tiny gold nails. For years I half believed they were made by elves or dwarves who worked at the back of the shop.

Two shops I recall with great affection from my childhood were Morrison's and McDevitt's. Positioned directly opposite in the narrow dog-leg of Duke Street they glared glassily at each other for many years.

I remember McDevitt's as a very brown shop. There were expanses of shiny khaki linoleum, brown mahogany counters and bentwood chairs for customer comfort. Great brown-painted radiators with claw feet gave off metallic-smelling warmth. Sliding trays of silk-lined leather gloves and lisle stockings slotted neatly beneath glass display cases and "serviceable wool afternoon frocks" were to be had from fifty-nine shillings and eleven pence upwards.

The windows were tastefully dressed with rigidly-posed mannequins exhibiting the very latest in quality outerwear. They had painted-on hair in a shingle bob and curious club feet. Staff addressed each other as "Miss", the customer as "Madam" and there was a resident seamstress with a pin cushion on her wrist in "Ladies Mantles".

Any number of garments were willingly allowed out on approval.

Regardless of the fact that we lived only 200 yards up the street, these were delivered by the shop boy on the shop bike and came in large brown pasteboard boxes with sepia labels and lots of thin, strong string. I was fascinated by that string, and how the most fragile of shop assistants could wind it round a finger and snap it with a single purposeful tug.

Even minor purchases were accompanied by a great deal of pencil work and carbon paper while account customers were dealt with in a twilit cubby hole upstairs by a lady with a velvet face (achieved, I discovered later, by the liberal use of Velouty Powder Cream).

A Saturday visit to McDevitt's had to be balanced by one to Morrison's. Morrison's was presided over by the patriarch of the firm – an immensely dapper gentleman with a neat moustache, a flower in his buttonhole and a black beret worn at a rakish angle. He greeted his favoured customers with a warm handshake and hovered near the front door counting how many of them subsequently paid a call to his rivals across the street.

For me, Morrison's had the edge over McDevitt's – it had toys. For years, what appeared to be the same bike stood in solitary splendour in a glass case of its own. Unfortunately, Morrison's also stocked school uniforms and a particular brand of thick school knickers which eventually alienated me.

There's a dual carriageway now where the master bootmaker, saddler, blacksmith, bakery and Morrison's and McDevitt's used to be, to allow us easier access to the supermarket. I often wish as I struggle home with the shopping, that in the midst of all this progress, they'd at least have held on to the principle of the shop boy and the shop bike!

I WAS EIGHT WHEN I FIRST SAW THE BICYCLE in Morrison's shop, its chrome gleaming through the panels of its own glass display case, inaccessible as the crown jewels. Sprightly Mr Morrison would pat my head and say if I was a good girl you never knew what Santa might bring. A snowball's surviving in hell would've been likelier than my getting that bike. Bicycles were dangerous machines and my sense of balance wasn't too good. However, despite falling off my scooter frequently and concussing myself regularly on roller-skates I knew I could master that bike.

At my country school, if you pestered the older children, they'd pass on their enviable life skills; French skipping, three-ball bouncy and climbing the forbidden chestnut tree. Their tutelage wasn't always entirely kind. They'd encourage you upwards with careful instructions, then run away, leaving you to make shift down again yourself. Thus it was that one day I was set upon somebody's ancient boneshaker, steadied for a few laps round the playground and shown where the brakes were. Then they launched me upon an unpaved laneway with a slight but definite incline. I was halfway down before an injudicious and terrified tug on the brakes hurtled me and the bicycle into a bed of nettles. My limbs were green with dock-leaf juice for two days but I had made my maiden flight.

After that it was a case of "Gwon, givis a go…" on other people's bikes till, at thirteen, I became at last the proud possessor of a burgundy-coloured Raleigh with straight handlebars.

So began what I recall as seemingly serial summers. Derry's hills, alas, are not the ideal terrain for a bike. You wheeled as much as you rode, though there were, in those days of little traffic, some exhilarating runs.

The great slalom of Creggan Hill created enough momentum to carry you, hair flying, wind whistling past your ears, all the way from Rosemount, down William Street to Waterloo Place and the Guildhall.

Alone or with friends, I roamed the city and countryside, cycling for miles on Famous Five-style expeditions with squidgy tomato sandwiches and bottles of lemonade. We had roses in our cheeks, callouses on our backsides and freedom. Real freedom – a sensation not experienced again till the day I got my first car. Whether our parents' hearts were troubled by our absence we neither knew nor cared. "Home before dark" was the only sanction. Few of us had house telephones and the intrusive, inescapable "mobile" wasn't even a twinkle in technology's eye. Oh, the joy of not being able to be found!

Of course it was safer then. Adults looked out for all children, not just their own. Good Samaritans mended our punctures and plastered our skinned knees. So the idyll went on, summer after summer till, one by one, we grew up, discovered boys and coffee bars and realised that turquoise eyeshadow accessorised with a bicycle is an incongruous combination. The bike was abandoned or passed on and with it went the kind of freedom that rarely comes again.

> "NOW, AS ALWAYS, THE MOST AUTOMATED APPLIANCE IN A
> HOUSEHOLD IS THE MOTHER"
> *Beverly Jones*

EVERY WEEKDAY MORNING my mother, armed with a stout string bag, set off to "do the messages". Such was the variety of shops in a triangle of three neighbouring streets she could buy everything she needed, from a ham hock to a half-set of china, in an hour's round trip.

She was one of a generation of homebound fridge-free wives and mothers, who daily shopped for fresh produce and made a social occasion out of necessity. Women like her were knitted into the fabric of their community in a way that their multi-tasking hyper-tense daughters can never match.

It was no small thing for my mother to be greeted by name by Albert and Eric in the grocer's, by Patsy and Harry in the butcher's, to have her bacon sliced to optimum thickness by Barney Callan himself and swap news with Mrs Orr as she swaddled the soup vegetables in several sheets of the previous night's *Belfast Tele*. It boosted her morale, as a valued customer, to be offered a bentwood chair in Morrison's or McDevitt's, and select a number of garments to be taken home "on approval" – "returns" collected next day and alterations done on the premises by a lady forever circling on her knees with a mouthful of pins.

I'd sit on the doorstep and watch for mother's return lugging the bulging string bag, knobbly with cabbage or oranges and maybe a surprise for me.

It was an era of service. The bread van stopped daily at the door. The fish man barked his Friday "Fresh herr'n'!" like a seal. The Braid Lemonade lorry pulled up with the clinking shudder of 1,000 bottles of whiskey-coloured effervescence. The less salubrious brock-cart trundled by, strung with buckets and piled high with stale food scraps whose sour smell lingered in the street long after it had passed.

The small or middle-sized shop, with its regular customers and idiosyncratic owner, nourished the community in more ways than one. It was at once a forum for exchanging opinion and a monitor and guardian of the status quo. The cautious camaraderie of the butcher's queue, the gossipy dressmaker's fitting room and the craic in the warm, wee home-bakery contributed to the cohesion of the society they served.

This social pattern survived into the early Sixties and I remember the day it changed. A local businessman fitted out his premises in American self-service supermart style. It was the talk of the town. Mother suggested we "give it a go". We skulked its modest aisles uneasily, feeling ourselves in alien "behind the counter" territory without permission. Behind the counter! That sacred space you'd no more trespass on than vault the altar rails!

Taking stuff off the shelves and putting it in a basket unsupervised seemed to us like shoplifting. Mother, deeply dismayed at this impersonal exercise in do-it-yourselfery, predicted the idea would never catch on.

She patronised Barney Callan's corner shop at the bottom of Chapel Road, where a majestic flitch of bacon occupied the corner of the counter, stretched in unhygienic splendour cheek by jowl with bags of washing soda and dusty liquorice laces. Bundles of kindling, bouquets of brooms and clatters of galvanised buckets cluttered the floor where the shop boy's rigorous sweeping vigorously rearranged the germs. The dust motes danced in the bacteria-filled air and overall swung a large sticky flypaper pendulous with corpses.

In brown shop-coat the proprietor, bald head glistening, expertly thumbed in the lugs of sugar bags or entered your "goods" in a lined accounts book with a stump of well-licked black pencil, prior to despatching it all to your door via the shop boy on the shop bike. Not a freeze-dried, vacuum-packed, plastic-bagged commodity in the place, but plenty of gossip and good-fellowship and a pink sugar mouse with a string tail for the wee one.

These days I get my meat from a real butcher and fish from a proper fishmonger. I applaud the resurgence of farmers' markets for creating an increased demand for quality, organic and local produce, but you pay extra for the authentic country muck on your spuds and carrots that we used to get for free.

The average 1950s woman had no concept of the idea of "leisure". Leisure for the working classes was only invented when films and television revealed to them how the other half lived and conditioned them into yearning for the gadgets and gizmos that would reduce the degree of their drudgery and give them time for themselves.

Women in the Fifties were virtuous victims of the "Little Palace" syndrome that had them out on their front step before 8am with a broom and the Brasso and a washing pegged on the line before 9.

They were victims too of early advertising that implied their degree of parental care was reflected in the whiteness of their children's school shirts. To be recognised as "house-proud" by their neighbours was to wear an invisible badge of honour. It made them graduates with distinction in the arts of scrubbing and polishing. For many talented women this was the only accolade they ever received!

Looking back from the safe distance of half a century and the other end of a rapid technological revolution, I don't believe we fully understand the sheer, hard physicality of housework then. I was a child in the Fifties and I never recall seeing my mother sit down in daylight. She rose at 7am, made porridge, tea and toast and delivered it on trays to the various members of her family still abed. This was not done entirely from altruistic motives. She just didn't want people downstairs "messing the place up".

Returning to reclaim the trays, clean clothes were hung over the bottom rail of each bed and she descended again to make the lunches. You were inspected head to foot in the hall, given your bus

money, clean hankie and put out to school while she washed up the
breakfast dishes, ran the carpet sweeper over the hall runner and the
hearthrugs, buffed the linoleum with a mop, made the beds and
dusted. On Fridays she came down the stairs backwards on her knees
with a dust pan and a stiff-bristled handbrush. The day she got a
Goblin cylindrical vacuum-cleaner out of Gilmour's of the Diamond,
she nearly wept with delight.

Perishables were stored in a kitchen cabinet with panels of pierced
metal mesh and in hot weather the milk bottles stood up to their
necks in cold water in the big soup saucepan by the back door.
Electrolux, where are ye?

The weekly wash was accomplished in a large porcelain jaw-box
(fashionably known nowadays as a Belfast sink) with the aid of a
Willis water-heater and a dinosaur of a mangle. Twice a year she'd
examine the sky, sniff the air and declare, "That'd be a quare day for
washing blankets!" It was my job to feed the sodden weight of endless
wool into the jaws of the beast without allowing it to twist.

All other domestic activities were temporarily suspended for the
making of "your father's dinner" (as if the rest of us weren't getting
any), all fresh ingredients of course and ready on the dot of 4.30pm.
My mother wouldn't eat anything out of a tin except for Ambrosia
creamed rice. The word "instant" was anathema to her, though
towards the end of her life she discovered frozen pastry, but her forte
was cake-making: egg sponge, Madeira, Dundee cake heavy with
fruit. There was always cake but it was always being kept "for
visitors". A thin slice for supper was delivered with the stern
admonition, "Remember you've another day to live."

My mother never went to bed without tidying the house. She had
a dread that she'd die in the night and wouldn't be able to be "waked"
in her own home because of the state of it.

It might be 8.30 or 9pm in the evening before she sat down and
picked up her knitting or crochet. She could run up an Aran sweater
and read the newspaper at the same time. In her spare moments she
painted and papered and was pretty nifty with a sewing machine. The
thing is, she was not untypical of her generation.

Yes, the women of the Fifties were probably fitter than today's fully automated housewife. In their prime they had energy, stamina and a highly developed sense of duty. But their prime was short. Many of them were old before their time, worn out by a relentless regime of repetitive toil, too many children and not enough money.

Worst of all, they were robbed of their intellectual potential. They may have been physically hardier but, I suspect, much less fulfilled.

WE GOT A WASHING MACHINE in 1956 when I was eleven and past the dirty stage. My mother always remarked with some bitterness that she got one when she no longer needed it – her family of five all reared, her constitution already wrecked and her looks ravaged by a lifetime's labour over washboard and mangle. I've no clear recollection of the washboard, but I do remember flinging all my weight on the handle of the mangle as the Witney blankets squelched through and watching the fourfold twill bed sheets with their wartime Utility mark emerge stiff as boards from its tight wooden lips. The scullery was a steamy, red-armed, chap-knuckled domain presided over by mother in three aprons; the washday pinny over the cooking pinny over the answering-the-door pinny.

A bowl of viscous blue Robin starch sat ready for collars and hankies and, in an enamel basin, the glassy flakes of Lux fell like snow into hand-hot water for stocking and smalls. Condensation ran down the fat bellies of saucepans on the top shelf and damp strands of hair were pushed behind ears with prune-wrinkled fingers.

The pulley-line's moorings creaked ominously. Its eight strands groaned with the overload of wet washing. My ten-year-old arms were almost yanked out of their sockets before the anchor cord was safely wound about the spindle and the loop hooked over in a figure-of-eight as insurance.

And then came technology in the shape of the twin-tub. The twin-tub was magic. It washed in one half, then the saturated clothes had to be transferred (by hand with ankle-deep sloshing) into the other half for rinsing. This task the machine performed while making a noise like a small foundry. It was also bent on escape, creeping constantly towards the back door with a furtive expression on its control panel.

Mother, having embraced modernity wholeheartedly, gave us no peace until she acquired a spin-drier too. The spin-drier's lid snapped shut with the clap of an alligator's jaw. Its mysterious centrifugal force terrified the water out of the clothes. We'd peel them off the drum afterwards like traumatised cartoon characters – long and thin and flat. The spin-drier had peripatetic tendencies too, advancing and retiring like a *Come Dancing* competitor.

I'd like to report that these appliances meant an end to my mother's toil and slavery. They did not. Not a moment was saved. Work merely expanded to fill the time available.

I HATE TO HEAR MYSELF SAY THIS, but in my day less did you. Though rationing was phased out by my time, choice was limited. You could take it or leave it. There were no alternatives.

You could have either a piece and butter or a piece and jam, but never the sinful extravagance of butter and jam together. "You can't have two kitchens" was the sharp reminder. The advent of guests rarely signalled a relaxation since mother operated a strict policy of "Family Hold Back". Generous chunks of Battenburg cake were served to visitors. Our slices were thin to the point of transparency. My brother observed with some bitterness that only in our house did you get a piece of window cake you could actually see through!

Whole days were coloured by the knowledge of what was for the dinner and were golden or grey accordingly. Running home from play, pressing the doorbell impatiently and thumbing open the letterbox to the rich aroma of gravy or the unwelcome pungency of cabbage. Thoroughness was the hallmark of Fifties cuisine. The dangers of underdone food (which gave you tapeworms) reduced most meat to fibrous grey flannel. Today's "al dente" vegetables would've been smartly returned to the pot lest they cause acid indigestion and every vestige of vitamin content was firmly boiled out of them. On particularly black days there were prunes for pudding.

The resourceful parents' task was to persuade you to eat the repulsive plateful. This was accomplished most effectively in our house by the simple expedient of calling it by a different name. Thus it was I reached the ripe age of fourteen before realising the French potato soup I supped with such relish every Saturday was, in fact, dreaded lentil. My father insisted that rice pudding disagreed with him, yet he ate it for twenty years with no ill-effect whatsoever. "Is this rice?" he'd enquire suspiciously of my mother. "Tapioca, dear," she'd reply soothingly. "Sure, why would I give you rice when I know it disagrees with you?"

IT'S A LONG, LONG CULTURAL ROAD all the way from cream cookies to ciabatta with the culinary landscape constantly changing on the journey, and there's no going back. No going back except with an evocative sniff over childhood's shoulder of that sweet and yeasty smell that enveloped you as you walked through William Street or Little James Street or Duke Street or the Rock, and thought of the shadowy army of men who rose at 3am on a winter's morning to give us this day our daily bread.

A brisk double knock echoes down the hall. "The breadman's here!" Saturday morning, 10.30. Skidding along the polished linoleum, snatching the shabby purse from the hall table in mid-flight and out to the bread van and the breadman in his brown shop coat and leather satchel slung crosswise like a child's schoolbag. "Stevensons" on the side of the van.

A deep breath and you rattle off your mother's order: "Sliced pan, a lodger's, a Vienna, soda farls, potato bread, a ring of donkey's noses and a snowtop for me, please." The doors of the van are thrown open upon a gust of warm air and the long trays hurtle out with a tremendous rattling screak and a puff of floury dust.

The child's eye takes in the mathematical precision of batch loaves like rows of brown bald heads, the roughcast cobbles of wheaten, glistening cookies stuck together in quilted clusters, curranty eyes agog; the lodgers side-by-side, regular as bobbins of honey-coloured yarn stored in a needlework basket. Last and best of all, the cloying perfumed sweetness of the pastries tray run out like a tapestried banner – an heraldic coat of arms in confectionery studded with jam-tart jewels.

The breadman's hands are big and dry with flour filling the grooves in the skin. He shakes the moneybag horizontally to rattle the change to the front of its mouth and the transaction is complete. I stagger up the steps with my precarious and precious load balanced carefully in my arms, hoping the kitchen will be empty so I can hoke a bit out of the side of the loaf with a crafty forefinger (despite full knowledge and previous experience of the inevitable maternal wrath). You never see children do that now, do you?

By 11am it's time for a drop of tea and a slice from the fresh loaf. Do I like the round-edged crust or the straight-edged crust better? No matter. Spread with satiny butter and the merest suggestion of a sprinkle of sugar, I have nothing left to wish for. Sitting in a patch of sunlight at the kitchen table I swing my legs and am happy.

IN THE DAYS BEFORE THE LOWER MIDDLE CLASSES aspired to dinner-parties, ham salad was the staple sit-down Sunday tea to which guests might be invited. It served several useful purposes. It showed a healthy degree of social ambition; it fulfilled social obligations and it was handy for vetting prospective marriage partners brought home for approval by a son or daughter. The enquiry "Were you in for your tea yet?" was a significant benchmark in the progress of the relationship.

The constituents of the meal rarely varied; moistly pink cooked ham with its strip of white fat and yellow crumbed rind delivered in thin shavings by the whirling, saw-toothed blade of the bacon slicer in the corner shop; the broad flat leaves of Dutch lettuce in an era before iceberg; quartered tomatoes – though social climbers cut them into castellated little points like petals of a water-lily; a scatter of chopped scallions and pale rings of hard-boiled egg like dead men's eyes. Occupying the centre of the table was a large plate of interleaved slices of ready-buttered bread and a paper "serviette" was folded in a triangle on your side plate. Condiments were mixed pickles (everyone wanted the onion, nobody liked the gherkin) and another of pickled beetroot. We had a proper long-handled pickle fork, like a miniature devil's trident with extra barbs to prevent whatever you speared from slipping back into the jar. And, of course, a big bottle of Heinz Salad Cream. There was an elaborate etiquette of passing things to each other. The pickled beetroot was the chief hazard, being both slippery and wet. Many a swain blushed to the colour of the contents of the jar at his own clumsiness as a puce-coloured stain widened on the pristine white cloth.

A special occasion might warrant an extra course of sherry trifle or tinned peaches and ice-cream eaten with round-nosed fruit spoons. Otherwise it was a slice of sponge-cake and hot sweet tea.

It was as predictable as taxes, as changeless as church on Sunday – a rite of passage as significant as graduating into long trousers. As children unfit for social intercourse, we were fed separately in the scullery on good plain fare – bread and jam and tea – and hovered hopefully around the kitchen door waiting for the leavings of the grown-ups. A brief glimpse of culinary Nirvana was fleetingly granted as the door to the parlour opened to admit a cosied teapot and the pungent greenness of salad stuff assailed our nostrils. It wasn't that we wanted the ham salad; we wanted the maturity of inclusion.

IN DERRY TERMS, my childhood was seriously disadvantaged. First I'd made the mistake of not being born of native parents. Secondly, by not attending a city school I was deprived of the annual experience of the all-singing, all-dancing, fiercely competitive "Action Song", and thirdly, by not taking singing lessons and choosing ballet rather than Irish dancing classes, I was excluded from the cultural loop altogether and the doors of *Feis Doire Colmcille* remained forever closed to me. In retrospect I consider myself fortunate. Whether or not their children have any natural aptitude in these fields has never stopped Derry parents or teachers from entering them in competition.

My nascent talent was eventually showcased in the annual pantomime. Pantomime defies analysis. Suffice to say, vital to any local production is the involvement of as many children as possible. Central to the entire show is the memorable scene set in "The Faerie Glade". The curtain rises to a concerted "Awwww!" of delight upon a stage thronged with endearing moppets in elven green and silver, charming all who behold them – chiefly their grannies. This is what the audience has come to see, not the superannuated C-list celebrity, nor the double-entendre comedian, but their little Jason or Jennifer in the spotlight, their names printed in the programme, "attendants on the Fairy Queen". Why otherwise would anyone turn out on a night of freezing fog in the teeth of Christmas?

It's actually much better fun to be in a pantomime than at one. I look back to my eight-year-old self in the days when the children's chorus was recruited from local dancing classes and I had my first heady experience of "the roar of the greasepaint, the smell of the crowd". Alas, the skinny kids with celery-stick limbs were put in tutus at the front, their bony knees thrown into famine relief by the footlights' glare. I had envisioned myself centre-stage in sequinned net, hair combed out like Moira Shearer in *The Red Shoes*, but we stockier citizens were issued with green satin knickerbockers and Noddy hats and told to stamp around a bit at the back. What a gunk in the self-esteem – but that's show business! With my fellow fairy folk, I marched and skipped clockwise, counter-clockwise, formed concentric circles and kept tight hold of Jacinta McPhilemy who skipped on the "off" beat and always went wrong in the chain.

The highlight was the grand finale when we waited in the wings for the "big walk down", two by two to the footlights, taking our bow to a growing crescendo of cheers, the rhythmic clapping of the audience and a last rousing chorus of Frank Carson's perennial pantomime conundrum, "Why does a brown cow give white milk when it only eats green grass?"

From elf or fairy, one generally graduated to the adult chorus, or, aptitude permitting, joined the "speciality dance troupe".

Regrettably, my meteoric stage career blazed but briefly, falling sharply to earth as my maturing figure and limited terpsichorean skills made it obvious my talents were best suited to radio and newsprint. Ah well. At least on radio or in the paper I get to do a solo, and I don't have to wear a Noddy hat.

"THIS IS THE BBC NORTHERN IRELAND HOME SERVICE. Here is the news and this is Duncan Hearle reading it." The beautifully modulated voice was recognisably northern, but starched, ironed and wearing a metaphorical dicky bow. Velvety-toned Michael Baguley, Ronald Rosser, synonymous with sport, and Havelock Nelson, with piano accompaniment, were the collective radio voice of a colonial outpost of Empire that was (as Margaret Thatcher later put it) as British as Finchley, where no vestige of indigenous culture was evident, save a spirited rendition by the Ulster Orchestra of "The Irish Washerwoman" in a concert programme. We received Received Pronunciation and were grateful. When it hit the airwaves, *The McCooeys*, an everyday story of working-class Belfast, held the province in thrall to our first folk soap opera.

I recall with affection *Children's Hour* hosted by "Aunt Cicely" where precociously-elocuted Ulster youngsters showcased their talents and performed little plays in the slot called *I Want to be an Actor!* I still have the book token (value, one guinea) that I earned for my starring role in *Anna and the Man in the Moon* in 1955. Many a BBC contributor would attest that the remuneration rates haven't risen much since. Smitten by the big wire-meshed microphones, the snaking cables, the terrifying adrenalin rush of live performance and the sound effects man with his creaking door, crunching footsteps and clanking galvanised buckets, this was the business! Hi-diddly-dee! An actor's life for me. I went home, honed my small talent and waited for the call. They got back to me twenty-five years later. Which only goes to show that speaking nicely does pay off in the long run.

The pictures generated on radio are created and coloured by voice. Whether or not you have the genius of Einstein coupled with the vocabulary of Dr Johnson, if people hate the sound of you, to put it colloquially, "you're bate". Voice creates an image, an expectation that may not be matched by the reality. I went to talk to a women's group whose president had heard but never seen me. "Oh! " she said with ill-concealed dismay. "You're fatter than your voice!"

We are the least euphonious on the ear of all four provinces of Ireland. Ulster's mouth-music reflects the historic disharmony of the Planter and Gael – the sostenuto skirl of Scottish pipes overlain with the shipyard's harsh metallic beat, underpinning the melancholy minor-keyed lilt of a Celtic inheritance – and every thirty miles or so, the change in inflection and pronunciation that takes one from the slow, soft musicality of Fermanagh's Lakeland to the staccato, sewing-machine swiftness of speech of shirt-making Derry and Strabane. Where speaking's concerned, the single most useful piece of advice I ever received was "Be proud to carry in your mouth the music of your own place, but polish it up for public performance!"

> "GROWING UP IS GOVERNED BY THE WILL.
> ONE CAN CHOOSE TO BECOME AN ADULT,
> BUT ONLY AT GIVEN MOMENTS"
> *Nick Hornby*

I GREW UP IN AN ERA before teenagers were a separate species in Northern Ireland. Teenagers were dangerous American things who ran about in long cars with silver fins, drank Coke and dated. Worse than that, they talked back to their parents and asserted their rights as adults.

Teenagers here wore what their mothers thought suitable, listened to the Top Twenty under the bedclothes and yearned silently for autonomy. Here one "adolesced" in decent obscurity, applied TCP to your acne in dead of night and existed in eager anticipation of a visit to the Borderland ballroom on one's seventeenth birthday. Had you muttered anything about rights in our house, you'd have got your head in your hand.

Looking back is like a boxer remembering the rounds he was knocked down in – an unpleasant but salutary exercise. I go back sometimes, probing the sore tooth of adolescence with the tongue of memory to see exactly how painful it was.

The first skirmishes in the sex war began at primary school. Boys could run faster, climb higher and take bottle tops off with their teeth. They were also better at cricket. Boys batted, girls fielded and that was that and since chauvinism hadn't been invented yet, it never occurred to us to resent it.

Every so often there was a quite deliberately engineered outbreak of sexual terrorism that consisted of the girls hurling insults at the boys, then running away as fast as they could through a large overgrown plantation near the school. Maddened with rage, a horde of crashing, yowling boys leapt in pursuit, wielding branches to beat the daylights out of us. The object was to get back to school unscathed. I'll never forget the delicious terror of plunging through that wood. I was every heroine in a diaphanous white nightie, running to escape a fate worse than death in a scenario framed by Hammer horror. (Well, I know now that's what I was when I started going to the pictures!) Then, I was just a terrified kid, knowing that the creatures behind me were both powerful and unpredictable.

Occasional minor casualties brought an investigation: "Why were you chasing the girls and beating them?"

"Please sir, they were tantin' us." Tantin' is the colloquial word for "tempting" or "taunting".

"Then you've only yourselves to blame, girls, haven't you?"

Yes sir, that's right, sir. Like everything else, we've brought it on ourselves. We'll take the rap. Only we didn't say it, because we didn't know it – then.

And then the serpent entered innocent Eden in the guise of half a bar of McCowan's Liquorice Toffee. We were all in Nicholson's Wood one day, half-heartedly looking for squirrels.

"Hi," said a big boy, "give you half a bar of liquorice toffee if you kiss Tony McAllister." He obviously got his kicks from voyeurism. I considered the deal. Tony, like Barkis, looked sheepish but willing.

"Go halfers with you?" I said.

"Right," he said – and I did.

As kisses go, it ranked rather low on the scale of eroticism, being completely unmemorable, except for a distinct clash of front teeth. The others fell back aghast! Had the words "Jezebel" and "trollop" been in our vocabulary, they'd have appeared on my brow in letters of fire. I gave two squares of the liquorice toffee to Tony.

Back at school, somebody told on us. We were arraigned before authority. I closed my eyes and the pictures of Adam and Eve with their strategically placed bits of greenery rose straight out of the pages of the Bible History and hung in the air.

"Please sir, please sir – she made me," said Adam. "The woman tempted me and I did eat," ran the caption under the picture.

"Is this true?" asked God.

"Technically speaking," said Eve.

"Does that mean yes?" asked the teacher.

I nodded. I was taking the rap, the age-old rap that is the lot of every female. I was ten-and-a-quarter and sentenced for life.

IN 1956 MY FATHER entered four pupils for the new-fangled Eleven Plus examination. We sat the test in the modern glassy strangeness of the Londonderry Model School for an arithmetic paper in the morning and an English paper in the afternoon. Utterly baffled by the last four problems on the maths paper, which involved baths being filled and emptied and trains leaving and arriving, to compensate I wrote a ten page composition on "A Policeman's Lot is Not a Happy One".

In between, Daddy took me out to lunch in Fosters Restaurant, which had linen tablecloths, silver service, three-tier cake stands and elderly waitresses with bad feet. I felt, even then, in my element among "the ladies who lunch".

Early August brought all four of us the fat envelope of the successful candidate, so it was off to Paddy Bannon's school outfitters in Butcher Street for the St Columb's College blazer or the Thornhill gym frock, a sad garment of stout navy serge topped by a royal blue blazer, bottomed out with thick black stockings and surmounted, like a cherry on a fairy cake, by a beret which suited nobody but Mandy Miller, the child star of a film that was very big at the time.

HOW THE DAPPLED SUNLIGHT DIMMED as the school bus rounded the corkscrew bend at the See House on Culmore Road and drove through the tunnel of trees to the main gate of the Convent of Mercy, Thornhill.

We travelled that road ten months of the year in all seasons save high summer.

The trees grew close. In spring the elephantine legs of beech trunks supported great fans of yellow-green leaves tender as tissue paper; chestnuts held up their pink and cream candles on spatulate fingers and the arthritic oaks played host to colonies of rooks' nests.

Advancing summer brought the sharp odour of evergreens – linoleum-leaved rhododendrons and the varnished green of laurel. In September we returned to school under a thinning canopy of ochre and gold and the breeze bowled the fallen leaves like spun pennies down the road before us.

For much of the year that corner was hazardous, slick with mud, leaves or frost. It was an accident black spot before the term had been invented. I recall in the aftermath of a great storm, the flat-faced Swilly bus chugging down the Culmore Road and coming to the Bishop's Corner, as it was known. It was totally blocked by a huge beech tree that lay like a dead dinosaur across the road. Beyond it, four more trees were stretched across the thoroughfare. Mature and massive, they constituted an insuperable barrier between us and education. A ragged cheer went up from all of us on the bus. "Yay! Free day!"

We had reckoned without the doughty Miss Armstrong. "Come, ladies. Out you get!" she ordered briskly. In a pencil skirt and high heels she shepherded us under and over, round and through the netted branches, twigs whipping our faces and snagging our black stockings, till we gained the haven of school. We, the Waterside girls, were the only pupils to make it. Busloads of Cityside wimps had taken one look at the obstacles and scuttled home. Must've been the wrong kind of leaves on the road.

I was left to field the flak from my classmates that it was my sister who cheated us of a day's dossing at home.

MY MOST VIVID RECOLLECTIONS of this stage of my education are of the things I didn't like or wasn't good at. They were many – but chief among them was Physical Education. My Enid Blyton expectations of jolly camaraderie and a crush on the games mistress soon evaporated. PE teachers were of two types. One stood on the sidelines with folded arms and advised us limply to "get on with it, girls". The other gauleiter barked commands from the hooded recesses of a snug anorak. Lord, how I resent the endless hours spent in goose-pimpled discomfort waiting for the pass that never came – musing on the utter pointlessness of getting a ball over, under or through a net.

Purgatorial pressure was stepped up when the team from hell came to play.

The team from hell were all six foot tall with blonde bobbed hair and long tan legs in tailored shorts. They exuded health and efficiency.

We faced them. We, acned dumplings in sad gym frocks hauled in about the waist like so many bags of chaff. The whistle blew. The Brunnhilde who was shadowing me had modelled for Hitler's idea of the master race. I stood like Fay Wray in the shadow of King Kong. She marked me so closely her bust could've been construed as an instrument of intimidation. Last picked because they knew I was a liability, if ever a team had a handicap, I was it. The public shame of losing the game was nothing compared to what your own team would do to you afterwards. It was time to perfect the twin arts of non-specific irregularities in the gynaecological area and the impeccably forged parental excuse note.

It came as a very unpleasant shock to discover that Phys. Ed. played a prominent part in teacher training for Early Years. I had foolishly thought that knowing the words of "Ring-a-Ring-a-Rosy" would suffice. Not so. As student teachers we were required to leap about barefoot in canary yellow sweatshirts. We were further required to hold hands and skip anti-clockwise singing, "I'm a Dingle Dangle Scarecrow with a Flippy Floppy Hat" – much to our mortification, in front of the painters who were touching up the skirting. Worse still, we were required to balance – and climb – and swing. "You can do it. You can do it!" encouraged the PE lecturer, who was herself pliable as a Bendytoy. I met her eyes as levelly as I could while dangling upside down from a trapeze. "No, I can't," I said quietly and got off. The unforgiving trapeze swung back, clouted me on the head and knocked me senseless.

BRILLIANT MORNINGS, golden afternoons, mellow evenings with people relaxing, soaking up the rays, but for one benighted section of the population these are desperate days. Cloudless May skies and rising temperatures mean only one thing to students – exam weather. It's a long, long time since I sat an examination but my stomach contracts with terror at the memory.

The examination hall, no matter what its dimensions, seems vast. Desks are arranged in regimented rows and you are number 981. The high windows admit light but no view. There pops unbidden into my head a line from Wilde's "Ballad of Reading Gaol": "that little tent of blue which prisoners call the sky". Steady on. This isn't an English exam. What is it then? History. Oh yes. History. Stewed like a mad thing till 4am this morning. Somewhat hampered by the fact you didn't have all your course notes. Ought to have attended more classes. Your Repeal of the Corn Laws is all mixed up with the Austrian Succession.

Who's the hatchet-faced harridan reading out the rules? The upside-down buff-coloured A4 booklet looks at you blankly. It is the key to your future. You stare at it with X-ray eyes, willing it to contain questions on topics you know something about. The invigilator raises her pebble eyes to the impassive countenance of the wall clock and announces, "You may turn over your papers and begin."

The dry rustle of turning pages settles to silence. A bluebottle fuzzes against a window pane. You sneak a desperate glance around. Linda is reading the paper with a half-smile. Julie tucks her hair behind her ears and begins to write. Helen frowns in concentration then scribbles furiously. There is nothing about the Corn Laws or the Austrian Succession on the paper. With a fervour not experienced since you were a child you begin to pray.

WHEN I WAS ELEVEN, the thing I wanted most in the world was a red racing-bike with drop handles. At fourteen I was eventually given a bike as a reward for passing my "Junior" but it was a girly bike with straight handlebars and no gears in a non-street-credible shade of maroon. Even at my youngest and most agile, I was never built for speed, but at least in those days my progress wasn't hampered by heavy traffic, lurking sexual perverts and those terrible pod-like cycling safety helmets that make you look like an alien extra from *Star Trek*.

Besides which, Derry wasn't a great place for a bike. For a start it was all hills and you spent as much time pushing the bike up steep gradients as flying downhill with the brakes firmly applied. A multiplicity of cobbled streets added a tooth-loosening discomfort to the ride. Still, it was liberation of a sort in a social climate that was a lot less dangerous than it is now. I trundled the town and its rural environs, from morning till night, through early teen summers when it never rained. Back then, you had your lungs aerated and your calf-muscles developed, but best of all, you got your first taste of freedom.

Over the hills and far away, nobody could keep tabs on you – so long as you were home in time for your tea – and the mobile phone was a dastardly, invasive nuisance far in the future.

The biggest advantage of a bike was that it allowed you legitimately to hang round boys in a chummy Enid Blyton sort of way – at least initially. The phrase, "the chain's come off my bike", uttered in a tone of pubescent helplessness, was a great catalyst to sudden sexual awareness in much the same way as the broken fan-belt facilitated more mature romances.

I was ill with adoration of a fella I saw cycling to school every morning. Blond hair, drop handlebars, he'd flash by the school bus and on the days he didn't look up, I lost the will to live. Years later I realised it was the bike I was in love with. Soon after, the discovery of high heels and hairspray relegated the bike to the dark of the coal shed where its dimming chromework glimmered at me reproachfully as I lifted a shovelful of slack. To be honest, I was never that nifty on it anyway.

THE FIRST TIME EVER I was asked for my phone number I was fourteen-and-three-quarters. The boy was fair, blue-eyed and

American. In a reckless act of social suicide, I confessed to having neither number nor telephone, at which the azure eyes of my transatlantic Romeo popped with disbelief, and my first romance was blighted in the bud.

It was a further 18 months till my father allowed that the infernal device might have some redeeming features, and the man came to install our social lifeline to the wider world.

Mother was troubled. Our front hall looked suddenly wrong. Out went the solid mahogany hall-stand with the curly brackets and in came a splay-legged "telephone bench" of vastly inferior quality with two drawers for the directory and your gloves and a buttoned velvet cushion to encourage prolonged conversation. Within weeks the traditional flowered wallpaper had been replaced by a smart neutral basket-weave and a mirror with a sunburst border of brushed metal framed the caller in flattering cameo.

Despite the fact that our hall was a perishing wind tunnel with a gale flattening the pile of the carpet from front door to back, I was in teenage heaven. Prolonged use of the new instrument led to my father stamping by, waving the newspaper and shouting that we'd all be in the poorhouse.

Mother answered the phone suspiciously in a tight high voice and suffered selective amnesia depending on the social desirability of the caller.

The whole point of getting a phone in, it was heavily underlined, was not so that people could contact you for reasons of business or pleasure, but in case anything happened. It was certainly not a means of conducting one's social life.

EITHER PUBERTY WAS DELAYED IN THOSE DAYS, or I was a remarkably late developer, but there was little pre-occupation with biological change until at least third year. And of course we were kept blissfully ignorant of the most basic sexual knowledge. Waking in blood-soaked pyjamas at fifteen, I thought I was dying. Periods were "something that'll happen every month from now on", and you were handed the equipment in a furtive sort of way that made you feel unclean and ashamed. It was not a thing to be talked about, but at least I wasn't told, like some of my contemporaries, that menstruation was "a gift from the Blessed Virgin".

THE MISSES VIOLET AND HESTER GALLAGHER, two maiden ladies of impeccable gentility presided over a discreet emporium at the bottom of Great James Street. Word had it that they catered for up to a 44 double "D" cup. The degree of patience and understanding shown by these ladies made their shop a veritable haven for harassed mothers who bundled in their unwilling and unshapely teenage daughters to be fitted and kitted out with the supportive underpinnings of adulthood. With many, it was purely a policy of containment.

Imagine the agony of the great bouncing adolescent taken by Miss Violet behind the beige curtain – the embarrassing removal of outer garments, the revelation of the battleship grey ill-fitting chain store bra at which Miss Violet is carefully not looking. "And what size is the young lady wearing at the moment?" she enquires. Not a tremor greets the muttered and unlikely response. The touch of the tape measure is like clammy linoleum upon the shrinking flesh. The unfortunate and accurate statistics are relayed in a polite murmur to Miss Hester, whose practised eye runs up and down her serried ranks of narrow cardboard boxes – lighting upon the one, the very one, "Though we might need to go up a cup size in this make."

A number of, shall we say, "serviceable looking" models are produced and oh horror, one is personally assisted into them. "Careful – it's not an overcoat you're getting into," smiles Miss Violet. Harness fastened, there is some gentle tuition in adjustment technique (very important, adjustment technique!). This involves leaning well forward whilst performing a discreet ladling motion rather like serving soup carefully into shallow bowls. Well, the whole thing is a mortification from start to finish.

With a final tweak Miss Violet steps back, satisfied. Miss Hester is called for a second opinion. "Nothing like basing life on a firm foundation," jokes the mother nervously. The Misses Gallagher nod approvingly. Yes – it has been an uplifting experience for all concerned.

TODAY THE WORLD IS FULL OF CONTRADICTIONS. Soap operas and reality programmes shown on prime-time television take a vicarious delight in pushing the parameters of taste and decency as far as they can. The later the hour, the more explicit the scene and the real thing is a mere mouse-click away on the internet. However, back in the happy family-friendly Hollywood film business, generously-bosomed leading ladies are having their "embonpoint" digitally reduced for the moral protection of younger cinema-goers.

One way and another we were always being digitally reduced in our youth. Who will ever forget the school film shows of the set works of the English Literature exam curriculum? Any tender moment on screen was hastily obliterated by a swipe of the black bombazine sleeve of a nun's habit, held there till moral danger had passed. We were digitally reduced on another occasion, I recall. We put on an historical play about the six wives of Henry VIII. Costumes were hired at great expense from Mutrie's in Edinburgh. They were padded, boned gowns in rich brocades, authentic in every Tudor detail, including low square necklines. At fourteen or fifteen in those late-developing days we had literally nothing to hide, but we made our stage debut in full royal fig, each incipient bosom decently covered in a dazzling white Irish linen dinner napkin.

By sixteen we'd discovered Littlewoods' lightly padded bra with the circle-stitched cups. The thing was, if anybody collided with you, the cups dented and didn't pop out again – but that's digital enhancement of a different sort.

WE ARE ARGUING OVER SUPPER, my friends and I, about the change in the social climate, the discarding of outmoded codes of behaviour, the disappearance of mimsy bits of etiquette about wearing stockings with formal dress and never choosing the most expensive item on a menu. Our generation has grown up with a healthy contempt for this kind of pretension. Once we discovered that drinking red wine with fish or chicken did not actually lead to instant social death and you could still give a party even if none of the crockery matched, we got dangerously bohemian, cooked big garlicky casseroles, put our elbows fearlessly on the table and dispensed entirely with puddings.

It is on just such an evening we recall with mirth and retrospective blushes our own juvenile *faux pas* and social solecisms. Who does not remember the teenage angst of their first formal dinner? The table an array of cutlery laid out like instruments of torture, with not even the kindly anaesthesia of drink to carry you through; watching under lowered lids what everyone else lifts first, getting it wrong, and the waiter's flourishing substitution of the correct implement so you don't have to eat your steak with a butter-knife, and catching his eye and dying of shame.

The catalogue of culinary pitfalls can be listed alphabetically – tackling artichokes, asparagus, bread (do you break it or cut it?), the disposal of fish bones, fruit stones, peeling a peach at the table. An inadequate response to any of these marks you out as surely as a paper serviette tucked in at the neck in a sea of linen napkins spread over the lap.

The same word has different connotations depending upon the company in which you find yourself. Take the word "picnic" – a childhood treat – eaten in the park or at the beach, its constituents unvarying: tomato sandwiches, Marie biscuits, heavy fruit-cake and a flask of Thermos-tasting tea. But at fourteen, lunch with a Cambridge academic teaches me our version is several ingredients short of a hamper.

She leads us into the garden. "Thought we'd eat alfresco," she announces. Some exotic foreign dish, I suppose. I wonder if I'll like it. From a triumph of Tupperware containers she produces lunch. I am handed a laden plate. "Sadly simple," she apologises, "just quiche, tossed salad, goats cheese and Greek olives."

I look at the plate. A triangle of solidified scrambled egg with bits in it; a palpable hum rises from the chalky chunk of cheese, beside it a small and equally pungent mound of rabbit droppings lies on a bed of mixed leaves glistening with some greasy substance. Is this the salad? Where are the careful quarters of hard-boiled egg, the green hyphens of chopped scallions, the dainty precision of tomatoes tortuously carved into water lilies and tastefully arranged on the compass points of the plate? And where is the Heinz Salad Cream? I am all dismay; the "alfresco", whatever it is, would've been better than this!

Ostentatiously smelling the roses, I tour the garden dropping bits of food down the backs of the buddleia bushes. "Finished already?" she barks. "You must have more!"

A friend once told me of the day he realised he was irredeemably lower-class. Visiting the home of a much better-off school friend, he noticed a large bowl of black grapes on the sideboard. Eyes wide with retrospective astonishment he recalled, "And there was nobody sick!"

TO MY MOTHER the convenience of convenience foods was somehow immoral. If you hadn't slaved over a hot stove for several hours, it wasn't worth eating. In her latter days when I looked after her, she took a notion for porridge. I burned the backsides out of several saucepans before I discovered instant porridge in a sachet. I hid the packet at the back of the cupboard but of course she discovered it and my deception. "Look at the price of that!" she said. "It works out at twelve-and-a-half-pence per serving," I said. "Twelve-and-a-half-pence! Two-and-sixpence! That's half a crown!" she said, scandalised.

We fifty-plussers were nearly the last to receive a thorough grounding in practical cookery, nutrition and sewing, since it was presumed, after a brief period as career women, we'd become wives, mothers and homemakers. But while we sat, heads bent over stitchery or stood by scrubbed wooden tables in calf-length cooks' whites, across the water, Sixties' skirt hems were shooting upwards with the rapidity of roller blinds. Nobody cared whether they were held up by invisible slip-stitch or Sellotape and Cap'n Birdseye was bringing home the first ever catch of frozen fish fingers.

Cookery lessons were fraught because there was no concealing the results of one's own ineptitude. We learned the basic tenets of good plain cooking with its emphasis on conserving vitamins and flavour, fiddling with the food as little as possible and keeping an eye on expense. My weekly triumphs, from First Year rock buns to Fifth Form ragout of beef, were borne home and fed to my father, who valiantly swallowed all with every expression of gustatory delight. My mother never set a tooth in any of it. As an ex-Domestic Science teacher, she knew where it had been!

The weekly cookery session saw us assembled in starched white aprons and a sort of 1920s flapper-style bandeau round the head. I think we might have had protective cuffs too – and woe betide you if you forgot any part of your kit. Under the magisterial tutelage of Mother Gertrude, of whom we were healthily terrified, we graduated by slow degrees from First Year fruit scones to the living horror of the Senior Domestic Science practical exam. This was the "hands on" element of "O" level, presided over by a lady inspector with the reputation of being a tartar. We christened her Hitler's Assistant. We stood staring at the grain of the bleached pine tables with our knees knocking, waiting for the signal to turn over the single sheet of paper upon which was written the names of the two dishes we must prepare. "Ladies," announced Hitler's Assistant, "you have two-and-a-half hours." I turned over my sheet of paper. "Cauliflower au gratin," it said and "lemon meringue pie." Ohgod-ohgod-ohgod! Two places down, the girl who got steak and kidney pudding with a suet crust turned blue around the lips, began to sway and was briskly told to get herself a drink of water. I went to choose my ingredients. The best looking cauliflower was the size of a football. Forty years on I'd know to cut it in quarters for faster cooking. Then, I engaged in a silent wrestling match with Margaret Bradley for possession of the largest pot, which she needed for vegetable soup. I lost the battle and boiled the cauliflower whole in an undersized saucepan out of which it kept bobbing like the blanched brain of some alien creature seeking escape.

Let me disabuse you at the outset of any notion you might have of permitted short-cuts. There weren't any. The white sauce for the cauli was made from scratch – a roux of butter and flour combined, thinned by the gradual addition of milk to a smooth pouring consistency – or in my case a milky whey with grey lumps that had to be sieved out. And all the while, time was galloping by and the lemon meringue pie still not started. Lemon meringue was a stinker to get in an exam. There were so many elements in it to go wrong.

Make a shortcrust pastry case that'll neither shrink nor crack when baked blind. Using fresh lemons and egg yolks create a curd filling to a consistency that will set and not run all over the place when the pie's cut. Separate egg whites and beat with a hand whisk in a scrupulously clean bowl to soft peak stage, knowing that a smear of grease or a single spot of egg yolk will prevent the whites thickening. And do all this under the gimlet eye and po-face of Hitler's Assistant who's writing notes about you. It was a *Master Chef* final, without equipment, filmed in hell.

"Ladies you have ten minutes to clear away and present your dishes." Ohgod-ohgod-ohgod! I must've boiled that cauli for an hour and it was still hard as the hob of hell. I drained it, heeled it into a tureen and emptied the white sauce over its head, picking the largest lumps out with a teaspoon. Then I grated cheese and a generous portion of bloody thumb over the top and attempted to brown it under the grill. It wouldn't fit, so I had to hold it under till the backs of my hands blistered.

Miraculously the lemon meringue looked alright. The pastry case had broken but I'd soldered it together with the gluey lemon curd and the meringue was perfect, glistening with glace cherries and angelica. I was always good at disguising disasters. As for the girl who got steak and kidney pudding with a suet crust? Her presentation looked like a face full of acne, but we all passed.

> "GIVE A MAN A FREE HAND
> AND HE'LL TRY TO PUT IT ALL OVER YOU"
> *Mae West*

THE FIRST FLUSH OF EXAM FEVER IS UPON US. I was talking to a young friend deep in the despairing throes of last minute revision for "A" level English. I smiled sympathetically, remembering the gallons of midnight oil I'd burned myself, wrestling with Jane Austen, Shakespearean comedy and the Lakeland Poets. "What are the set books this year?" I idly enquired. "Oh, Tennessee Williams, D. H. Lawrence and James Joyce," she said. I was somewhat taken aback. Strong stuff for impressionable young minds! Lord, how times have changed, I thought, ruefully surveying the yawning gap between her schooldays and mine. It speaks volumes for the changing moral climate in education. They were very hot on "morality" in my day, and such authors as Tennessee Williams, D. H. Lawrence and James Joyce came firmly under the heading of "dirty books".

It seems like only yesterday we sat choking with giggles as Miss Johnston attempted to skim lightly over the ruder verses of Chaucer, none of us daring to ask enlightenment about the naughty bits.

Our musical studies of Tchaikovsky (another moral suspect!) were illustrated by ballerinas in tutus, carefully pencilled in by Sister Veronica to a modest ankle length. Whatever knowledge they intended us to gain, none of it was to be carnal they made sure!

OH WHAT AN INNOCENT AND NAÏVE BUNCH WE WERE – but it didn't

save us from wholesale condemnation as moral reprobates of the lowest kind. We were declared beyond redemption on the famous occasion we absconded, mitched from school en masse – the entire Sixth Form, save one – on the day before the A-level English exam.

Unobtrusively we slunk off the buses, scrambled over the school wall (to the detriment of our black stockings) and ran in a semi-crouch through the thickets of rhododendron and laurel down to the river. It was a bleak, overcast morning with a bitter wind. The turgid waters of the Foyle lapped over the muddy stones and the smell of sewage effluent would've felled horses.

Somewhat inexpertly we built a fire and daringly despatched the boldest of our number to the nearby village of Muff with instructions to buy ten cigarettes – though a quick whip-round had produced a halfpenny short of the required amount. Having taken turns to stand in the putative footprints of St Columba incised in a rock, there wasn't a lot else to do. We shivered miserably, ate jam sandwiches and tried to pretend we were enjoying ourselves, each of us privily thinking it wasn't a bit like the Chalet School adventure stories.

The hours dragged by. It was almost a relief when divine retribution arrived in the shape of the black habit and immaculately starched veil of the vice-principal. Margaret Barr had broken under interrogation and sung like a canary. Like prisoners of war we were frog-marched schoolwards where, before the whole community, all 22 of us were ceremonially stripped of our badges of rank, head girl, prefects and all – and summarily expelled.

Expelled, but not dismissed. Oh no – we were immured in a small attic classroom until 8.30 pm that evening and fed prison rations of weak tea and cream cookies. In chastened silence we wrote thousands of lines and listened to a lengthy diatribe about our wickedness and moral turpitude, while the caretaker bicycled round 22 sets of bemused parents to inform them of our grievous sin. Funnily enough, I have no recollection of the ensuing row at home. I dare say it's overshadowed in my memory by subsequent and worse ones about make-up, bad companions and hot-pants – for having set foot upon the primrose path to perdition, I went steadily down it at an ever increasing trot.

Of that 22 miscreants implicated on that day, four became staff members of the old school, where they were held in terrified respect by a new generation.

And I saw Margaret Barr the other day with her two adolescent daughters. The elder is studying Tennessee Williams, D. H. Lawrence and James Joyce for "A" level English – which must be a source of some distress to her poor mother!

TO THE MODERN GENERATION the devil looks a bit like Jack Nicholson and is just about as innocuous. These young ones reared on a liberal theology based on "sharing love", with sin relegated to the back-burner, have no idea of the prominent position the devil held in our childhood lives. The devil was a lively and living part of our religious upbringing, for ignoring the countless other billions in the world, he kept a perpetual, specific and exclusive watch on you.

Like all young people of my generation, I was fascinated and terrified in equal measure by the devil and his dominion; the lake of fire that burns eternally yet does not consume, and me in it for nicking sixpence off the hall table! Even at a tender age I was remarkably well-informed. By eight I could've done *Mastermind* with Beelzebub as my specialist subject. I found the story enthralling – Lucifer the brightest angel in Heaven before he fell, a victim of his own intellectual arrogance. Well, I didn't know the bit about the intellectual arrogance then, but I've often thought since it was rather a pointed warning to people who reason themselves out of their religion.

Henceforward, apart from a bit of part-time torturing with the trident, Satan was fated to hover at my left shoulder, a source of constant temptation to wrongdoing.

People with no history of religious belief might balk at the image of a child weighed down by both guardian angel (standard issue) and an evil spirit, one on each shoulder, engaged in a perpetual brawl for possession of his will. No wonder we kept our heads down and envied people who only had a chip on their shoulder!

The battle of good and evil was waged daily with conflicting messages whispered in the ear. When you did the right thing, your guardian angel dealt the devil a severe clout with a brawny wing. The devil leapt hissing away, muttering, "I'll be back!" If, however, you succumbed to sin, the devil danced with delight and your angel's light dimmed, he wept and his wings went limp.

Things became more complicated once puberty reared its acned head, and hearts, hormones and various other things began to throb. Now the full import of phrases such as "the devil roams about like a ravening lion seeking whom he might devour" was borne in upon us. Armed with the protective literature of Catholic Truth Society pamphlets, we embarked upon a tentative and fearful sexuality. The pamphlet quaintly entitled "Keeping Company" inferred that on a date with a boy there was always a threesome – you, the boy and the devil. It gave crisp directives for keeping both at arm's length. When dancing, for example, it advised, "Leave enough space for the Holy Spirit to slip between you." What with the guardian angel on one shoulder, the devil on the other and the Holy Spirit between, this dance floor was getting kinda crowded!

One was constrained, too, to remember the devil always presented himself in attractive guise. So grew the urban myth of the handsome fellow with the cloven hoof reputedly seen in every ballroom in Ireland. He must've been knackered, dancing every night of the week! It was a well-known fact that guardian angels didn't like dances, or pubs, or the pictures, walks out the Prehen Road, St Columb's Park (particularly down by the railway line), secluded lanes, sand dunes or parked cars. It was just about safe enough to walk up and down Strand Road in broad daylight.

Of course, if you did drift a bit, there was always the Annual Retreat to haul you back from the brink of damnation – a week of spiritual retrenchment, repentance and shriving. A succession of missionary priests took time out from converting pilgrim Africa to come to godless Derry and draw lost sheep back to the fold. They worked in pairs usually, like Special Branch detectives, a lovely wee priest and a grand big priest, one sincere and low-key, the other a showman. Both spoke in impenetrable brogues in either a magisterial bass or a high nasal whine. It was pure theatre. The grand big priest swept onto the altar, removed his cape with a twirl and fixed us with gimlet eye.

The substance of their sermons has been well documented by better writers than I. It was years before the negativity of their approach dawned on me, with its emphasis on the sins of the flesh, sacrifice, duty and punishment. It portrayed a God of justice rather than compassion and of love, joy and human fulfilment. Pious, scrupulous people who led blameless lives were told, and believed, they were sinners. As for the clerical attitude to women and their role in the home, society and the church – well, don't start me!

But that was then, this is now. There's been an explosion of evil in the world with new cruelties and horrors perpetrated every living minute. Whether you choose to ascribe these to the selfish bloody-mindedness of human nature or the work of the devil and his agents, is immaterial. Satan's days as a serpent in the garden are over. Today the devil is on the internet. Whether you believe in a biblical Beelzebub or you don't, may you never find out – in this world, or the next!

DRIVING INTO PORTRUSH, one feels still a frisson of nervous anticipation as the familiar silhouette of the big wheel rears up on the left and the flickering neon sign announcing "Barry's Amusements" comes into view. Without doubt, at a certain age and stage, the main attraction of Portrush wasn't the beach, the promenade or the Knickerbocker Glories, but the kaleidoscopic colour, pulsating energy and braying music of the funfair.

It happens twice in your life perhaps, the first time governed by six-year-old timidity that has you clinging terrified to the candy-twist pole as the brightly-painted gallopers with their flared nostrils and flying manes rise and fall and revolve forever. Mammy waves and applauds every circuit of the carousel and tells you how brave you are when the music and motion slow to a standstill and the man lifts you down jelly-legged, just as you're beginning to enjoy it. The serial terror continues with a bird's eye view of mum's anxious face from the lonely top of the towering helter-skelter and the corkscrew journey downwards, seated on the scrubbing brush bristles of a coconut mat, sped on your way by someone else's feet in the small of your back. There follows a tooth-jarring session on the dodgem cars, all except yours driven by psychotic child-haters. The remark "We'll give the ghost-train a miss this time" is murmured over your head and you're glad of solid ground under your sandaled feet and candy-floss stuck to your face by an errant breeze.

At 16, in the dusk of a summer's evening, Barry's is scary in a different way. Bathed in an ever-changing rainbow of light and the blare of fairground music, bolstered by the bold glamour of turquoise eye shadow and the safety of numbers, our budget is limited, but the world's our oyster.

Admiring eyes are on the teenage roustabouts, most of them students doing holiday jobs. They leap sure-footedly about the moving rides, collecting money in a busman's bag, ostentatiously checking the safety bars and showing off for our benefit. Our collective bravery knows no bounds. We spin and scream on the Waltzer to such good effect, its handsome curly-headed attendant gives us an extra two minutes, but the rollercoaster ride reduces us to trembling wusses and we have to be helped off individually by the blond Germanic-looking boy, who turns out to be from Maghera. A smell of hot metal and phosphorescence draws us to the dodgems (never called anything but "the bumpers" in Portrush). We tight-squeeze into the battered cars with their bulky rubber buffers. The rods connecting us to the overhead metal mesh begin to spark and, in a mass exhibition of traditional Norn Irish gallantry, every young fellow on the floor drives purposefully towards us for a head-on collision.

Time and money drain rapidly away. There's just enough left of both for a trip on the ghost-train before dashing for the real train and the journey home. Crouching self-consciously in ridiculously small wagons, our 16-year-old sophistication is suddenly dented by such juvenile indulgence. One decides she's "too scared" to go, but is persuaded by the brown-eyed boy with a big smile who offers to sit beside her. The silly little train gathers momentum. We hit the black wooden doors with fearful blatter and plunge into pitch, wailing darkness and cold. A greenish glow illuminates rubber webs and fabric ghosts; toothless witches loom, skeletons rattle and dance, and skulls leer at us to a squealing soundtrack. We roar out again into fluorescent brightness, white as sheets, except for one who's suspiciously pink and her lipstick's vanished.

For my generation Barry's tawdry magic was part of childhood and adolescent summers. Whatever it became in latter years, we remember with affection its louche atmosphere its grubby glamour and air of contained danger. Innocence lasted longer then…

WE POST-WAR BABY-BOOMERS have always regarded the accident of our birth as fortuitous timing. Born into an era of forward-looking legislation, it guaranteed us free milk, immunisation, decent schooling and growing prosperity, free of the shadow of conflict. Little did we realise we were on the cusp of a social change so rapid, so far-reaching that, in the space of 15 years, the pattern of our lives would alter radically. In our dark brown draught-ridden homes, carpet replaced linoleum, wallpaper and textiles erupted in a riot of pattern and fashion forsook Forties angularity for the Fifties look of the full-blown rose. For the first time in history, "design" was within the grasp of the common man.

Wartime technology transmuted into labour-saving devices and a raft of feel-good films from across the Atlantic fed our new hunger. No serious study has ever been made of the sociological effect of Doris Day movies on a generation of scullery-bound housewives, who watched her swan about a palatial kitchen in a lacy negligee, juicing oranges and cracking eggs in extravagant half dozens, straight from a seven-foot fridge-freezer. Guests were offered alcoholic drinks, olives and pretzels. A far cry from tea, egg and onion sandwiches and a wedge of Victoria sponge. We felt we had a way to go.

But the most pervasive post-war influence was the music. My friend Una, aged twelve, toured Stateside with the Little Gaelic

Singers and came back with a goggle-eyed account of being on the same Ed Sullivan show as a raw-boned young singer suffering severe involuntary spasm of the lower limbs and mumbling incoherently about somebody being "nuthin' but a hound dawg". Bill Haley's oiled kiss-curl had already wrought havoc, not least upon the sensibilities of the City Fathers, who foresaw rock 'n' roll as the precursor of a moral apocalypse. "This must stop!" they said. Too late! We were all tuned to Radio Luxembourg and the musical genie was out of the bottle. On Saturdays we haunted Phillips' music shop where there was a listening booth. One or two coffee bars installed a juke-box. The Decca Dansette was on everyone's Christmas list and the 45 rpm single was the only legitimate teen currency.

BURIED IN THE TELEVISION SCHEDULES of a wet summer Sunday was a little documentary called *Goodnight, Safe Home, God Bless – A History of Irish Showbands*. What a programme! It sang, it spoke, it smelt of a rite of passage that was part of all our youth.

Every element was there – the whiff of perspiration, the quiff of brilliantined hair, the metallic bray of saxophones wielded in a vigorous nodding routine that brought its own round of applause. And in the memory, the apprehension of an adolescent launched into a sea of seasoned socialites, none too sure how to stay afloat.

Each of us has our own Ballroom of Romance. This was mine.

Borderland is a country ballroom which at the height of the showband era brings dancers from all over the province. It is strictly run, serves nothing stronger than tea and the ubiquitous "minerals", but to my parents it is a pit of perdition and I'm not going and that's all about it. On my seventeenth birthday, they relent.

I stand gazing at my reflection in the spotted cloakroom mirror, striving to look 21. The door slams open to admit a gaggle of older girls – "regulars", who, rumour has it, are hot stuff on the floor, breaking with impunity the "no jiving" rule. In a flurry of net petticoats and cheap scent they commandeer the mirrors, smoking and shrieking, swigging from the quarter bottle in their handbags, slinking their hands down over their aggressively pointed bosoms and shamelessly adjusting the threepenny bit serving as suspender button for their stockings.

Later, one will see them in the slow dances, draped around a partner, a ten packet of Park Drive and a box of matches clutched firmly in the hand about his neck, jaws working rhythmically on a cud of chewing gum and hard eyes over his shoulder, ever alert for a likelier mark. They are creatures of impossible glamour and dance every dance.

The boy who asks me is quite good-looking but has damp hands. There rises off him the musty odour of a good suit worn one day in seven and stored the other six in camphor balls. His footwork, like my own, is far from dexterous. "Whaddya think of the band?" he mouths over the din.

The gleam of their electric blue stage suits is reflected in the greasy sheen of their complexions, their nylon shirts adhesively transparent with sweat as they work themselves into an apoplectic frenzy persuading us to "do the Hucklebuck". The girl vocalist's plump midriff is straining through her crocheted mini-dress like semolina escaping from a string bag. The floor is a leaping lunatic mass. There was more room in the black hole of Calcutta.

"Will ye come up for a mineral?" he asks. The fizzy orange is served at room temperature. Near the door, knots of young men come and go regularly, returning, faces ruddier each time, from the Squealin' Pig pub next door.

"What do you do?" he asks.

"Actually, I'm still at school," I reply, guilelessly.

"Oh," he says. "Excuse me, I'm just going to the toilet."

I nurse the warm orange for a long time. The band breaks into "Save the Last Dance for Me". The boys at the door head purposefully, if unsteadily, for the nearest passable-looking female.

From my vantage point on the balcony, the crowd revolves slowly, like stirred porridge, upturned faces livid with leprous spots of pink, purple and green light.

On the far side I suddenly see him. He's dancing with a blonde. She has a ten packet of Park Drive and a box of matches clutched firmly in the hand about his neck.

## "TO BE AN ADULT IS TO BE ALONE"
### *Jean Rostand*

I WAS NEVER AWARE OF THE FACT that I had a privileged childhood. Not in the material sense, though I wanted for nothing, but I was carefully shielded from any of the more unpleasant aspects of life. I often wonder if this was deliberate, or merely a side effect of living in a houseful of adults where certain topics were not discussed "in front of the child". I remember being sent out of the room if scenes of a mildly erotic nature appeared on television. Since this was 1956, they couldn't have been any too startling.

Scrupulous care was taken over every aspect of my development, from piano lessons to the purchase of the *Children's Encyclopaedia*. My father taught me in primary school, my elder sister taught me in grammar school – everywhere I went there was somebody belonging to me. I walked the edge of the deep dark pit of life, my hand securely held. And did I appreciate it? Not a bit! Like a recalcitrant donkey, it took the whole family with the judicious use of carrots and sticks to pull me through school. When I was accepted for teacher training there was an audible sigh of relief. Of course I was going to be a teacher – everybody else in the family was.

Thus I was dispatched to college in a very good quality tweed suit with the luggage of my short life – a holdall of small successes and smaller disappointments and a very large vanity-case full of quaking insecurities. Of real life I knew nothing and understood even less. Like the young Queen Victoria before her accession, I had never been alone in my life.

"This is yours," said the second-year student. Anaesthetised by horror, I surveyed my six-by-six-foot cubicle which contained an iron-framed bed, a clothes cupboard, a basin and a jug. "Number 64," she intoned flatly. The salmon pink curtains screening it from the other 63 inhabitants of the dormitory didn't quite meet. I sat down in my cell, sick with revulsion.

The evening passed in a bafflement of bells and bed-making and ended in mugs of warm milk and coconut snowballs which lay like lead shot in the pit of my stomach. I rebuffed all overtures of friendship, adopting an air of snooty disparagement. I heard somebody say that we would be let home in six weeks time for Hallowe'en. My veins turned to ice. I made wild resolutions – to find somebody in authority, take them by the elbow and say, "Look, there's been a mistake. I've changed my mind. I don't really want to be a teacher. I can just manage the last train if you'll be good enough to get me a taxi."

The ubiquitous bell clanged again. Bedtime. In the September twilight the dusty trees fronting the Falls Road muffled the sound of traffic. Ordinary people going to ordinary places. I leaned out of the window as far as I could, desperate to hold on to normality.

Behind me 63 young women aged eighteen and over chattered happily and obediently donned their night attire. It was 9.30pm and home was as inaccessible as Outer Mongolia. At exactly 10pm the lights went out. We were left in Stygian darkness. I had never slept without a light of some kind.

This was the last straw. Every shred of dignity deserted me and I rolled on the lumpy bed in an agony of silent grief, biting the pillow. When the first paroxysm had passed, I made up my mind. I'd sneak down and ring home. "Daddy will send for me in the morning," I thought, "no matter what Mammy says." My scalded eyes watched the tiny hands of the brand new travel alarm clock creep round snail-slow.

At 12.10am I felt my way through alien territory. All around me the steady slumber of healthy well-adjusted young women – these crass and unfeeling creatures. Down and down I went, teeth chattering with terror and hiccupping with misery in the dark.

The dim security light of the back hall barely extended to the phone booth. I dialled the number by touch, my heart suddenly light. Daddy wouldn't make me stay in this awful place another day. Far away, a telephone rang and rang. Then "Hello," said my father's familiar bass voice. "Hello? Hello? Who is this, please?"

I quietly replaced the receiver and stumbled back upstairs to face the Spartan contours of the bed in cubicle 64 and the long nightmare of becoming an adult.

I BOUGHT A LARGE CALENDAR at rock-bottom price, since there were only three months of the year left, and religiously ticked off each day. I developed small elaborate rituals to measure time, and discovered a bitter affinity with the early works of Edna O'Brien, who truly understood suffering. And all the time, waking and sleeping, in a locked box in the pit of my stomach, lay the feel and smell and the image of home.

And then suddenly it is Friday, 29 October, and the train is pulling out of York Street Station. I sit with my back to the engine watching the purplish contours of Napoleon's Nose recede. My chest is tight with excitement. In two hours and ten minutes I'll be home.

Halfway there, the tackety-tack of the train wheels change key as we rattle metallically west across the River Bann. The Israelites could not have passed through the Red Sea with more relief. The landscape becomes familiar – the stepped face of Benevenagh Head looming out of the mist, the cold bleached strand at Downhill, the dun-coloured sloblands of the Foyle Estuary and then the spires of the two cathedrals. Look up, look up to the left. There's my street, my house, my own bedroom window, and in it a waiting hand wags a yellow duster. Daddy's at the station, his speckled tweed overcoat smelling of school and Gallaher's Blues. "My God, you're failed off the face of the earth," he says, hugging tight.

Two minutes from home. Up the street, inhaling the intoxicating whiff from the bonded warehouse. The leaded-glass canopy of the

Midland Cinema declares "continuous performance from 2pm". Past the Bat and Ball Bar and Bridie's confectionery and tobacconist – with Bridie in the window nodding and smiling and arranging her presentation boxes – past the scabby railing of the old church. Nearly there now. Two steps, two white pillars, a black front door, the brasses bloomed with damp. The door opens. I'm enveloped in an aroma of hot soup, Mansion Polish and Parozone bleach. "Sacred Heart, you're like a skeleton," my mother says. "Excuse me," I say, "I'll just take my case upstairs."

Up in the attic, the little blue room looks cramped and fussy. I feel a jag of embarrassment looking at my pin-up posters and the grubby rag-doll on the bed. I open the wardrobe to hang up my clothes. Inside the door is a full length mirror. For the first time in seven weeks, I see all of myself. A grown woman looks back at me.

THE TERM "STUDENT" has always been synonymous with "poor". Part of the rite of passage from adolescence to adulthood is to be far from home in cheap, sordid digs, eating irregularly and blowing what you have on a ticket for a pop concert or a second-hand leather jacket. Years later, you remember with fond nostalgia the all-night cramming sessions for exams, the prodigious celebratory hangovers and surviving an entire weekend on a single packet of custard creams. But it was not good fun at the time.

A brief and generous window in the government's wallet opened during the Sixties when student grants, based on a parental means test, were available. I was granted the princely sum of £106 per term and the first thing I did was buy an Italian leather handbag for three guineas in Robinson and Cleaver. I still have it.

Liberated into society in our second year, five of us shared a freezing flat. We lived on porridge, coffee and Dolores Ward's mother's Dundee cake and kept the saucepans in the wardrobe. Instead of buying a bag of coal, we'd go to the pictures to keep warm, then get into bed with our coats on. Every so often, somebody's dad would have to be rung up and the advent of a brown envelope with a white fiver in it literally saved our bacon. We were heedless and carefree and owed nothing to anybody but a gratitude that was seldom expressed. Sense and sensibility would come time enough, with graduation and a real job. In the meantime, we bought Etam out of pink gingham underwear the minute it opened its doors.

IT WAS OUR GOOD FORTUNE to be college students in the Sixties – an era in which even the sedate Northern Ireland skirt crept shyly above the knee and the favoured student look was the unrelieved black with curtains of hair like Juliette Greco, or the bright and brief op-art attire of the early Lulu period. The college principal patrolled the aisles of the First Year examination hall noting the names of girls whose skirts were too tight or too short. I'm proud to say I headed the list on both counts.

Ironically, the two items of clothing which could've solved the problem were expressly forbidden. Opaque black tights could not and would not be countenanced. They drew attention to the lower limbs, would inflame young men's passions and, besides, were exclusively the province of showgirls and streetwalkers. Trousers, quaintly referred to as "slacks", were inappropriately masculine. They silhouetted the figure in a manner that might prove detrimental to male chastity and probably lead to outbreaks of gross beastliness. In either garb, we were walking occasions of sin.

Meanwhile, the most foolhardy of us were flaunting ourselves around Belfast in trousers as closely fitting as two coats of matt paint, ruthlessly and illicitly tapered on a Home Economics department's sewing machine, or stalking the streets, our liquorice-black legs attracting lascivious glances and maddening the entire male population.

All of this was achieved at considerable personal risk since we had to smuggle the offending garments out of college in a brown paper bag, change into them in the cramped confines of a coffee-bar toilet and, like Cinderella, change again before skulking back in civil tweed.

Nothing could be more awkwardly designed than tights and trousers for getting into or out of in a small space whose surfaces were hygienically suspect. An apocryphal tale is told of a resident second year who, stripped to her underwear in an unlit phone box, was interrupted by a policeman. The situation being explained, he understood perfectly and drove her back to college in a police car, in her modest grey flannel skirt.

These being the halcyon days before the Troubles, we shopped on the Shankill on Saturday mornings because we happened to live at the top of it, beside the Ardoyne shops. We were almost the last students to enjoy a "normal" student life in Belfast.

Teaching practice was a nightmare. My first experience was a large class of infants in St Mary's Primary School, Divis Street. To complicate matters, the class teacher was an ex-girlfriend of my brother. You can imagine with what warmth she welcomed me. Compounding the felony further was the daily playground flak I took from the big boys at the Christian Brothers' school across the road whose English teacher I was going out with. "Hi, Cilla!" they'd shout through the railings at my modish Vidal Sassoon bob. Subsequent postings were more comfortable, except for a gloomy school in the incongruously named Sunnyside Street, which signally failed to appreciate my talent or expertise. I shook its dust off my stiletto heels within a week and begged college for a transfer.

The year's residency rolled relentlessly on, the only frisson of excitement when a young and good-looking Father Tom Toner was appointed student chaplain. Student attendance at morning Mass leapt dramatically.

Like all educational establishments, St Mary's had its fair share of eccentrics. There was a west-of-Ireland biology lecturer too shy to raise his eyes in class lest the effect of our combined female pulchritude drive him insane. That was our theory anyway. There was Paddy O'Neill, senior Geography lecturer, who arrived from running a very tough boys' school to teach the flower of Norn Irish Catholic womanhood. He called us by our surnames, threw things at us if our eyes strayed in the course of his teaching and, if our answers weren't satisfactory, he showed us the door with the recommendation that we take up bell-ringing or horse-shoeing. He was an appalling chauvinist, but we adored him and worked our socks off for him.

Miss Mona Kearney was a different kettle of fish. She taught cookery, nutrition and needlework, all intrinsic elements of "Infant Education", as it was known then. Always impeccably groomed, she entered the room, took off her tailored jacket with a flourish and hung it over the back of a chair, its silk lining and Frederick Starke label clearly visible. She was an absolute tyrant who found fault with everything. Pathologically incapable of doing anything till the last minute, I fell badly behind with my practical needlework and enlisted my mother, a trained Domestic Science teacher to help out with my book of stitchery specimens. "Unpick! Unpick!" directed Miss Kearney, pointing a manicured nail at one after another. My mother threatened to come up to Belfast and throttle her.

Submissions for our final exams included a rag-doll constructed from scratch. Ever ambitious, I decided to make mine in the persona of Captain James Hook, the villain of *Peter Pan*. I consulted costume books and bought velvet, brocade, lace and fake hair. I cut and sewed and stuffed for days, sitting up all night to hand-stitch his fine leather top-boots. Hollow-eyed, with punctured and bloody fingers, I presented my masterpiece for her critical appraisal. "That looks a bit thrown together," she said.

Some years later I went back as a mature student on a Nursery Education course. Linking her arm in mine she proudly showed off her modernised facilities and confided that "the calibre of student these days is vastly inferior to your time".

I OFTEN SAY THE MERCY NUNS gave me my educational grounding but the Dominicans finished me off. The ethos of St Mary's Training College was geared to producing Catholic lady teachers. And indeed they did. Whether we were trained for what we were about to face in the rapidly-changing world of the late Sixties, and an even more rapidly-changing climate of approach in education, is another thing altogether. Suffice to say, what they fostered was a sense of vocation, of dedication and duty to the children in our care and a scrupulous sense of doing our best by each child. It was an archaic institution, but the values it taught have never left me. Graduating in 1966, I went back in '72 as a mature student to discover they'd let male students in and ruined the place entirely.

I returned again in 2005 to do some creative writing classes with the students and, turning in at the front gate, raised my eyes to see the shade of Mother Ailbe stop in her perambulations across the Nuns Corridor, peer through the big plate glass windows and say, "Who is that red-haired student lowering the tone of the place by walking hand-in-hand with a young man? Send her to me in the Blue Parlour immediately!"

I'M A LATE STARTER in the holiday job stakes. I only ever have one. My college mate Delia has washed dishes, picked raspberries and canned peas. She also looks responsible, so my mother grudgingly consents to let me go to London in her charge on condition that I ring home every day and write twice a week. "Mother, I'm twenty years old!" I protest. She dismisses this irrelevance with pursed lips. "You never know," she says darkly.

Delia and I disembark at Heathrow and look around. With one accord we head for the airport shop, buy a packet of needles, a spool of thread and repair to the Ladies. We emerge ten minutes later, our hemlines a full six inches shorter, ready for anything. It is the summer of 1966. Swinging London is pulsating with people. The mini-skirt has reached danger height and World Cup football tickets are quadrupling in price daily. We find digs in the bosky environs of Cricklewood and employment in a distinctly upmarket establishment at Marble Arch which sells continental patisserie and hand-made chocolates. I dutifully report back to Head Office. Mother is mollified, a "nice" job and so central. What opportunities for the theatre, art galleries, museums! I forbear to tell her that a ten-hour day plus travelling time leaves us fit for nothing but a crawl back to Cricklewood and collapse. However, they do feed us and every Friday put into our calloused little hands the princely sum of eleven pounds, seventeen shillings and sixpence.

Rules are few. You can eat whatever you like so long as you don't chew in the customers' faces. Within two days I am cured forever of my addiction to coffee creams. One's counter display is to be at all times complete. This is a full-time occupation since people simply reach over the glass panels and help themselves. "Just tasting," they trill, and walk away.

The art of selling hand-made chocolates is not an easy one. Under the customer's beady eye you have to make up the box, put in the liners, dividers and corrugated papers, fill it up with their choice of centres using a dinky pair of silver tongs, then tie up the completed selection with thin gold string. The whole lengthy process is beset with pitfalls for the cack-handed. I end the first day ankle deep in strawberry fondant with my till returns hopelessly wrong.

Our clientele are very definitely drawn from the upper income bracket. Guests at the hotel next door pop in for "presentation boxes", bouquets or gift-wrapped gateaux. Occasionally some common ignoramus presents himself at the counter requesting a sixpenny bar of Cadbury's. "Sorry sir," we sneer pityingly, "we only stock French or Swiss at half a crown."

So the days go by, and I become adept at flourishing my tongs, coping with my "corrugateds" and frittering away my eleven pounds, seventeen shillings and sixpence, less rent, in Carnaby Street boutiques. Once mother realises that I am too perpetually exhausted to fall into moral danger, she relaxes. Too soon!

One morning I am called back from a tea-break. A Brazilian gentleman wants to buy chocolates. He has no English but a little French. Could I help? Could I what?! He is about forty-five and looks exactly like Rossano Brazzi in *South Pacific*. Phwoar! He comes every morning at the same time. While I make up his two-pound box he goes to the flower shop for a single red rose which he presents to me with a bow. From the distant ranks of rum babas, guardian angel Delia glares ferociously at this touching tableau. Back home, mother's novena leaflets flutter in an invisible breeze. "I have 'teekets' for the World Cup semi-final," he says one morning. "Perhaps you would do me the honour?" Delia stands, arms akimbo, eyes glittering dangerously behind the Black Forest gateaux. "I'm sorry," I say

modestly, lowering my double set of false eyelashes. "It's impossible."
He shrugs charmingly, in that inimitable foreign way. I tell Delia.
"How dare he? – the – the – the – philanderer!" she says indignantly.
"Him and his 'teekets'! He's probably a white slaver. You'll end up in
a packing case in Argentina!" she splutters with a fine disregard for
geography. "I'm going to ring your mother!"

Something tells me when he subsequently invites me to the
World Cup Final that I should invent a large, violent husband and
two permanently ailing children, and I should not mention it at all
to Delia.

I often think with regret of the only holiday adventure I nearly
had. I'll never know now whether I might have had an alternative
career dancing in a feather head-dress in a nightclub in Rio. Just as
well really, since the outstanding legacy of the holiday job was a large
and throbbing varicose vein!

IF EVER ANYTHING PROVED that what goes around comes around, it's
the current debate about what is, or is not, "cool". I remember "cool"
from the first time round when it meant original, authentic, ground-
breaking and, well, cool. Today's "cool" is only a term for short-lived
fashion. To be perfectly honest, "Derry cool" was a couple of degrees
warmer than our cosmopolitan counterparts. While West Coast USA
chilled out into laid-back bohemianism and Swinging London
swung to the hectic beat of a happening metronome, we in the
Maiden City merely hoisted our hemlines a demure distance and
persuaded single males into velvet flares and Cuban heels. There was
an extraordinary amount of hair on both sexes, mostly parted in the
middle – and that basically was it. Frankly, we were a couple of years
behind the zeitgeist, few of us had experience of mood-altering
substances and anyway, our mothers didn't allow us to stay out all
night. It was all a bit Babycham really, till the last reverberations of
the Sixties youthquake rippled outwards and finally reached our
stagnant little backwater.

Since there was so little of it about, we were deeply pragmatic in
what we considered "cool". If a fella had a car, even if it was his dad's

five-year-old Hillman Minx, he was cool. If he had a sports car, no matter how clapped out, it made little difference if he had the personality of a piece of ectoplasm and a face like a busted cushion, he was Simon Dee. A motorbike was nearly as good because then you could pretend to be Marianne Faithfull on the pillion.

Girls were extraordinarily girly. On a Saturday night you ironed your hair under a sheet of brown paper, stuck on two sets of false lashes and struggled into a new doll-sized dress from "She" boutique in Pump Street. The overall look was Pan's People crossed with a shop dummy.

It was seriously uncool to chatter. We cultivated an attitude, a remote detachment that we fondly thought of as enigmatic but was frequently mistaken by our elders for a vacant stare. It was counter-productive actually, since the most extraordinarily stupid but beautiful girls got off with the best looking fellas, and we intellectual wallflowers were left to blush unseen.

The concept of cool changed depending on whose company you were in. College cool was jazz: Sidney Bechet, Chris Barber, Humphrey Lyttleton, with Charlie Parker and Dave Brubeck for those too sophisticated to need recognisable tunes. To reveal your secret passion for bubblegum pop-viz Hermann's Hermits would've been social death.

Cool uniform was head-to-foot black, accessorised by a thick and obscure paperback, usually unread. Frothy coffee was the beverage of choice – a melamine cup seven-eighths full of vile brown suds. We aspired to the pale, studied nonchalance of Juliette Greco but more frequently attained the image of Morticia Addams.

"Cool" was then, as it isn't really now, about the crowd you ran about with, the places you went, the daft and irresponsible things you did. It was about the flexing of decision-making muscles, about autonomy and feeling the centre of your own universe, when to be young was heaven.

"TO TEACH IS TO LEARN"
*Japanese Proverb*

THE FIRST OF SEPTEMBER marks the real beginning of most people's new year. There's a general air of tidying away the languorous days of summer along with the holiday tee-shirts and cultivating a brisk autumnal energy. Like falling leaves, through the letter-box come brochures, prospectuses and programmes for those bent on self-improvement. Schools are back and the streets awash with the twice-daily tide of the uniformed and uninformed young. Normal service has been resumed.

However it's all a bit stressful for the novice. There'll be a lot of exhausted young people recovering from the new beginning they've just made and realising, however dimly, that it was merely the start of a process that stretches into the foreseeable future.

Sign of the times – an ex-colleague tells of being approached by an eloquent four-year-old at 10am on the first day of term. "Hi," he said, "gwon ring me mammy on 'er mobile an' tell 'er tae come 'n git me. Ah doan like it."

A vast amount of sympathy is expended on school starters. Our hearts are sore, our eyes moisten as we witness the annual sacrifice of parents delivering their little ones and watch this year's quota of mixed infants disappear into the great maw of the beast called Education. Almost as emotionally affecting is the experience endured by our pre-pubescent eleven-year-olds, separated from their friends, crouched inside their oversized blazers, confused by bells, lost in corridors, terrorised by seniors, bewildered by a plethora of subjects and an antipathy of teachers. This is the initiation rite known as "transferring to big school".

There is, however, one other group to whom my heart goes out, whose trauma is possibly worse and longer lasting. Each September, a flush of newly-qualified teachers walk into their own new classrooms, their own new classes and the full autonomy of being a real and responsible teacher. No more the student practising the craft for three or four lessons a day with the class teacher comfortingly in the background, ready to quell trouble at a glance, help out with group work and step in when that ill-thought-out lesson on fractions goes down the tubes. "You're on your own now, Sunshine!" Do you remember the day you passed your driving test and went for a wee celebratory spin? Halfway down the road you realised for the first time you were totally and completely alone and in charge of the car? It is at once as heady and terrifying to find yourself suddenly "Miss" or "Sir", with thirty-odd pairs of eyes looking expectantly at you, the Fount of Wisdom, dependent upon you, the Source of All Knowledge. For some new teachers, it's a daily "Daniel in the lions' den" experience; for others a challenge they seize with imagination and relish.

But no matter how thorough and excellent your training, it doesn't furnish you with the real skills you need in a classroom. There are no college courses in how to spot, in time, the child going green at the gills, about to throw up into a boxful of expensive science equipment, get it out of its seat and its head over a sink without breaking stride in teaching the principle of osmosis. Is the pupil constantly asking to be excused suffering (a) a urinary problem, (b) fear of hard sums or (c) just swinging the lead? Do you risk (c) only for someone to pipe up "Please Miss, Michael's wet the floor!"? These tips and wrinkles I learned from senior colleagues of many years' experience. Now there's barely a body left over fifty in education. Those wise mentors also taught me that the two most indispensable members of staff in a school are the caretaker and the secretary. Without one or the other it ceases to function efficiently. Without both it descends into chaos. Despite the huge changes in curriculum, methods and emphasis, the central core of education remains essentially the relationship between the teacher and the taught.

On the first of September 1966, I walked into Holy Child Infants' School, Central Drive, Creggan, in a pearl grey suit and green suede shoes. It was my first job. I was twenty years old, newly qualified and I knew everything there was to know about education.

Holy Child was a unique establishment. With an enrolment of 1,000 children under the age of eight, it operated in two shifts like a coalmine. Teachers worked from 9am until 2pm or 11am 'til 4pm, overlapping in the middle so that each class had the benefit of two pairs of hands for creative and expressive work and structured play. On the day I began my teaching career, 365 Primary One children were admitted to the school and ten new teachers appointed to cope with them. There were five Mrs Dohertys on the staff. The induction policy then was, get them all in quick and get the bother over. Parents were discouraged from lingering. Class sizes were large, forty-plus not unusual. I was corralled in a classroom, my back against the door with 48 mixed infants hell-bent on escape and all caterwauling at once for their mammies. I damn nearly cried for my own. The sobs and snotters gradually subsided, except for Winnie, who rolled round the walls in an ecstasy of vociferous grief. Winnie had a wail like a professional keener and, as I discovered later, could keep it up indefinitely. One boy climbed onto the windowsill and arms extended, flattened himself against the glass, howling for release in a scene reminiscent of Dustin Hoffmann in *The Graduate*. It didn't look good from the street.

Lulled by their exhausted torpor into a false sense of security, I let one of them get away and found myself pounding the streets in hot pursuit, a pencil skirt and three inch stiletto heels carrying the child, screaming and resisting back into school.

Then suddenly within a week, they were settled. I was their mammy and they were my children in our bright Wendy-house of a classroom with its pictures and toys and books. I combed the country for birds' nests, conkers, beards of barley, ears of corn and sea-sculpted pebbles – things strange to city children. We grew mustard and cress in eggshells with faces drawn on them – little men with green hair. We painted and sang and danced and had stories galore. I had most of the curriculum covered and this teaching lark was a bit of a doddle. It's amazing how, the older you get, the harder it becomes.

In that happy era before the shadow of suspicion fell on all adults in charge of children, I took upon my knee, nursed and hugged the neglected and sick, the sad and the hurt and put my mind to devising original and stimulating ways to create bright shining days and make learning a pleasure. What a privilege it was. And, despite everything, what a privilege it is still.

"NOBODY FORGETS A GOOD TEACHER," was the slogan adopted by the Labour government some years ago in a desperate attempt to staunch the steady haemorrhage of overworked, underpaid and undervalued teachers leaving education in droves. Some who stayed did so only at the behest of their principals, who appealed to their loyalty that the quality, stability and expertise within the school not be diluted or lost.

It is much more difficult to assess what makes a good principal than what makes a good teacher. In the old days, long time-servers were rewarded or brilliant class teachers appointed to headships. With doubtful managerial skills, sometimes unsuitable personality quirks and no training, they frequently made a complete bamdoodle of the job, but some were born to it.

Holy Child's principal was a lady ahead of her time. Miss Mary Duffy's ethos of education marked her out as a groundbreaker. Working in an area of high unemployment and social deprivation, the school was a haven of quality experiences, sound teaching and fun. Though class numbers were high, there were few discipline problems, children were obedient and their parents supportive, believing that education would open the door to opportunity and better prospects.

Mary Duffy was a "hands on" principal. My classroom door

opened each morning and in she came. With a mission box and a yellow duster under her arm, she talked her way round the children, whose breed, seed and generation she knew, praising the diligent and scolding the miscreants, wiping surfaces and dusting shelves as she went, her gimlet eye taking in exactly what was on your walls, on your blackboard and in the children's books. Nor was she dilatory about telling us young, newly-qualified teachers that our skirts were too short, our heels too high and a chat with a more experienced colleague might help the quality of our teaching of decimal coinage or basic fractions. Parents held her in awe, respect and cautious affection, as did her staff. She was a remarkable woman whose sterling work for education was recognised by the Carlisle and Blake Blue Riband award for organisation and excellence in 1963.

Miss Duffy had scrupulous notions of economy. In order to get what you needed in the line of stationery or equipment, you had to request twice as much. She saved the Department of Education hundreds of thousands of pounds by her prudent parsimony and the parish a great deal more by the simple expedient of having the teachers clean the school. The "morning" teachers did the insides of the windows, the "afternoon" teachers the outsides and we all, she included, washed the walls. Nor would we have dreamt of refusing. What a field day the unions would have had with that one! No matter, Miss Duffy minded us like a mother hen and her like will not be seen again.

"AND DON'T FORGET TO BRING IN YOUR PENNIES for the black babies," was the teacher's daily hometime reminder. Lent saw a great push to save countless black souls half a world away, from the unnamed evils that were the result of paganism. The "mission box" grew gratifyingly heavier day by day as our big, brown pennies dropped clinkingly into its thin-lipped slot and gobstoppers, Black Jacks and everlasting toffee remained resolutely un-bought. Rumour had it that for half-a-crown, you could buy a black baby by proxy and give it a name – but that was thirty brown pennies and a sweet-free future too bleak for a Derry wean to contemplate. Not until I was woman-big and went to Africa did I discover that my Rhodesian in-laws had brought their pocket-money to school to save Chinese children from the curse of Communism.

The ubiquitous mission box was still extant when I became a teacher, for, despite all our self-sacrificing efforts, poverty remained endemic in the Third World and despite our increased commitment to its eradication, is worse today than ever it was. It always struck me as ironic that the most generous givers were those with the least –it's been proven year after year by Trócaire statistics for the relief of poverty abroad, when the need was, and is, on our own doorstep.

I know that a significant proportion of the children I taught in Creggan in the mid-Sixties came from houses where each day tested the ingenuity of their parents to feed and clothe them. I know that a sizeable number of the children I taught in Carnhill in the mid-Seventies were being reared on the very edge of the economic margins. A recently published report reveals that in forty years little appears to have changed. Such areas are as poverty stricken as ever – only now it's more distressing to be poor in a climate of pseudo-prosperity where expectations are high and the twin spectres of credit and debt sit nightly on the bed posts of parents trying to do their best for their children. I find particularly poignant such statistics cheek by jowl with stories of an £85 sandwich on a London lunch counter and Master Wayne Rooney negligently running up £100,000 worth of gambling debts. Were it not for the magic in his feet, young Rooney might have been just such a social statistic.

I'm reminded of the mother of a past pupil years ago who told me with tears in her eyes that she hadn't been able to afford to send her son on a football trip. Promising youngsters from local schoolboy teams were being offered the chance of a weekend's coaching with professionals under the eye of talent scouts. He'd been nominated, but she simply couldn't come up with the money. And what was this inaccessible sum? £20.

WHISPER IT LOW, my unfavourite part of the National Curriculum is Physical Education whether it be dance, gymnastics, skills practice or games. There are (if you will pardon the pun) two schools of thought about team games. One view is embraced by hearty types in purple shell suits who, without extra pay, bellow from the sidelines at a motley crew of chap-kneed adolescents every wet Saturday. "Team games will teach them co-operation," they'll tell you, "unanimity of purpose, a sense of fair play, graciousness in victory, dignity in defeat," and various other rah-rah and ultimately empty sporting clichés. That most of these sentiments are utterly fallacious must have occurred to them, as they observe with equanimity the illegal foul, the unprofessional tackle and both sides' resolute refusal to mingle at orange-sucking time, but they choose to ignore the obvious and blindly continue to protest the honour and validity of "team spirit". The other school of thought about team games is encapsulated in a quotation from that most definitive of literature's teachers, Miss Jean Brodie. "Team spirit," she remarks witheringly, "where would team spirit have got Pavlova? The corps de ballet has team spirit."

Now, the notion that there's only room for one on the podium smacks uncomfortably of elitism. But this is not a concept that troubles any other nation in the world. Only we feel the need to apologise for being successful and shamble backwards into the limelight, awkwardly deprecating our own achievements.

I dread the twice-weekly PE session with its limitless scope for serious injury and the energetic recklessness of children determined to do themselves grievous bodily harm. I watch the clumsy and unpopular, cruelly left till last and try to counteract it by apportioning team places myself. "Awww, we're gettin' Jason," who'll drop the bean bag, run the wrong way, trip on his shoelace. But I'm watching the shy, the unwilling being drawn in, forgetting themselves, becoming part of the group – achieving. I'm entranced by the perfect physical co-ordination, speed and grace shown by an eight-year-old who can barely write his name. Called back from my reverie to arbitrate an offside dispute between two cardigan goalposts I think of that flannel phrase so often used in school reports, "a good team member". Not to lead, but be led; not to soar, but to plod; not to dream but to exist. Yet look at Suzanne arching over the jumping horse, landing sure and steady as a Soviet gymnast. Look at Kevin, perspiring with happiness, in proud control of the ball. He's Michael Owen surveying the pitch while ten pairs of imploring eyes will him to pass the ball to them. Sweaty and breathless, we trail back to the classroom. The post-mortem lasts well into the afternoon. A red-faced Jason presents himself at my elbow. "Hi teacher. Is Thursday our next PE day? I can't wait!"

A COUPLE OF WEEKS into the new academic year you could nearly put a date on the first press report of some pupil or other being sent home for a breach of school rules about appearance.

A version of this pantomime is enacted every year in nearly every school in the province, often with the parent of the alleged "victim" unwisely weighing in, in defence of outré haircuts, hair colours, inappropriate footwear or unacceptable body piercing.

From the point of view of the student, it is the business of authority to make young people's lives a misery with stringent enforcement of pointless and outmoded regulations. They think school is like the army – only you go home for your tea. From inflexible authority's viewpoint, standards must be rigorously upheld, lest the ethos of the place be diluted and anarchy prevails. School is like the army – they want nobody out of line.

Punishment doled out to the culprit, intended to make him feel the weight of himself, frequently has quite the opposite effect and before you can say "Mohican" the media has got hold of the story. The young offender is photographed for the local newspaper with a soulful expression on his face that was last seen on Confirmation Day. The television camera finds him, unnaturally tidy in branded sportswear, on the sofa in the protective crook of his mother's arm, while dad stands behind, an Edwardian paterfamilias looking solemn.

The dialogue is predictable – the fond mother with a weak smile says, "He just lives for that hairstyle." The father, truculent, mutters about his son's right to education; the principal stands on principle; the miscreant himself is monosyllabic. Everybody comes out of it looking seven sorts of an idiot. Among his peers, the young offender's street credibility soars, he's cock of the walk.

The democratic concept of a uniform is a sound one. The point of uniform is uniformity – subsuming one's individuality into a common identity for a common purpose – that of creating a sense of community and fostering the idea of belonging. I never knew a young person yet willing to take this aboard. They're far too busy trying on identities, like clothes in a dressing-up box, and haven't yet decided what fits or suits them. If forced into sartorial sameness, they'll sneakily subvert it with the anarchic addition of dreadlocks or lip-gloss or a row of rings down the edge of the ear like a spiral bound notebook. These say to authority, "You may have put me in this geeky gear, but I'm cool, I'm me, and you're not going to make me take it out, and if you do so, I'll get me da up to you, so I will." And the grim reality is, dad will come. Like his son, he too will fail to grasp the idea that external discipline and the discipline of small things breeds internal discipline in the individual.

But bucking the system is nothing new. The art of customising the standard school kit is ingenious indeed, and manifests itself in shirt-tails hanging out, shoelaces undone, tongues of trainers lolling over the feet like sick pups, and ankles thickened by great concertinaed socks. We mustn't forget either, the universal phenomenon of the pelmet-style skirt (one turnover of the waistband for each year of seniority) till the Sixth Year look more St Trinian's than Britney Spears in schoolgirl mode.

Ah, the artifice of the Sixth Form girls! Forbidden make-up, jewellery and nail-varnish, they are tanned, tinted and buffed like Baywatch babes cantering by on rocking-horse legs, tossing manes of professionally highlighted hair. It's a far cry from our Clearasil-daubed complexions and primitive experiments with neat peroxide in the science lab.

Come now, don't tell me you've forgotten your own subversive schooldays. Travelling to and from school and on the street, we were forced to wear a beret. Now a beret is a singularly unflattering piece of headgear on anyone other than an onion seller. On a pudding-faced, acned schoolgirl it is nothing short of tragic. It was the era of bouffant hair and mine was a mop-head chrysanthemum enamelled into position with hair lacquer, stiff as a Tiffany lampshade. Nor was I going to put a dent in it to accommodate the loathsome beret. Sister Mary Dorothea was at the school door as usual, inspecting us for flaws from the feet up as we came in off the buses. She was smiling, but the thing about Sr Dorothea was the wider she smiled, the more bother you knew you were in. "Anita Armstrong," she enunciated, "where is your beret?" Wordlessly I bowed as if to royalty. There, adhering to the back of my head like a jammy pancake, was the beret, tenuously secured by hairgrips. "Insolent girl!" she said, but I had her on a technicality.

It's in the nature of the young to push back the boundaries and the old to attempt to strengthen the fences. It comes out even-stevens in the long run, since the boundary breakers eventually grow (faster than they think) into the fence builders and suffer the same selective amnesia as those who went before them. The difference is, we were dismissed as nuisances, mere "notice-boxes". The new subversives enjoy the helium high of widespread notice on everybody's box, and boy, do they love it!

CHILDHOOD IS A WORLD APART – a place to which each of us inevitably loses the key as we step over the threshold into puberty. It's a world with its own structure and governance, strict as any civic state, which can be at one and the same time moral and unjust, noble and cruel. It's a world at once despotic and anarchic, a world of rituals and rites of passage, both tender and savage.

Along with the key, we lose the art of communication, the ability to decode the mystery and, regrettably, the capacity to understand. From the distance of age we smile fondly back at the small terrors of childhood, the irrational fears and empty myths and see them for the paper tigers they were. But they growled authentically and fiercely enough from the shadowy corners of our own youth and the biggest and fiercest of them all was the bully.

Today, more often than not, primary teachers spend the twenty minutes after lunch performing what we call the post-mortem. A line of playground miscreants awaits the judgement of Solomon and all notion of maths or geography is postponed till we get to the bottom of who kicked whom first, who called so-and-so a bad name (and their mother!), who menaced the girls and took their ball away. One could unhappily spend the whole afternoon in this Star Chamber of claim and counterclaim, denial and blame and be no wiser after the event than before it.

Bullying, they tell us, is endemic in our schools and it is our duty to investigate (exhaustively) every accusation. This creates a dilemma. When does the rough-and-tumble of the playground, the casual name-calling and taunting that is a normal part of the fluctuating friendships of the young, turn into singling out, picking on and victimising? The sensitive little soul boo-hooing because somebody called her "Gingersnap" or "Googly Eyes" is assisted tenderly indoors by the one with the persecution complex who has business of her own. "It's Jason. He keeps looking at me –" is her complaint, " – with his eyes."

Are these what used to be known in the old days as telltales and cry-babies? Little girls are particularly adept at causing pain. Where two or three are gathered together, one will be left out. Oh, the social death of being excluded! The one not invited to the party! But is this bullying? There are such things as natural victims, born to be put upon. Forlorn children, shunted from school to school by their parents, no happier in this one than the last. Within a week of their arrival, the others' antennae are tuned in and the pattern begins to repeat itself.

The hardest part of dealing with bullying is deciding what bullying is. And the second hardest thing is convincing a parent that their child is guilty. Everybody's child is a victim, it appears, but nobody owns the perpetrator. Parents don't like to be reminded that children absorb their manners and morals from home, that values are caught, not taught and a child imitates what he sees. In a world of conflicting images it's not surprising he chooses the most swaggering and macho, whether borrowed from screen or from life. The first thing the modern bully seems to learn from a fairly early age is that he can behave thus with impunity and there's not much anybody can do to stop him – certainly not the school with its Mickey Mouse sanctions. This lends a certain heady element to his excesses.

Children are troubled souls, pulled this way and that in the tug-of-war that is peer-group versus parent. "Be different. Stand alone. Do the right thing," preaches the parent. "Be in with the crowd. Be part of us. Belong," urges the gang. No contest really, is it? Don't we still, as adults, long for the security and kudos of being part of the in-crowd?

Children are primitive souls whose animal instincts have not yet been buried under several veneers of social convention as adults have. Like all young creatures, they are trying their strength, seeking their own place in the pecking order, establishing their identity – all of which is necessary and natural. It's unfortunate that they exhibit some animal characteristics more markedly. Animals turn upon those of their own they perceive to be different, the albino, the runt, the maimed. Humans do it in a more sophisticated way, home in on those with a different accent, culture or religion – or the wrong brand of trainers.

The "me" generation of the Eighties has spawned an even more unpleasant breed of self-centred young who play to a subtle agenda concealed from authority and bound by a code of silence to which we have lost the key. We, who need to know, are the last to know and tragically often cannot reach the casualties in time.

ALL ATTEMPTS AT AMATEUR DRAMATICS are beset with pitfalls, hedged about with disaster. The odds increase exponentially when children are involved. The idea that children are natural actors is a fallacy. Put someone else's dialogue in the mouth of a child and you need dental pincers to get it back out. Children, boys especially, never know what to do with their hands. They make feeble penguin-like motions while muttering half-remembered lines in a monotone. They also shift uneasily from foot to foot, have no sense of rhythm and constantly look skyward for inspiration – and those are the talented ones. I had an unfortunate experience once with a wobbly maypole and a group of mixed infants who bound one of their number hand and foot to the central shaft in the course of their simple terpsichory. However, nothing daunted, schools do school shows with a cast of hundreds. In our heart of hearts we know a week from today the magic will have worked, the teachers misty-eyed with pride, the parents clapping like mad, seeing only their own wee one third from the left at the back. Meanwhile, rehearsals are at a crucial stage, nerves are frayed, tempers short. There is a pervasive air of gloom.

"THIS ELECTION SCENE NEEDS SOMETHING to dress it up," says the producer in the last stages of exasperation, with the school show. We are doing *Thompson in Tir-na-nOg*, that celebrated slice of orange and green political life, and things are not going well. "Lots of colour with banners and posters," he says. "And flags to wave, plenty of flags." I make a resigned scribble on my notepad. As props mistress it is my job to find the flags. "Where would you get flags?" I muse, looking gloomily out the classroom window. Two hundred yards away an enormous Irish tricolour flaps in the breeze over the Sinn Féin advice centre. I need advice.

The young fellow in the Sinn Féin advice centre looks at me as if I've fallen out of a tree. "Flags," I say, "where would I get them? Wee ones," I continue, "on sticks, the kind you wave." I waggle one finger feebly. He disappears to consult higher authority. Subdued muttering is followed by hoots of laughter through the half-open door.

Later that afternoon I make my way to the shop he recommended. I go in and look around at the usual tourist paraphernalia, linen tea towels, delph leprechauns, miniature shillelaghs and a selection of porcelain plates bearing Irish blessings of varying degrees of fervour. A pale dignified lady looks at me from behind the counter. "Excuse me," I say, "I was told I might buy Irish tricolours here." The lady says nothing. "Wee ones," I say, "on sticks, the kind you wave." I waggle one finger feebly. Without speaking the lady slowly sinks below counter-level. There is a discreet rustling and up she comes again, smoothly, as if on a pulley with a great anonymous paper bundle. "How many do you want?" she enquires conspiratorially. "Two dozen," I say. "Two – four – six," counts the lady. I look at the Irish tricolours. Small rectangles of heavy duty PVC in violent Day-Glo shades of green, white and orange affixed to plastic sticks with a little knob on top. I pick one up. "Made in Taiwan," it says in the corner.

The lady parcels them firmly. "How much is that, please?" I ask.

"£12," she says.

"WHAT?"

"50p each," she says.

Stunned by the price of patriotism, I pay up.

The following day sees me treading the red, white and blue bordered pavements of a street on the other side of town where I am assured the emblems of the opposite persuasion can be had.

The shop is presided over by a motherly-looking lady in a blue nylon overall.

"Yes, love?" she says. "Excuse me," I begin tentatively, "I believe you stock Union Jacks." "Indeed," she says, non-committally. I don't know whether to interpret it as an affirmation or not. Her eyes swivel in the direction of the far wall where, piled to the ceiling, are enormous cardboard cartons proudly labelled "Ulster Goods". "Now, what was it you wanted?" she enquires, dragging forward a set of folding steps. "Just plain Union Jacks," I say, "wee ones, on sticks, the kind you wave." I waggle one finger feebly.

"Hmm," she says casting a considering eye along the shelves. "Just plain Union flags – we don't call them Jacks," she corrects me over her shoulder. I jump guiltily, aware that my antecedents are showing. "That's right," I gabble, "plain Union flags. I need them for a show we're doing."

Thirty minutes later we've been through every permutation of loyalist conviction from the Red Hand through God and Ulster, Charles and Diana and Her Majesty on horseback. The nice lady is exhausted, her complexion mottled, her breathing laboured and her varicose veins visibly throbbing. At last, in the very bottom of the very last box on the very last shelf we strike lucky – plain Union flags.

We rejoice together. How many do you want love?" she asks. "Just two dozen," I say apologetically, feeling I ought to buy the lot after all her trouble. "Six, eight, ten," she counts out. I look at the Union flags – small rectangles of heavy duty PVC in Day-Glo colours, mounted on a plastic stick with a little knob on the top. They are identical in every respect to the Irish tricolours I bought the previous day, right down to the "Made in Taiwan" label.

"How much is that please?" I ask, delving for my purse.

"That's £2.88 love," she says, bunching them together with a rubber band.

"What?"

"I'm afraid they're 12p each," she explains.

I wind my way homeward with the bunch of flags like a bridesmaid's bouquet before me, musing on the cock-eyed economics of political ephemera. "What price allegiance nowadays?" I think.

Artistic triumph behind us, we look forward to letting our hair down on a big night out. But…

IT'S THE SAME EVERY YEAR. Nobody wants to organise the staff do. Thus, around November's end goes up a querulous chorus of, "Aren't we doing anything / going anywhere to celebrate?"

Now to me, the word "celebrate" means having a good time with people you're fond of, or have something in common with. These two criteria may not always be met in the case of a staff do.

The press-ganged organiser makes a provisional list. Debate waxes over the merit of bringing partners. Those who live in a state of single blessedness naturally feel miffed; those whose marital relationships are long established aren't in favour on the grounds that they don't want the Loving Spouse to see a facet of their character so far unrevealed at home. So, in favour of partners you'll have only the youngest, most lately married and dewy-eyed member of staff saying:

"I wouldn't enjoy it unless my Jimmy was there."

That decides it. No partners. The organiser amends the list.

Choice of venue in theory depends on how many want a decent meal and a bit of entertainment versus those who're out for a booze-up and a rave. Choice of venue in practice at seven days' notice means wherever will take you. Of the three restaurants that will, one is too far, one is too near and the third has, on a prior occasion, given somebody food-poisoning. The organiser opts for number three.

The prospective bill of fare is the next vexed question. The staff gourmet won't go unless there's salmon on the menu. Yes, there's salmon.

"Oh, but is it wild salmon?"

"I don't know," says the organiser, "but your attitude could make it very irritable."

Everybody wants to know is it a dressy-up-do, or will the standby black frock suffice? All the fellas, of course, want to come casual, i.e. acrylic jumpers and baggy cords. The ladies object vociferously about their *lamé* and lurex lights being hidden under a bushel of ordinariness. Retrospective grudges are aired about the pint of lager that was spilt down somebody's velvet cleavage last year and "Really, it's madness to buy something new to go out with a parcel of glipes. Anyway the sales start in a wee while and wouldn't you kill yourself if you saw it reduced after you buying it at the full price?"

The rival style queens privately resolve to attend dressed to the nines and turn the sartorial knife in its smiling sheath.

The organiser spends every waking moment refining lists and copper-fastening every detail of venue, menu, times and places of collection and setting down, seating plan, individual itemised bill totals (including tip), drinks list, wines and liqueurs list, kitty for drinkers, kitty for non-drinkers, a special plea from the sole vegetarian, and two awkward cusses who want their prawn avocado without the prawns and without the avocado respectively. The resulting document is big as a roadmap and complicated as double-entry book-keeping.

The great night arrives. The organiser shepherds us aboard the coach like a border collie. Groomed and gleamin', we embark in anticipation.

Later, much later in the ladies' loo, the consensus is it wasn't the organiser's fault the restaurant had overbooked and we couldn't all be seated together. It wasn't the organiser's fault that the cabaret was a blue comedian who mortified the sensibilities of two of our starchiest members of staff. Nor was it the organiser's fault that the modest nouvelle cuisine-size portions made one of the fellas loudly threaten to send out for a Chinese take-away. Not at all! The organiser had done a great job – in fact should do it again next year.

The coach is waiting, engine throbbing in the car-park. It has been there for forty-seven minutes. The driver, after three fruitless pleas for passengers, tilts back his seat and slots in another Daniel O'Donnell tape. The organiser, who has stayed sober, paid the bill, kept the kitty, taken personal responsibility for underdone steak and overdone vegetables, soothed the stroppy management and broken up fights – where is the organiser now? Laid out across the back seat – the labours of Hercules accomplished, head on a folded coat, the organiser sleeps the sleep of the just.

Back inside, beaming, dishevelled and perspiring, we're all out doing the Birdie Dance together. We're all gonna regret it in the morning but in the meantime, Happy Christmas everybody! Happy Christmas!

AT RISK OF INCURRING THE WRATH of the Derry Mothers' Mafia, I must dig up an annual bone of contention that is gnawed and worried over for a few weeks only to be buried again and excavated year after year.

We've had a gap recently in the Derry diocese, a year in which we were mercifully free of flounced petticoats, frilled ankle socks, diamante tiaras, satin bags, crystal beads and fringed parasols. In moving First Communion up to Primary Four, the Catholic Church is hoping its recipients will have reached the age of reason. If it hoped their mothers have done the same, it is doomed to disappointment. Of course, First Communion is an exercise in iniquitous extravagance but I must own that I do understand why. It's all to do with the psychology of motherhood and the glorious gift of a daughter.

I'm a mother myself and every woman sees her mirror image in her daughter and all her sublimated hopes and dreams that may have been thwarted or disappointed or impossible, are projected onto that little replica of herself with the fiercest ambition. It begins at birth. Who has not seen the poor infant flounced to within an inch of its life, sitting bolt upright in the pushchair like a crocheted crinoline lady on a toilet roll? Who has not registered a moue of distaste at the kewpie doll travesty of its meagre tuft of baby hair secured by a winsome bow, its gold-bangled wrists, its innocent earlobes pierced already with jewelled studs. A little solemn icon to perpetual mother love. A living doll.

As more and more daughters grow earlier and faster away from the influence of their mother, the latter seems to sense that their role finishes sooner and sooner. Confirmation has become studiedly casual. A chino-clad army of soldiers of Christ. What daughter nowadays even consults her mother about her wedding? Or allows her parent the merest suggestion where arrangements, venue or style are concerned? Many daughters dispense with nuptials altogether and, in the most unfeeling way, deprive their mother of her only legitimate excuse to wear a hat.

So First Communion is probably the last occasion in a girl's life where what mum says goes. And boy, do the mammies take advantage of it! They push the boat out on a Titanic scale. We learn the skills early. It is no accident that girls are preoccupied with dolls. In that role-playing activity, we unconsciously develop our mothering instincts, our decision-making processes and our emotional tyranny over an inanimate object shaped like a baby. How natural then that we should project it onto our female flesh and blood at the earliest opportunity.

I remember clearly my burning jealousy of little friend Elaine's shop-bought dolls' clothes which made my dolls' homemade ones look crude and ugly. Though they were knitted and sewn with maternal care and skill, I was just mortified by them and screamed out my shame. My mother's sacrifice of time and love meant nothing to the ungrateful little beggar that was me.

Sacrifice is a word no young person understands but every mother does. It is the gradual relinquishing of self that creeps up on us as our daughters grow and mature and take centre stage, until they launch themselves upon the world with hardly a backward glance at the woman to whom they owe so much. Years of small self-denials for most of us, but some mothers indulge it to a martyred degree.

My own mother may not have approved of either the place I was going or the company I kept, but would stand for hours sewing and pressing so I'd look well when I got there. Other mothers endure years of stringent economy so their daughters might have the best. Some put themselves literally in hock to transform their beautiful child into a travesty, a creature, at once herself yet not herself, a doll, richly dressed and remote as the effigies of the Virgin carried in third world religious processions.

I understand perfectly the bafflement of people who view these mothers as feckless fools, running themselves into debt over a few hours' finery. I understand perfectly the anger of people who accuse them of profaning the sanctity of the occasion by gross materialism and empty vanity. I understand, because to this day her father does not know the price of our daughter's First Communion dress. I understand, too, that there is no use whatsoever in asking any mother to have a sense of proportion about her own child. At worst she is only guilty of loving too much. In an uncertain world she's ensuring for her darling one perfect golden day as princess-bride, a day she may never see again.

JUNE – THE TIME OF YEAR when teachers come home every day and have to take two tablets and lie down. This is the time of year when schoolchildren from four-and-a-half upwards are already imbued with the holiday spirit. Attempting even to contain them for the last fortnight of term is like sitting on the lid of a boiling pot. Actually teaching them anything is impossible.

This is also the time of year when the school report lands upon the domestic doormat with a dull and foreboding thud. A time to be dreaded by all parties concerned, unless the subject of the report is closely related to either Einstein or the angels in Heaven. A time to be dreaded by parents with an inflated set of expectations; by the teacher who has to write the unpalatable truth about their wee Johnny; and by wee Johnny himself, who frequently wishes he hadn't acted the maggot for most of the school year. Once upon a time Johnny's progress was monitored informally over the frozen food cabinet in the local supermarket, "Mrs H, would you ever take him by the scruff of the neck and put him over his reading at night? He's falling behind." Case conferences were conducted against the jamb of the classroom door. But now the Great God of Record-keeping rules education in a welter of photocopies and computer printouts. Children are expected to fit neatly into boxes. They are pigeon-holed on paper; level two; working towards level three; good, average, poor. Average? Would you care to define average?

Jargon rules: "Through lack of practice Johnny's poor word-attack skills result in faulty comprehension and lack of expression in his reading." In plain language, Johnny's still guessing every word as he goes along, because you're doing sweet damn all to help him! Once upon a time, teachers were a lot less mealy-mouthed about disruptive children. "Your son's a bloody nuisance," parents would be told. "Take him home and put manners on him!" Now it has to be phrased, "Johnny needs to listen and concentrate more. He is inclined to distract others." What you yearn to add is, he's the way he is because there's no consistent pattern of discipline at home. Johnny's attitudes are unco-operative because you have told him, dear parent, "The teacher can't make you do anything you don't want to." And Johnny's predisposition to beat the head off all and sundry in the playground? – "You stand up for yourself, son!"

Perhaps the value of a written report at an early stage is questionable. For the unhappy child whose personality clashes with this year's teacher; for the low achiever who isn't praised enough for his limited success – will the next teacher be unduly influenced by an unrelenting litany of apparent backsliding, insolence or academic failure? What all children are good at is meeting our expectations of them.

The danger of pigeon-holing children is that it deprives them of the will to break out of the pigeon-hole. The danger of categorising them negates their capacity to be drawn either outwards or upwards. In a particular pigeon-hole of the bureau in my house is an old brown envelope. Inside is a report form with the glorious 28 per cent I achieved in algebra at the age of thirteen. I still have it, and the maths teacher's despairing letter to my father that accompanied it. It is entirely due to that report that I became a teacher of infants, so that I need never again have to contend with X equals 2Y squared – since with infants you rarely have to go past twenty and there's no algebra either!

But despite my reservations, I suppose the report system does offer protection. For, once upon a time, there were children who remained in a state of unspoken and abject terror throughout their entire school careers. A conspiracy of silence shrouded the petty brutalities and criminal neglect perpetrated in both classroom and playground. It was a system bravely borne because there was no appeal. Contemporaries of my own relate with white-faced venom the bitter tyrannies of teachers who were thugs, bullies and snobs, who left physical weals and emotional scars – and against whom there was no sanction. In writing reports this week, I'm trying to appraise concisely the character of the child who has sat before me all year, and the quality of the work he or she has done. As I write each carefully chosen phrase, I remember two things. I remember my father, a country school principal for forty years. His advice to me on my first day of teaching was "Be scrupulous in anything you commit to paper about a child. *Verbum scriptum manet* – the written word remains."

JUNE. THIS IS THE MONTH FOR SCHOOL TRIPS, when coachloads of schoolkids take to the road in the name of education, or, more dangerously, enjoyment. School outings! What fond memories I have of preparing the little ones for the treat. First, the note home to mammies: "Sensible footwear please, packed lunch (no glass containers) and a £2 limit on pocket money." Not a whit of notice do they take of it. In the kids come, in strappy First Communion sandals and their best clothes, bags bursting with E-additives, clinking with bottles and a small fortune in their pockets. The night before I've spent packing a large box with tissues, toilet roll, sun-cream, anti-sting spray, spare knickers, plastic bags and a bale of newspapers. The great day dawns as ever, bright and clear, for we have taken the precaution of asking someone to put the Child of Prague statue out on the windowsill overnight to ensure fine weather.

Nobody's late for school on the day of the trip. First task is to field the mammy-sezzes: "Mammy sez will you mind my camera/money/my good cardigan?" No. Look after it yourself or leave it in school. "Mammy sez if I'm sick will you give me one of these wee tablets?" No dear. You should've taken it at home under her supervision. Anyway I have the infallible remedy for all ills – an anonymous but very medical-looking foil-wrapped card of spearmint Rennies, which work psychologically for everything from migraine to diarrhoea.

Two by two, chattering like magpies, they file out of school and up the high steps of the bus to sit three to a seat on scratchy patterned plush. Coats, bags and stuff safely stowed in the overhead racks, we are a hands-free bunch of happy trippers. The engine turns over. To ragged chorus of "The Wheels on the Bus Go Round and Round" we're off. A bevy of mammies with pushchairs wave us out of sight of the school.

First patrol of aisle and headcount involves ruthless confiscation of gameboys, puzzle books and coloured pens. "You'll discover more by looking out the window, dear." This is a phenomenon of the rising generation. They're not interested in the journey, only the destination. They cross the Foyle Bridge without a notion what river it spans. Nobody tells them what they're seeing. They've no idea where they are. I recall mentioning to the class that en route to Portrush we'd be going "over the mountain" to Coleraine. I had a demented mammy at the door next morning saying she'd been up all night with Caroline who was terrified of going over the mountain and could she sit beside teacher in the bus. The afflicted child kept her eyes scrunched shut all the way from Ballykelly as far as Coleraine.

There are two things that'll make a child throw up on a bus. One is excess excitement and the other is unlimited access to sweets and fizzy drinks. The order of the day therefore is "NO EATING ON THE BUS". I've taken a bit of a stick over the years from colleagues who accuse me of running a kind of concentration camp outing, but I notice they're the ones mopping up the vomit with paper towels and standing in road side sheughs with mixed infants spewing up a feed of rubbish. Anyone on my trip looking even vaguely green about the gills is given a double page of the *Daily Mirror* to sit on. Mind you, it needs to be the sporting rather than the feature pages, since the sensational tone of the latter can lead the kiddies into an unhealthy interest in tabloid journalism. I don't know where or from whom I heard it, but a child sitting on newspaper will not get sick. Try it. It works. A quick foray to the back of the bus to check if anyone's bringing the name of the school into disrepute by making faces (or worse) at the traffic in our wake and we can congratulate ourselves on being alright so far. The boys' fitful renderings of "The Sour Apple Tree" clash with the girls' determination to sing bubblegum pop songs. They have shrieked themselves hoarse already.

IT COMES AS SOMETHING OF A SHOCK to realise that my teaching career is bounded almost exactly by the beginning and ending of the Troubles. Only the first three years could be said to have been untainted by fluctuating violence, mistrust and hatred. Schools, by some miracle, managed to remain oases of calm normality in the midst of the escalating insanity that passed for living here. We didn't go in much for political debate in Primary Four, so it was with some apprehension in November 1993 I broached preparations for a Day of Peace with my class of eight-year-olds, many of whose parents didn't even remember what peace was like.

Anxious to avoid Technicolor accounts of recent atrocities told with the breathless relish of a horror film plot, I simply asked them, "How do you feel about what's going on and what d'you think can be done about it?" then sat back and let them at it. Their responses were fascinating. Definitions evolved. "Peace", it was agreed, was a

state of "just bein' ordinary". Conflict was interestingly defined by
Richard. "Fightin' in the playground was a wee war," he explained;
big war was the same, but with better equipment. Katherine, with the
sagacity of Mrs Mary Whitehouse, wanted harrowing television
coverage banned because "It only shows people how to kill other
people and gives you bad dreams." Lisa reflected the gloomy
hopelessness of the average citizen. "My mum thinks it's ridiculous,
so she does, and far worse to come." Brian adopted a moralistic tone.
He was fed up with people murderin' each other and they'd soon find
out when they die they won't be welcome in Heaven! Going back to
first cause, Johnny wished they'd never invented guns and bombs in
the first place. Jimmy philosophically pointed out that, without
weapons, people would batter each other to death by other means.
Robert, with the true egotism of the young, was desolated by the
cancellation of the Hallowe'en fireworks in the wake of the Greysteel
massacre, until stopped in his tracks by Nicola who's related to one
of the victims. "I've a pain in my heart thinkin' about him," she said.
And through all the discussions from every quarter, the relentless
melancholy retrain, "It's not fair! It's not fair! It's not fair!"

Not for the first time I became aware of the burden of the
criminal responsibility my generation carries for the future of these
children whose lives are destined to be limited by fear and blighted
by bigotry. I felt depressed. The debate was running out of steam.
Then Rebecca, shining-eyed, shot up out of her seat like Archimedes
from his bath and announced, "Why don't they all just stop – right
now??!!" Rueful glances were exchanged among the others as if to say,
"Why didn't we think of something as obvious as that?"

As to how a cessation of violence could be brought about, they
were less clear, so a democratic decision was taken to inform God
firsthand of the seriousness of the situation. With much chewing of
pencil ends and furrowing of youthful brows, the task of storming
Heaven began. Jennifer's somewhat peremptory missive turned out
to be fully comprehensive. "*Dear Enemies,*" she wrote, "*I write to say
stop killing on behalf of everyone in this world. They do not like to have
to wake up in the morning and see that their son or daughter is dead.*

*And now I write a prayer to God Himself.*

"*Dear God, I don't like seeing everybody upset. Including you. Could you please forgive everybody? Thank you. Dear God, I wish the world would be a better place. If everyone would pull theirself together it would be much better fun. If everyone got good, there would be no more killing and we will all live happily everlasting.*

"*By Jennifer, Aged 8.*

"*Thank you.*"

Would that there'd been a place at the talks table for a very capable young lady from Primary Four.

THE SCHOOL YEAR IS A SHORT ONE, and however relieved some teachers (and all children) are to see the end of it, it induces feelings of regret in a few of us more sensitive souls. There is nothing so forlorn as the sight and sound of an empty school, recently vacated for the summer holidays. The hollow ring of footsteps in deserted corridors, the mathematically unnatural tidiness of empty classrooms, the still tangible atmosphere, compounded of milk, gym shoes and small hot bodies.

While its erstwhile population take to the streets and parks and torture their parents, we, the teachers, wander around, picking up the debris of their presence. There's Robert's lost book which must've slipped down behind the cupboard weeks ago. Here are Michael's missing *Star Wars* men, all mixed up in the tray of plastic animals. I shall miss those two kids. I shall miss them all. It's remarkable how attitudes change in a few short months. I daresay most teachers would secretly confess to positively disliking their new class. The relationship has to be built from scratch every year. I recall last September when they came to me. An unprepossessing-looking bunch all told. A dozen timid little girls and a veritable swarm of large noisy boys whom I despaired of ever getting to sit down, let alone learn anything. And so immature, such babies really. I don't know at what point interest and affection are engaged, but it never fails to amaze me how deeply involved one becomes with children, their joys, their sorrows, their little triumphs and tribulations.

For a year you are the most important person in their lives, often outranking and surpassing in affection and authority even their parents. "Mummy, that's wrong. Teacher says we have to do it this way." You urge, cajole, nurse them along. You worry about them. Some you drag by the scruff of the neck through the educational process, muttering through gritted teeth, "Someday you'll thank me for this." They never do.

I wonder, will next year's teacher love and understand them as well as I do? Probably not. How will she know how well shy little Fiona has adjusted and come out of herself; how quiet and responsible Gary has become after swinging from the light fittings for most of the first term? I must remember to warn her about Billy's stubbornness and Sandra, who fizzes with energy and needs to be sat upon from time to time.

For a year you are the most important person in their lives. Suddenly the bond is broken. Next year they will greet you indifferently in the corridor. Two years hence, they won't acknowledge you at all.

## "…THE DISNEYFICATION OF CHRISTIANITY"
### Don Cupitt

SEAN RETURNS FROM AN ERRAND to another classroom. "Hi teacher!" he announces, eyes round with indignation, "the P Twos are gettin' makin' pancakes!" Indeed, wafting on the air accompanying him from the corridor is the unmistakeable aroma, sweetened with sugar, sharpened with lemon, of hot fresh pancakes. Pencils suspended, juvenile noses probe the air and anarchy breaks out. I am besieged by little pleaders. "S'not fair! G'on let us too. We never get anything nice!" In vain they plead. I do not yield. I will not relent. Pancake Tuesday or not – no pancakes for the P Fours.

In the past 25 years primary education has become a branch of the entertainment industry and teaching a performance art. In the cause of "learning through discovery", I have harboured flea-ridden hedgehogs which stank, hosted a colony of snails which ate the library books and suffered the company of newborn baby goats who left minute but authentic souvenirs in the dressing-up box. All these I have endured, but I will not cook in school. Particularly not pancakes. Despite the televisual tips of Delia, Jamie, Nigella, Paul, Gary, Keith *et al*, the principles of batter defeat me. The simple combination of flour, fat and liquid into a smooth cream turns into a gloopy wallpaper paste the colour and consistency of orphanage gruel, or else a clotted sticky sludge which drops heavily off the spoon to lie sulking in a puddle of hot grease, slowly developing acne over its pasty complexion. The sad and misshapen result has the look of a coated tongue, the texture of a bath mat and adheres to the roof of the mouth with all the persistence of a rubber plunger.

I thin the batter and try again, ever in my mind's eye the picture of my Belfast-born sister-in-law who greets the unexpected visitor with unmixed delight and promises, "I'll just toss you up a few wee drap scones", uniformly golden and perfect in their symmetry. Or the other vivid image – my mother rattling the big spoon round the crazed delph baking-bowl where seemingly random quantities of ingredients obediently blend. "This is a crumpet recipe you know, not pancakes at all," she says every time, but she never tells me what the recipe is. I watch her, a heel of hard margarine in her hand, anointing with quick strokes the blackened old cast-iron pan.

Dollop! A single creamy disc appears in the pan, another, a third, precisely placed as domino dots. Mother stands sentinel, watching the surface dull and bubble and the edge turn to golden lace, her wand of office an ancient fish slice worn razor-thin. Dollop – flick – rub – over and over again in perfect economy of effort. You could set it to music. It's culinary choreography.

As chief assistant I build the crazy tower of finished pancakes. They are thick and velvety, deliciously yielding to a pressed finger; butter, sugar and lemon juice between. We eat as many as we stack. "You can have the wee wonky ones," she says and misshapes a few on purpose. We laugh and rub our greasy fingers on a damp cloth.

She belonged to a generation who cooked by rule of thumb, whose measures were handfuls and pinches and nips and shakes, whose ingredients were rarely the same, twice running, and who had the courage to experiment. Frequently that courage was born of necessity, eking out slender means with the judicious addition of extra onion or potato. What she could do with three cold spuds and a cooking apple to produce apple fadge, at once savoury and sweet; leftover mash and a bit of flour and fat made potato cakes light as air; stale sponge cake transformed into trifle and the heel of the loaf, bread pudding.

As I throw the surplus vegetables in the bin I feel her eye upon me accusingly. Waste was criminal, waste was sinful. I laughed at her hoarding a spoonful of peas in a saucer. "You'll follow the crows for it yet," was her dark rejoinder, doling out portions of egg custard and prunes. The man of the house was shown due difference. He got six prunes, we got four.

And so she lived and died and never wrote any of her recipes down except the one for Christmas cake for my sister who lived in Africa and I've been trying to recreate the taste since.

On the way home from school I stop by a bakery. They have those big thin fancy pancakes – crepes they call them. I'll do something interesting with these, I think, to make up for them being bought.

"They look like table mats," says Daughter Dear. "Taste like 'em too," she adds. And indeed, they are peculiarly resilient, as if made of some rubberised material. I'm sure they contain a percentage of Lycra. I fiddle about with fillings and a creamy sauce. The end result on the plate looks like a row of small vulcanised bolsters. "What's this?" asks the Loving Spouse. "Savoury pancakes," I say, "for the day that's in it." "I've just eaten a stack of homemade ones," he replies ruefully, "up in my mate George's granny's."

WE'RE HELL-BENT NOW on emulating the Americans in celebrating ersatz feasts and festivals dreamed up to part us from our cash and manufacture a market for the kind of goods nobody needs anytime of the year – golf-club muffs, ceramic pot-scourer holders, infantile soft toys for adults. An entirely new "tradition" has begun, turning Hallowe'en into a major festival tourist magnet and, by way of a bonus, giving the local hospital's A and E department its busiest night of the year. The young beneficiaries of this elaborate, firework-fizzing spectacular are curious about the past. "What was Hallowe'en like when you were wee?" they ask. The truth is, it was no big deal. I recall no singular celebration apart from a cardboard mask, a few nuts and apples and a couple of Jumping Jack bangers let off recklessly in the street by corner boys. I never saw a firework display till I was woman-big and only bold children went round doors asking for things.

Instead, we stayed at home with an unwontedly full fruit bowl, eating apple tart and thinking about the Holy Souls. The apple tart was, I must admit, the more enjoyable element. My mother put in Halloween favours wrapped in greaseproof paper – a button, a thimble, a sixpence, a ring – and after it had been impartially apportioned, so that I got the sixpence, it was time for bath and hair washing for the Holy Day of Obligation on the morrow.

From a tender age I realised that we were put on this earth to suffer. Neither bathing nor hair washing was a sybaritic experience in an unheated bathroom. After the blue goose-fleshed ducking came a rough towelling fit to dislodge your brains. Then the scalp was scoured with a vigorous fine-combing over a page of *Ireland's Saturday Night* in search of what we called "boos". I was always faintly disappointed when no livestock fell out. My mother lived in social terror of the nit nurse and kept a bottle of yellow sulphurous stuff handy, just in case.

Restored to the warmth of the kitchen, part two of the torture began. Awaiting me on the table were eight ominous paper spills made of the tightly folded pages of Oxendales catalogue, eight strips of rag torn from old flannelette sheets and eight long strands of thick knitting wool. In minutes my head was hung with rigid white pods like the chrysalis cases of some repulsive insect. I was to have curls for All Saints Day, eight fat bouncing corkscrew ringlets to delight the eye of the passing parishioner and the purgatorial night I must endure to achieve them; well, I could just offer it up for the Holy Souls in Purgatory, couldn't I?

You hear remarkably little these days about the Holy Souls in Purgatory. Rather like Limbo, Purgatory seems to be on a spiritual bus-route where the service has been discontinued. But the last generation was a great one for the Holy Souls. Any unpleasant task or experience was transformed at once into a meritorious act to shorten the period of punishment the poor souls spent there. Thus, porridge, cod liver oil and fetching a shovel of coal in on a wet night were all offered as surety to the Almighty in a bid to get early parole for the incarcerated. Getting papers in my hair was the weekly bail instalment I paid for some unhappy soul.

I never questioned the logistics of it. I never discovered if, by a blitz of good works, you got somebody off or out, was the surplus credit transferable to someone else? Rather like a snooty bank manager, you didn't like to bother the Almighty with these trifling matters regarding your account lest he began paying your spiritual affairs an uncomfortable degree of attention. You kept a low profile and got on with the business of living. "Be sure your sins will find you out" was graven on my infant heart, and the detection rate an infallible 100 per cent. God was distant, yet horribly near. His love was to be earned by self-denial and suffering. His grace was a kind of golden gravy which permeated your whole being like a second bloodstream but ran out the bottoms of your feet when you did wrong, and his inexorable sense of justice allowed only the unspotted into Heaven.

Those poor souls who departed this life mildly grubby in the spiritual sense were designated a place like a station waiting-room where the blue therms of the Londonderry Gaslight Company roasted them slowly without consuming their flesh until all trace of sin was erased.

Heavily influenced by a combination of *Lives of the Saints* and the Brothers Grimm I came up with a beezer idea for helping them. On a freezing night I crept out of bed and arranged myself, arms crossed piously on my breast, on the ice-cold linoleum. I would be discovered, like the Little Match Girl, in the chill light of dawn, frozen to death for love of the Holy Souls who would all be redeemed immediately. On being found in this recumbent posture, however, my insensitive parent gave me a clip round the ear and a dire warning that the exercise was not to be repeated.

Years later I came upon a little picture portraying the Holy Souls in Purgatory. They seemed to be exclusively female, wearing tattered shifts and resigned expressions rather than tortured ones. And the other thing I noticed – they all had long poker-straight hair. Not a ringlet among them!

PEOPLE WHO SUPPOSE there are only twelve days of Christmas, as the traditional song suggests, are poor mathematicians. From 29 August, when Christmas cards first appear in stationers' windows, to 31 January, when the last day of the last Blue Cross sale furnishes the prudent and parsimonious with heavily-reduced goodwill and half-priced gifts for Christmas Next, there are no fewer than 155 days, 154 of which are profitable, but you'd never get all of them into the lyrics of a seasonal song.

I wish I could feel warmer towards the type of person who stockpiles joy, has her greetings cards addressed by Hallowe'en and one or two little multipurpose gifts laid by for the Unforeseen Circumstance. I admire much more the feckless friend who at the last minute wraps all her presents in newspaper, binds them in garden twine and passes them off as a style statement.

"HAVE WE ANYTHING LEFT IN THE HOUSE to dry dishes with?" asks the Loving Spouse forlornly. "Sorry, love," I say, "I need all the clean tea towels for the shepherds." He looks at me blankly. "Shepherds," I repeat, "in the Nativity play. Nearly every class in the school does one for Christmas." "Oh," he says, "and I suppose that's where my pyjama jackets have gone?" I nod. Now is not the time to tell him that his father's silver-mounted walking stick is serving as a shepherd's crook as well. He's very generous, the Loving Spouse. Would give you the shirt off his back (and I have taken it), but he does like to be asked, ever since the famous occasion he sat in the audience at a play and saw his new tweed hat enter stage left on somebody else's head.

Daughter Sarah eyes the growing pile of garments and household effects stacked in the hallway. "What're they for, mummy?" she asks. "For the Nativity play in school," I say, adding a chocolate box, a perfume bottle and a tin tea caddy to the heap. "See, these are the gifts the wise men bring the baby." "Didn't Santa bring him any presents then?" she enquires. "Sarah, isn't your class doing a little play about the Baby Jesus?" I ask. "No," she says. "Aren't any of the classes in your school doing a little play about Baby Jesus?" I say with growing anxiety. "No," she stoutly insists. "Sarah, you do know the story of the Baby Jesus don't you?" I ask in alarm. She doesn't answer, but runs upstairs to play. I make a mental note to embark on a crash course of theology at bedtime and stagger out to the car with my pile of props.

Later in the day providence decrees that *Blue Peter* is entirely given over to the making of Christmas crib figures out of scrap materials. An anonymous pair of hands is swaddling a pipe-cleaner infant in bands of kitchen roll. Cotton-wool sheep look on stolidly. Sarah is transfixed. This is a heaven-sent opportunity. I gather her onto my knee. "Look mummy, there's Mary and Joefis!" she shouts. "What was Joseph's job?" I ask her. "He was a carpenter," she says with great conviction. "But what did he do all day?" I say. "He made carpets of course, out of wool," she says scornfully. "Oh," I say.

"Aaah, look at the wee donkey," says Sarah. "Why did they need a donkey?" I ask. "'Cos they had to go to Befflehem to write their names in the king's big book. You see," she adds by way of qualification, "the king wanted to know how many people were sleeping in his castle." "I see," I say, "and what happened when they got to Bethlehem?" "D'you know, mummy, it was terrible," says Sarah solicitously, wearing her middle-aged face. "It was packed out and they had to go to a stable. It was horrible 'cos the cows were doing smelly poo-poos in it. YIK!" She shudders exquisitely. "And guess what, mummy?" she continues, getting up a fine head of narrative steam. "The baby was inside Mary's tummy and in the middle of the night HE CAME UP!" "Really?" I say, hoping to side-step the theological minefield such statements imply. Sarah nods vigorously and goes on, "And Mary made a wee nest for him and put wee panties on him. He was snug as a bug!" "Wasn't that lovely," I say. "Did anybody come to see him?" "Lotsa people – angels and things," says Sarah, absently concentrating hard on the television screen where horns are being applied to a pipe-cleaner cow. "Anybody special?" I ask. "Oh yeah, three wise owls came and brung him golden money," says Sarah. "I shall bring you a picture book tomorrow with the story in it," I say. And I do. It's well written, beautifully illustrated and accurate, but alas, it doesn't have the charm of the Gospel according to Sarah.

CAMERON MACKINTOSH AND ANDREW LLOYD WEBBER could not put more into a West End production than teachers put into their annual Nativity plays. Getting the casting right is first priority. Contrary to popular opinion the starring role is neither Mary nor "Joefis", but the narrator, upon whose six-year-old shoulders the burden of responsibility lies. You want a self-confident child with a clear voice and a good memory to keep things moving. From the moment you pick the narrator you never have an easy moment as you watch him or her for signs of flu, tonsillitis or chicken pox. Mary is another difficult choice. She must look both beautiful and meek, yet be able to motivate Joefis if necessary, since boys are the ones most likely to "rust" on the Big Day. Wise Men and shepherds need leadership and co-operative skills in equal measure and a good sense of direction. Vying with Mary in the glamour stakes is Chief Angel Gabriel who gets to boss the minor members of the Heavenly Host as they stand in a row on a bench at the rear in prayerful attitudes and tinsel wreaths, forming a living backdrop to the play. Sustaining a pious tableau is too onerous a task, so after their big number, "We are the Christmas angels, doing little jobs for God", they spend their time hoking at themselves, picking their noses or waving to their mammies, who are to a woman, weeping with pride.

In thirty years every permutation of disaster has occurred, from Mary going down with mumps to Joefis belting the innkeeper, to an empty manger when somebody's toddler in the audience made off with the Baby Jesus and wouldn't give him back; but I remember with great clarity the year we borrowed a real baby, who bawled and kicked till he dislodged himself from the straw and rolled slowly downstage into the front row of the audience while his fond father videoed the event for posterity.

WE HAVE DEVELOPED A MISPLACED SYMPATHY for men at this time of year. The poor souls see themselves very much surplus to requirements in the run-up to Christmas. Women are fully occupied with the minutiae of the festive season, scouring things, stirring things, stuffing things. Many men sensibly feel they'd be far better off out of the house. This accounts for the huge number of displaced male persons staring gloomily into pint glasses in pubs and wondering when it'll be decently safe to go home. Nowhere is the ancient demarcation zone between men's jobs and women's jobs seen more markedly than in late December. Men's jobs: trawling the countryside in semi-darkness for holly with berries on it, erecting the Christmas tree (invariably in a spot too small and unstable to hold it safely), the decent disposal of turkey entrails to oblige squeamish females; the sudden rearrangement of all the furniture in the spare room to accommodate the far-flung members of the family who have suddenly decided to come home for Christmas and the surreptitious concealment of black refuse sacks full of tricycles, bicycles, pedal cars and Barbie houses in roof space, garage or outhouse.

Feeling he's redeemed himself by the accomplishment of all these Herculean labours, the man of the house trickles off to the local before he's asked to peel sprouts or put a lick of paint on the landing skirting board.

Whether single or spliced, his sixth pint brings the sudden sweaty recollection that he's bought nothing for the woman in his life, be she sweetheart, wife or mother. Hiccupping gently, he adjourns to the nearest shopping mall. Painful, sexist and politically incorrect as it is to say so, where gift buying is concerned there is little evidence of "the new man". Sadly, most men have not got a goat's notion and are defiantly proud of it. Devoid of taste, originality or imagination, they fall easy prey to the unprincipled wolves of the retail economy.

Shop assistants are trained to spot this vacant-eyed Forrest Gump standing hesitantly in store, and guide him tenderly towards those products specifically designed for the female Christmas gift market. You know the sort of thing – the kind of thing no woman in her right mind would ever buy – strange bondage-type undergarments in scratchy lace that leave lumpy undulations under clothing; hold-up stockings that create twin tourniquets round the tops of the thighs and whose glossy finish gives female limbs the greasy sheen of sausage skins. Totally ignorant of such details as measurements, fit or style, he buys whatever it is in red, or else leopard-skin print. "Aaah – about your size," he mutters vaguely, casting a lary eye upon the assistant, whether she be model slim or matronly stout.

"Could I suggest fragrance, sir?" chimes the ever-helpful assistant. "Pardon?" "Perfume, sir." With a single squirt she envelops him in a scented cloud of eye-watering pungency, powerful enough to strip pine. "A limited supply special offer, sir," she adds. The reduction makes the price now merely exorbitant. Bemused, he rocks a little on his heels like a stunned boxer.

The brash gilt of costume jewellery catches his attention. Earrings! She likes earrings. "Pierced or clip sir?" enquires the assistant. "Eh?" "Has your wife got holes in her ears sir?" The shop lady's tone is getting a bit shrill. A small Everest of possibilities has grown upon the counter. In an agony of indecision he'll take the lot. With reckless resolution he signs away January's salary on the credit card stub. Anything to bring this purgatory to an end.

Laden with gift-wrapped frippery he makes his way back to the pub. Later, much later, he inserts his wavering door-key into the unsteady lock and makes his way upstairs with exaggerated stealth. Only as he fights a losing battle with the second sock does he recall the pile of presents carefully stowed under the bar-counter for safe keeping. "Ah well," he thinks with the supreme optimism of the truly intoxicated, "she'll understand. After all, it's the thought that counts!"

WE NEVER DECORATED EARLY. Indeed one of my abiding childhood memories was my mother's annual threat not to decorate at all. "Nothin' but a plaster," I hear her saying. "We'll not bother this year. Sure you're getting too big now for a Christmas tree and all that stuff." And my stomach contracts with disappointment, for every year I believe her, and this might just be the year it's true. Thus Christmas Eve finds me moping about the house doing my impression of a deprived child and getting under people's feet.

Out in our tiny kitchen, which my father has christened the witness box, my mother and her two sisters are grating breadcrumbs, making stuffing and colliding with each other. The three Geoghegan girls, reunited for Christmas and reminiscing. Auntie Mollie reaches up and grasps the turkey firmly by its leathery ankles. It has dangled from a hook on the back door all the previous week with its lolling head and mad eye, like a newly-hanged man. "Do you remember," she is saying, "how Nita, God rest her, used to perform miracles with bones and black thread to make sure all the children got a drumstick? Sure wee Brendy thought for years that a turkey had five legs!" Auntie Mollie's distinctive laugh can be heard all over the house as she plunges her hand into the innards of this year's bird.

My mother's voice calls up the stairs. She is standing in the hall with a ladle in her hand. She has relented. In the gloom of the fast-falling afternoon, I am despatched to the attic to root around for the box – the large dusty pasteboard box with its faded label, "McDevitt, Duke Street, Ladies Mantles and Millinery". It is tied with thin shop string in a double bow, and on one side is written in my mother's curly copperplate, "Xmas Decorations". Without lifting the lid I know the contents of this box to the last item. The top layer is tangled lengths of tarnished, hairy tinsel. Directly underneath, three boxes of spun glass tree ornaments in individual tissue paper nests. Each year I find that one more has fallen silently into powdery shards. Beside them, the old fashioned and hazardous fairy lights, the wall-eyed angel and the big Christmas star.

In a smaller box at the bottom lie scarlet and green ropes of plushy stuff which will be gracefully swagged across the chimney breast with pendant silver bells on either side. My heart yearns for twisted multicoloured streamers looped from corner to corner; my soul thirsts after bunches of balloons and pleated paper Santa Clauses – but no. These constitute what mother calls "a plaster". We have discreet clusters of holly and mistletoe highlighted with gold and silver paint. We have "taste". I feel more deprived than ever.

"Give that child something useful to do," directs my mother. Me and Auntie Beenie change my sheets for Santa coming, turning and tucking in practised harmony, tweaking the corrugations of the candlewick bedspread straight as winter furrows. I watch her shoulder the bolster like a homecoming sailor his kitbag and feed it into the long starched chute of its case. My new Christmas pyjamas are stiff in their folds and smell of the shop. They lie beside the wide-meshed stocking that in the morning will have a silver-wrapped tangerine and a sixpence in the toe – and what else? Don't hope too hard, for Santa is an infallible greed detector.

Downstairs the turkey huddles in the cold oven, its knees under its chin. Over its head, the battered enamel pudding basin with its neat pleat of greaseproof paper and stoutly-corded handle begins to hop gingerly in its bath of boiling water. We're as ready as we can be.

In the wet and windy darkness we set out for midnight Mass. The Spartan country church smells of ploughed earth and potatoes. The canopy over the altar is supported by two arthritic angels. "*Gloria in excelsis Deo*" issues in golden letters from the mouths of their wooden trumpets. Our breath hangs in the air before us.

Up in the choir, my father treadles the wheezing harmonium into life and turns round to conduct us with one hand. "*Gloria in excelsis Deo*," we carol enthusiastically, the square black notes of the small black hymn book dancing before our up-too-late eyes. Not one of us is over nine years old. Flurries of hailstones like thrown gravel at the windows punctuate our praise, "*Et incarnatus est*", and the word was made flesh.

The thin clang of the church bell in the tower above our heads confirms – to the world at large and the parish in particular – that Jesus is definitely born.

WHERE CHRISTMAS IS CONCERNED nowadays I favour the modern minimalist style – the discreet statement of a simple but effective table centre composed of three pine cones and a candle, the small silver tree erected late on Christmas Eve, the single bough of mistletoe suspended on a silk ribbon, and something original to eat for Christmas dinner. All in terribly good taste and (most important) no bother at all.

I had an unfortunate run-in with tradition one year. One Christmas, Daughter Dear revolted. "Other people's mothers," she observed, watching me extract the brandy-laced rich fruit cake with marzipan and royal icing from its Marks and Sparks carton, "make

their own Christmas pudding and the whole family stirs and wishes."
"Mm-mm," I said. "Other people's mothers," she went on, "let them
decorate the living room with paper chains and bunches of balloons
and accordion-pleated Santa Clauses." "Do they?" I said. "Other
people's mothers give their families turkey and ham and Brussels
sprouts for Christmas dinner." "Really?" I said. "Other people's
mothers make gravy," she added slyly. That did it. "Right," I said,
"you want a traditional Christmas? Boy, are you going to get one!
Now where's my mother's recipe for stuffing?"

Christmas Eve turned out bitter, stormy and wet and that was just
the weather. We returned from the traditional midnight service
sodden and chilled. "Right," I said, flinging open the fridge. "We
always had a fry after midnight Mass." "I don't want a fry," said the
Loving Spouse. "Neither do I," said Daughter Dear. "We are having
a fry," I said, "It's traditional." The ensuing heated exchange resulted
in Daughter Dear departing to bed in floods of tears and the "Santa
Run" being done by self and Loving Spouse in icy silence. It is
extraordinarily difficult to bring a full-size bicycle down a cast-iron
spiral staircase silently at three in the morning after a bottle and a half
of Cabernet Sauvignon.

Christmas morning came. Determinedly full of the Christian
spirit, I rose early and within minutes was presenting the Loving
Spouse with a laden breakfast tray of bacon, egg, sausage, tomato,
black pudding, white pudding, potato bread – complete with dainty
napkin and a seasonal sprig of holly.

Propped on four pillows and beaming broadly, he flourished his
knife and fork in eager anticipation. I left him to it. Returning for the
dishes I found the plate satisfyingly empty and His Nibs in a
soporific state, murmuring, "Great stuff! That was great."

What a nice Christmas it was going to be! Even the turkey co-
operated. After wrestling with it the best of three falls, I'd come out
marginally ahead on points and my mother-in-law had made the
gravy.

Four o'clock and the light fading fast, I was enjoying the
traditional Christmas afternoon occupation of most wives and

mothers, standing by the sink, when a furtive figure slunk past the kitchen window, a plastic carrier bag suspended from one finger. As I flung open the back door he froze in his tracks, the bin lid arrested in mid-air. "What are you doing?" I enquired. "I didn't want to offend you," he said, "after you'd gone to so much trouble, so I scraped it all into a carrier bag and dropped it out the bedroom window…" his voice trailed off. I looked in the carrier bag – bacon, egg, sausage, tomato, black pudding, white pudding, potato bread and a seasonal sprig of holly.

WE WAKE ON BOXING DAY to flannel-white light, the palpable silence of falling snow and our cat, belly-flopping down the back garden slope in a state of high agitation. Our cat does not understand snow. Our cat, like snow, is beautiful and thick. About twelve centimetres of the stuff has fallen. I open the back door and measure it with a school ruler. That's about four and a half inches in old money. We peer out the windows at our cosmetically-enhanced garden gowned in velvet, the branches of our little trees glamorously furred with rime. I expect the opening bars of "Walking in the Air" to strike up any moment. We are like the Little House on the Prairie – all the appearance of a rural idyll, yet only two and a half minutes drive from Tesco. Within the hour we discover it might as well be two and a half miles over pack ice because, of course, nobody expected this.

Snow in late December? People are astonished! The province is at a standstill. Trains, boats, planes are delayed or cancelled. The urgent tone of the radio newsreader advises us "not to travel unless absolutely necessary. The Glenshane Pass is being kept open with difficulty." For cryin' out loud! Glenshane is only a 1,000 feet above sea-level. It's not the bleedin' High Andes. You could keep it open with a coal shovel if you started early enough. Surely we've advanced beyond the stage of weather forecasting with a wet finger? Somebody must've known this was coming. There's not a lot of point in sending gritters out to treat the roads after the accidents happen.

An eight-year-old can tell you the world climate is gradually changing. We glean evidence of it daily in television pictures of plucky south-of-Englanders sandbagging their doorsills against floodwater in true Dunkirk spirit, the skeletal images of the drought-stricken African poor, the unexpected Alpine avalanches that wipe out the European rich.

But we're never ready, are we? No more than we're ready for a heat wave, when the first two things we do are run out of sun block and introduce water rationing. Three days of sub-zero temperatures and we're in chaos, literally paralysed with the cold. Half the civilized world lives in northern latitudes with up to six months a year of severe weather. Do any of our city fathers or other public representatives ever go to Canada or Scandinavia and see how they cope, with a view to introducing some simple, cheap but effective ideas? An investment in one or two bits of machinery that could be speedily shunted round this postage-stamp-sized province must surely make sense. Failing that, let's have men – lots of men in yellow coats with a song in their hearts and a shovel in their hands.

Our personal sense of civic commitment seems to have declined sadly over the years. Time was, neighbourly spirit made light of the job. Using a stiff yard brush, preferably wielded by a sturdy ten-year-old, you cleared your front, or at least a path to your door and another parallel to the house for passing pedestrians. These walkways were kept clear with a scattering of salt or cinders. In our street, a house without a man in it would find the job anonymously done. On the morning of my father's funeral, I woke early to a swept and salted pavement and saw Robbie McCarter from No 16 tiptoe away without a word before it was fully light.

While harsh weather lasted it seemed children stayed out till all hours, snowballing and sleighing even by lamplight. How the hands stung with the unbelievable ache of returning circulation. How the chilblains on your heels itched and throbbed as you ran about in your stout belted overcoat, a pixie hood tied firmly under your chin and man's socks over your school shoes to make sure you didn't measure your length in the slush. The socks were rolled in a wet ball in your pocket when you went to have a go on the slide – the black glittering slide, lovingly polished to a lethal gloss by the big boys with judiciously poured buckets of water.

A tottering run-up, semaphoring arms and a terrified Tarzan yell before your feet went from under you and your backside hit the ground with tooth-jarring force. Up you got without a murmur, the hot salt taste of your own blood in your mouth from a gloriously busted lip. Now, you daren't let children out in a school playground on a snowy day in case they get wet or cold or injured and their parents take legal action. By a curious irony some of these same youngsters manage, out of school hours, to create serious public nuisance by snowballing buses, cars and pensioners with impunity.

I can't remember when snow stopped being fun and I started caring more about clothes and dignity and learned to be afraid. I have to be "lunk" round icy pavements now by the Loving Spouse – as a Belfast friend of mine so vividly describes it, "swingin' on his arm like a bucket of refuse".

EASTER IN DERRY is synonymous with one thing only – *Feis Doire Colmcille*, commonly referred to with a fine disregard for the music of the Irish language as "the Faysh". At fourteen or fifteen, under the guise of legitimate pursuit of our native culture, it was a legitimate means of meeting boys and an improvement on swimming galas where, though you saw them with fewer clothes on, you stank of chlorine and your hair went flat with the humidity. Entries for individual feis competitions were so numerous that it was not unusual to be there till a late hour and a season ticket was a passport to an entire week's illicit delights. In half a century, despite the addition of fake tan, full make-up and Harpo Marx wigs, its ethos remains entirely unchanged.

Every year in Easter week there may be spotted in great numbers that breed indigenous to Derry City, the feis mothers. Abandoning their spouses to a diet of chips in a neglected house, they congregate in large flocks at the Guildhall where they spend a week twittering, squabbling and grooming their young.

As a species they are easily recognisable, generally having the well-developed calf muscles of the early Irish dancer, immensely strong kidneys and the iron digestion of a city council refuse truck. Also stoicism of a high order to sit unfazed through 78 infant renditions of "Baidin Elemi" with the critical certainty that their wean is the best.

The feis mother pays for one seat but occupies three. This is necessary since she carries her temporary nest-building materials with her at all times. These consist of a capacious handbag containing throat lozenges, Junior Disprin, kaolin and morphine mixture, half a toilet roll and three emergency pairs of split-new dazzling white ankle socks. Her even larger holdall is crammed to capacity with mousse, gel, lacquer, pins, clips, rollers (foam and spiked), tail combs (steel and plastic), brushes (various), bobbles, toggles, ribbons, hair slides, a battery-operated hairdryer and a gas-powered hot brush.

Over her other arm are draped two or three coats and cardigans, while from her index finger is suspended the zippered portable wardrobe-bag containing "the feis frock".

The feis frock used to be a relatively simple garment. Now it would take the eye out of you. Lined in satin, stiffened with buckram, it's a riot of quasi-Celtic motifs picked out in fluorescent thread and further embellished with little bits of mirror glass. Despite the exquisiteness of its artistry, it is always too short, giving rise to ribald remarks from the louts in the lower balcony when its wearer has passed the age of puberty.

The feis mother is generally accompanied by one or more small children whose enormous knobbly heads are swathed in pink nylon scarves. You see, feis children are not prepared for competition in the comfort of their own homes where every modern facility is available. Not at all! Instead, they are garbed, titivated and rehearsed in the main thoroughfare of the Guildhall known as "the corridor".

In the corridor we witness the wholesale destruction of the ozone layer. A palpable fog of hairspray hangs in the air. The aroma of cheese and onion crisps permeates the atmosphere. Every second adult inhales deeply and thankfully on a cigarette. Giggling clusters of teenagers are strenuously ignoring the fellows they will have got off with by the time the next competition's over. There is barely room to stand; the noise is deafening and little boys in mustard-yellow kilts are sliding merrily through the melee on the shiny parquet floor, shuttling empty Coke cans as they go.

In the midst of this bedlam, the feis mother has set up her temporary nest. Every available nook and cranny is choked with children being tweaked and teased into perfection. God be with the days when it was all done with a pocket-comb and spit – though the serious feis mother, it was said, used a secret recipe of sugar and water to stiffen petticoats and hairstyles to a uniform rigidity. It was also said (with whatever truth) that Ursula Doherty won every competition on the strength of her totally symmetrical ringlets, which bounced like bedsprings in perfect unison as she danced.

For the twenty-second time the pianist breaks into "The Rakes of Mallow". On stage a tiny figure, arms clamped to the concrete folds of her feis frock, points a pre-pubescent toe.

Under her chair, the feis mother's feet dance every step with her child.

I walk down the Guildhall stairs with the feis mother and her friend. "See thon adjudikitter," snorts the friend, " all he's tist's in he's mouth so it is! He's fer nathin. Our Sharon got two seconds and a first in Moville, so she did. What about your Donna?" The feis mother sadly shakes her head. The friend's mouth turns down, all sympathy. Then she rallies. "Ach sure it gets ye outta the house, so it does." She turns to me. "Does your wee girl not do nothin'?"

> "ALL HUSBANDS ARE ALIKE, BUT THEY HAVE DIFFERENT
> FACES SO YOU CAN TELL THEM APART"
> *Anon.*

"THE ORGANISED BRIDE," the book said, "retires early the night before the big day with a nourishing cream on her neck and two slices of cucumber on her eyelids." Well, I couldn't because we were boiling my wedding petticoat in a saucepan till 2am.

"Could you not have got married in white like everybody else?" asked my mother despairingly, lifting it out of the dye with a wooden spoon. We were on our third attempt and the sorry-looking garment was now the colour of a used dishcloth. The shade we were aiming for was "delicate beige" and so far we'd missed by a mile. By 2.30 we had it the colour of Rich Tea biscuits and were dunking it in bleach. By 2.45 I'd given the wedding shoes a second coat of Holt's car paint spray – shade, Metallic Mushroom. They smelt awful but were a perfect match for the dress. "That's everything I think," I said. "Right, well, goodnight then," said my mother, as though it were any night.

"Goodnight Mammy – and thanks," I said, as we made our ways to our separate rooms.

I'd looked after my mother for seven years since daddy died and we'd developed that kind of relationship which every single daughter of an elderly mother will recognise – though we talked incessantly, we told each other nothing. As I got ready for bed on my last night in my own home, filtering up from the floor below came the familiar noises I'd known all my life – the clink of her water glass, the rattle of her pills, the screak of the little drawer where she kept the four pink foam rollers she put in the front of her hair.

I went downstairs and fetched out the sherry bottle and two glasses.

We sat side by side on the edge of her bed like two pensioners on a park bench. The bedside lamp made a puddle of light illuminating the clock which said 3.05am. We both sipped our sherry looking steadily at the opposite wall. Above the mantel hung the framed papal blessing on my parents' marriage. It had been for them a 45 year guarantee.

"What do you remember about your own wedding day, Mammy?" I asked. "I nearly didn't go," she said. "I went out to empty the tea-leaves round the rose bushes and I looked down the hill and saw people arriving at the church and I thought I'll not bother." "Mother," I thought, "this is not what I need to hear eleven hours before my wedding." But of course she did go – and after the second glass of sherry came accounts of the gold satin flapper dress and the pointy shoes from America and the cloche hat that looked just like a chamber pot. "My hair was shingled," she said. "It looked a bit like yours." Her voice broke. "It'll never be the same again after tomorrow."

"Of course it will," I lied, patting her shoulder.

"I don't know what you want to go rushing into this for," she sniffed.

"Mother! I've known him twelve years!" I protested.

"And leaving me alone," she continued.

"Mother, we've bought a house five doors up the street and installed a telephone extension." She was not to be comforted.

By 3.40am we both had had some more sherry and a good cry. I held her hand till she drifted over to sleep. Eventually I stumbled to my own room where, with eyes like two pickled onions, I read magazines till daylight. "Groom vanishes on wedding morn. Jilted bride maintains, 'I love him still.'" "A monster from the moment I married him: How a man can change the minute the knot is tied." It was elevating stuff.

The wedding day dawned, overcast, chilly and threatening rain. We had chosen to be married in a church renowned for its architectural excellence and utter inaccessibility. From a vantage point in a lay-by, the bridesmaid and I sat and had a quiet smoke. While our driver pushed his peak cap to the back of his head and sang country and western numbers, we watched our friends' cars criss-crossing a complicated pattern of by-roads in a desperate attempt to reach the frustratingly visible church before we did.

"Where the hell were you? Come on for God's sake!" said my eldest brother, anxious to give me away with unflattering alacrity. He hauled me out of the car and up the very short aisle. I was at the altar before the organist had eight bars out. I looked at the man waiting for me. He was the right one. When the ring was put on my finger I got a terrible urge to say, "Well, that's that."

We were motioned forward a few steps to the inner sanctuary and the service continued. An altar boy nipped in smartly behind us and swung together a little pair of golden gates. They closed with an infinitesimal click. I looked back once over my shoulder. Mother was on the other side.

"TILL DEATH US DO PART" – every word weighty as lead. I'm sitting up in bed staring into the dark. Beside me, the Loving Spouse, immovable as a rock, is occupying two-thirds of the available space. I'll turn on the light perhaps, and switch on the radio very softly, or go downstairs and get a snack. Then I remember. In the polite deference of newly-wedded bliss, my civil rights have been eroded. You have no irritating habits, thank heavens – just "little ways", like disapproving of people eating crisps in bed and playing the radio all night and sleeping with the light on.

I sigh a great sigh and think about it all. This is what we got married for, to be together always. We've been married a fortnight and the togetherness is killing me.

Now I'm haunted by the presence of another body in the house. No matter where I turn, there you are. I feel crowded, my personal space invaded and I resent it. And yet, what can I say? Inside my head I shout, "Go away! Go away and let me breathe! Let me have an hour, a day, a week to myself. Let me see past you!" Outside my head I say, "Could you please not stand directly behind me when I'm putting on my make-up? It's very distracting."

"And they too shall be one flesh." I've never understood that. In this first two weeks of married life it has struck me several times that you are a complete stranger to me. After all, you're not family, are you? I'm only related to you by marriage.

Meanwhile we're playing Wendy houses. There is a pile of once-worn shirts lying on the landing. Your mother picked your shirts up and washed them. I'm thinking if I pick them up once, I'll be doing it for the rest of my life. Your shirts lie amorously entwined with my own laundry. My mother picked mine up and washed it. We have a stalemate situation. Despite comprehensive training in domestic science, the strain of planning and providing something different for the dinner every day is exhausting my culinary ingenuity and limited repertoire. I have acquired my mother's habitual expression of harassment within a week.

We've had our first row. Surprise, surprise, it's about money. What's yours was yours, what's mine was mine – now everything is ours, and there isn't enough of it. I go out to buy dining-room curtains and come home with a new dress instead. We have a full and frank exchange of views about economic priorities. Whatever happened to "with all my worldly goods I thee endow"? Is this what they mean by "for better, or worse"?

I remember a useful piece of advice from my friend Joanie: "When you have a fight," she said, "make sure you get to bed first. Then you won't be the one sleeping on the sofa."

You did that one night – sleep on the sofa I mean. I forget why we were having "a little coolness". You were mad when I pointed out that there was a fully-furnished spare bedroom where you could've sulked in comfort. Oh, I remember. It was the evening I said I'd just run down the street and get something from home. "You mean your mother's house?" you said. "What?" "This is your home," you said.

Uh-uh, Freudian slip. Why does it not feel homely then? Why hasn't it an identity, a character, a smell? When does raw newness blur to reassuring familiarity? When does it become a home? When does the raw newness of this marriage translate to comfortable ease?

You stir in your sleep and half waken.

"What is it?" you ask. "Are you worrying about something?"

"Nothing at all," I say. "I'm perfectly happy."

"I love you, you know," you say.

"And I love you." I lie down in the crook of your arm and, snug as two spoons, we sleep.

I'D MET HIM IN A COFFEE SHOP and "took agin" him on sight. I was going out with his Best Friend. An evening came when Best Friend rang to say he couldn't make our date but, sooner than disappoint me, he was fielding a substitute. The substitute arrived. "Oh, it's you," I said.

It was customary in those days to invite your evening's escort in for coffee and a light snack. "Were you in for your supper yet?" was a litmus test of the state of the relationship. Abandoning him to sit uncomfortably in the good room, I ran to the kitchen. With lightning speed I buttered bread, sliced bananas and spread the merest soupcon of lime marmalade to enhance the flavour of the fruit. I carried in the plate of sandwiches.

Back to the kitchen for energetic combining of chopped dates, walnuts and cream cheese with brown bread. I carried in the second plate of sandwiches. There was nothing left of the first save three crumbs and the doyley. "Very tasty!" reported the new swain. Returning with the coffee pot, the date sandwiches had all disappeared too and the new swain was ostentatiously dabbing his mouth with a napkin. "I'd sooner keep that fella a week as a fortnight," muttered my mother.

Reader, I married him and we lived happily ever after. He never told me for ten years that two things he can't abide are dates and marmalade. He'd filled his pockets with the sandwiches and threw them out the car window at intervals all the way home.

I'M GOING TO BUY one of those pedometer things that you strap round your ankle and it records how far you walk in a day. I'm sure I'd amaze myself even if I monitored nothing more than the distance between the points of the eternal triangle of sink, worktop and cooker that leaves you at the end of the day with arteries standing out like ships' hawsers and pain that persuades you have deep vein thrombosis. Like most women, I haven't sat down in twenty years. All day, everyday, I traipse, I trail, I plod. Like Felix the cat, I just keep on walking. Rather like summer swifts who do everything in the air, women have a tendency to flit about tweaking, adjusting and pecking at the fabric of their lives. Ever restless, even when ostensibly off duty, women must constantly pace out what belongs to them, just to make sure everything is where it should be and everybody is where they ought, or at least said, they would be.

Being a successful wife and mother is like being a competent teacher. The secret is discipline and order. Arrange your classroom so that you can see all your pupils' eyes. If you can't see their eyes you've lost them. This is equally applicable to husbands and children in a domestic setting. Keeping on the move is the second secret of success. Like a factory overseer or a fairy godmother, they shouldn't know where you'll pop up next. Your movements must be arbitrary with no discernable pattern, otherwise they'll cultivate the appearance of industry while in fact doing nothing. There's no point in issuing commands from an armchair. It's necessary (see rule one) to get up close and personal, eyeball to eyeball, speaking slowly and distinctly, "I want that bathroom ceiling painted. Now!" One or two may attempt to desert on the pretext of buying more paint or a pint of milk. Be merciless. Stand over them till the job is done. Show no sign of weakness. Remember – a woman on her feet keeps a man on his knees! It is a noble thing to wear out one's shoes without going anywhere. There was no seat in Queen Maeve's chariot! The woman who sits down to iron is lost! (I thought you might relish these epithets from the book of Modern Female Irish Martyrs). Women, it has been proven, are more adept than men at multi-tasking.

Let me illustrate. Attach pedometer to one leg and follow me.

Bedroom. Start to plump pillows and straighten duvet. Find two library books, three newspapers and paper hankie on his side. Note one book overdue. Leave in hall beside empty plastic bag. Drop paper hankie in bedroom waste bin. Bin full to overflowing. Fetch plastic bag from hall. Bag rubbish. Take to utility room bin. On utility room floor notice heap of washing. Sort into darks, delicates and hot whites. Hmm – not quite a load. Scour rooms for grubby things. Note peculiar stain on daughter's bedroom carpet. Rush for spray stain-remover. While kneeling to zap stain, discover two crusted cereal plates and coffee mug growing its own penicillin under bed. Carry to dishwasher. Dishwasher full of clean crockery. Unload into cupboards. Notice sticky sauce bottle rings and spilt herbs in top cupboard. Turn out cupboard. Discard elderly looking packets and cartons. Ah, tarragon. Remember promising Anne a recipe for that chicken thing. Open recipe drawer upon a yellowing blizzard of magazine cuttings and grease-spattered cook books. Turn up all kinds of interesting things, including the lost recipe for Mother's boiled cake. Ring sister and dictate down telephone line. She'll make it. She has time. Fold dry tea-towels with one hand while phoning, opening drawer with foot. Remember wash not started. Remove eleven damp towels from garage line to leave room. Re-organise airing cupboard to accommodate them. Discover good silver and salad servers wrapped in a napkin and entirely black with tarnish. Spend a happy afternoon standing at the draining board restoring them to their reproduction splendour.

Suddenly, he's home and hungry. He heads down the hall towards a shower and a shave, tossing rhetorical questions over his shoulder, "What did you do all day? Have you started dinner yet?"

The backs of my legs are aching. He stands stock still in the bedroom doorway with a look that says, "You might at least have made the bed!"

Men have a very poor grasp of economic reality, particularly in the domestic sphere. They couldn't tell you off-hand for example, the price of a pair of children's shoes, or a pot of jam. They could not attempt an educated guess at the cost of a carpet sweeper; a car, yes;

a cooker? Possibly. Curtains, no. Curtains are just dangly bits of coloured material. The average man wouldn't notice if you hung flour-bags at the window.

The average man, truth to tell, thinks there's something a bit "big girl's blousey" about taking an interest in (let alone appearing knowledgeable about) interior design or personal style or the fixtures and fitting that lend quality to family life.

It's his mother's fault, of course. She has trained him from childhood to pallid indifference about such things. These are her domain. She it is who has laboured long over his trouser creases and colour coding his socks until the day sartorial responsibility for his matching tie and hankie is handed over to his new bride at the altar rails.

This "learned helplessness" in men is rooted in history, a legacy of the conspiracy of silence perpetuated through the ages by generations of women. My father lived and died and never knew the real price of anything. My mother believed it would only upset him. In the course of a 44-year marriage she took scrupulous care to preserve his ignorance by ensuring that he rarely if ever darkened the door of a shop and thus risk a coronary by reading a price tag.

It was relatively easy then when food-buying was a corner shop, women-only job performed daily with the aid of a stout string bag. Clothes-shopping was equally simple. In those enlightened days of home approval, shops would let you have three of anything for as long as you liked. Father stood awkwardly before a mirror while garments were hung upon him, his economic innocence protected by the simple expedient of detaching the swing ticket before trying on. In the unlikely event of his enquiring the cost, my mother had a fictitious but realistic figure hovering on the tip of her tongue.

This skill she'd acquired the hard way after several embarrassing experiences with him. On the rare occasion they did shop together, my mother always came home puce with embarrassment, the bow on her velvet hat quivering with indignation. She would never, she swore, go anywhere with that man again. He had "shown her up" by haggling in the shop. "Glory be to God!" he'd say, dropping the sleeve of a sports jacket in disbelief. His ancestors must've been cattle dealers or similar, since my father stoutly affirmed the named price was merely a starting point and he was entitled to a hefty reduction on the grounds that (a) he was a decent fellow and (b) surely that wasn't the best the unfortunate retailer could do?

Meanwhile, my mother operated a highly successful black domestic economy, making every penny do the work of two and juggling the demands of a growing family with miracles of creative accounting. Public opinion corroborated the fact that she kept us lovely. "Heh! Heh! We'll be in the poorhouse over this," she'd giggle as the crackling brown paper carrier bag was stealthily smuggled past the oblivious occupant of the living room and rushed upstairs to the back of the spare room wardrobe.

An unspoken agreement has existed among women across generations – there are some things men never need to know and how much a woman really spends is one of them. Men are psychologically incapable of taking such information aboard. This is proven by the variety of their response, from incredulous rage to baffled despair to profound depression when they inadvertently come into possession of the truth. I taught my daughter the importance of preserving this particular facet of the feminine mystique.

All went swimmingly, I told her, until Adam's applecart was upset by Eve's espousal of feminist frankness, that the fall of man was in fact brought about by telling the truth. Adam awoke from slumber one warm afternoon in Paradise to find Eve prancing about in a very natty leaf-green outfit comprising bikini bottom, matching bustier and cape. He eyed her designer fibres with suspicion. "Zeebub Designs," said the label. "B.L. Zeebub." "How much did that snake in the grass charge you for that?" asked Adam. Eve hesitated. She and B.L. had discussed her husband's possible reaction to the price and had arrived at a reduced but credible sum. He'd thrown in the birch bark bangle for free. Eve looked into the clear trusting eyes of her loving spouse. She couldn't deceive him. Eve told him straight and true. "My God!" he shouted, tearing his hair. "You'll have us put out of house and home! We'll be paying for this for the rest of our lives!"

And from that day to this, no woman has ever told a man the true price of anything.

A RECENT POLL SUGGESTS that the single most frequent cause of arguments between married couples, in restaurants and cafés, occurs when she leans across the table and steals his chips. This I refuse to believe. The restaurant offers many more fruitful opportunities for full-scale marital battle, all the way from booking the table to paying the bill, with no guarantee of getting to the pudding stage in a state of armed truce. People pay extravagant sums to go out and squabble and not enjoy their dinner when they could disagree more cheaply at home over a pizza and a bottle of plonk. You've all seen them, the couple by the restaurant window, with their straight backs, deadpan expressions and exaggerated courtesy in helping each other to vegetables. An atmosphere of tension hangs over them, palpable as a bad smell.

He has a genius for taking forever to choose the dullest thing on the menu. Her dish arrives. It looks interesting. His arrives. It looks disappointingly undistinguished. "Mmm, this is delicious," she says. "How's yours?" He looks lugubriously across the table. "Mine's a bit on the bland side. I *was* going to have what you're having." "Oh!" she says, smitten with guilt, as if it's her fault he chose the wrong thing. "Have a bit of mine." "No," he says. "Come on," she says. "No, really." In the ensuing fencing match with the cutlery, the generous forkful lifted across the table falls in the butter dish. From thence the evening goes rapidly downhill following an unvarying pattern of dialogue beginning "Why do you always...?" Like the waiter, let us tiptoe quietly away.

Subjects that create arguments between couples are many indeed; they range from the mundane to the bizarre, from the sublime to the ridiculous. Random examples: hoovering with great energy and little skill, welting the head of the vacuum cleaner off the skirting boards and chipping the paint; washing the pots but not drying them and leaving them stacked wrong side up with half an inch of water still lying in the bottom of them; dropping dirty clothes on the floor despite the close proximity of not only a laundry basket but a laundry bag.

Clothes and the care of them are one of the chief bones of contention between couples, especially if one is a hanger-upper and the other a draper-over. (You lay the outfit you've just taken off over the back of a chair to cool before putting it away and, as the days pass, the garments just seem to pile up until the chair falls over.) This last seems to be a feminine failing, though men are the worst hanger-uppers in the universe. The world's most gifted male mathematician cannot grasp the geometric correlation between a hanger and the shoulders of a jacket. The science boffin with a PhD in the molecular structure of natural fabrics will still hang a lambs-wool sweater on a wire hanger or throw it over a coat hook where it will develop a hump like Quasimodo's.

Men rarely hang out public washing, except when their wives are recovering from childbirth and it's the look of the stuff on the line, pegged-out all higgledy-piggledy in front of the neighbours, that galvanises so many new mothers into speedy recovery.

Now none of these little, shall we call them, "idiosyncrasies" would matter if both parties in the relationship could keep quiet about the other's failings, but "always the bitter word". In a recent cold snap the Loving Spouse dug out a sweater he'd not worn for some time. I was intrigued to discover that, wearing it, he seemed to have developed two decidedly prominent but peculiarly placed nipples. Did I say a word?

"IS THERE ANYTHING WRONG, DEAR?" he enquires mildly in the cab on the journey home. "Nothing," she responds with the hard-edged smile, the enigmatically expressionless eyes that say, "Boy – you're in trouble!" "That's alright then," he says, lulled into a false sense of security by a glass too many of George and Ella's excellent Cabernet. "I enjoyed myself." "Indeed you did," she says in a brittle voice that, were he sober, he'd realise bodes ill for the rest of the evening. Only the presence of the taxi driver, listening with the very stubble on the back of his neck, is saving him from the wrath to come.

Men are literalists. Tell them there's nothing wrong and they believe it. This drives women mad. Women start by denial, but expect to be coaxed towards revelation. Instead, a man takes the statement at face value, settles down to read the paper and is astounded when, five minutes later, a weeping harridan snatches the sports pages from his relaxed fingers and shrilly berates him for perceived slights, omissions and lack of sensitivities he's totally unaware of. Men don't do "subtle".

Men are emotional infants who must have what a woman wants, needs or means, spelt out to them in block capitals on billboards. This is not the view of a rampant feminist but the result of a Scottish university's psychological study based on recognition of facial expressions of emotion. Men's poor grasp of the more subtle gradations of feeling call their accuracy and sensitivity into question. They can identify "happy", "sad" and "surprised", but score low on recognising "anger" and "disgust" on pictured female faces.

It's many years since anthropologist Desmond Morris gave us the term "body language" to describe how we betray ourselves a thousand times a day by stance, movement, gesture and expression in a non-verbal language as eloquent as any oral expression. Women prove apt scholars, their intuition giving them a head-start. Adept at assessing atmospheres and interpreting silences, they're also more used than men to picking up non-verbal clues from children who manifest their moods in facial expression and body movement. It's a fact that fathers deal less efficiently with the temporary occupation of a teenage daughter's personality by an alter-ego who's a cross between Morticia Addams and Marilyn Manson. He seeks in vain his lost little princess behind Goth velvets, dead white make-up and a predilection for music with violent lyrics and no tunes. But it's chiefly between husband and wife that one observes every nuance in the almanac of non-verbal arts.

A significant percentage of young couples still confess their eyes met (figuratively at least) across a crowded room and they knew they were destined for each other. This, I venture to suggest, is a "once-in-a-lifetime" moment of male perspicacity that rarely recurs. With the typical woman of course, the catalogue of tips and wrinkles for keeping her Significant Other in order evolves automatically from the moment the engagement ring slips on her finger and soon develops into a handsomely bound first volume on Man Management.

Nothing however beats the seasoned performance of a couple whose mime-artists' skills are as good as a cabaret. When in company, sit opposite the wife and watch her telegraph unobtrusive signals across the table to her hapless partner. Deprived of her full vocabulary of body language, she employs a kind of shorthand – an infinitesimal narrowing of the eyes, the tiniest tightening of the lips, a flare of the nostrils, a barely perceptible nod – all of which serve to remind him of the taboo topics of the Northern Irish dinner table: religion, politics, money and sport, and warn him off inappropriate anecdote and suspect humour. You may well intercept the killer glance that says, "I warned you before we came out." Best of all is when, emboldened by alcohol, he embarks on the kamikaze route to social death by telling the one about the drunk, the dead tortoise and the meat pie.

Most wives, if they're honest, institute themselves a one-woman policing board of every social utterance that passes their husband's lips. I'm fortunate in rarely having to employ these tactics with the Loving Spouse, who, drunk or sober, is the soul of discretion. One lift of an eyebrow from me and he does and says exactly what he pleases.

AN ALLIED HAZARD OF HOME-OWNING is the unspoken obligation to the bit of ground that goes with it. Neighbourhood expectations are high.

You are nearer to God in a garden, they say, than anywhere else on earth. I remain agnostic. Like you, I watch gardening programmes with consuming but dispassionate interest. As with cookery books, devoured voraciously, but I'm still dining out (or in) on half a dozen faithful old recipes. Horticulturally, I can admire the finer points of a hedyserum coronarium with the best of them but I've never grown so much as a nasturtium.

That's not to say we haven't a healthy show ourselves. Bristling three-foot nettles, dockens like banana leaves and thistles of a ferocity to make you whistle. Sulucks stud the lawn in great flat plates like veruccas with roots reaching down to Australia. An invasion of foxgloves, celandines and clover has colonised the back. "It's a wild garden," we explain, "for the butterflies and the bees, you know." It fools nobody. Our rockery has nothing in it but rocks. We soon learn to dread our visitors' cutting remarks. "Must pot up a few cuttings for you," they offer. "In no time at all you'll have cushions of colour." "No thank you," we never have the courage to say, so subsequent visits bring dozens of dinky little containers and enough instructions to rear a child by. Some of the little green things up and die while some just expire on the spot. "I'm afraid they don't 'do' with us," we say, not meeting the donor's sceptical eye. "We think it must the acidity of the soil."

We're just not gardeny people but we live in an area where folks creep about on all fours at all hours in all weathers weeding, feeding and talking to their garden plants.

A short stroll up our road in the cool of the evening reveals the substantial posterior of the greater spotted housewife rising roundly out of a riot of blooms as she mulches her ranunculas. Her mate, the lesser-striped businessman, wields an assortment of impeccably maintained accessories or pilots a state-of-the-art mowing machine skilfully between unusual species without visible perspiration. Edging tools, gleaming seccateurs, gardening gloves and kneeling pads lie upon the barbered sward in careful disarray. They're not out with kitchen scissors, a broken plasterer's trowel and an old bath mat, like us.

Our mower is of a cantankerous temperament and bronchitic disposition, grumbling under its breath and stopping every one-and-a-half lengths for a phlegmy wheeze. Our epileptic strimmer belches forth a foul-smelling stream of black smoke and gives the grass a finish like a prison haircut. We grudgingly admire our neighbours' stamina. They always finish the job, signalled by the scented whorls of smoke burning garden waste, curling obediently upwards. We cleared an area of undergrowth once and left the pile of debris so long it re-rooted. The neighbour who mows his lawn at 7.30am once directed people to our house: " – the one with the weeds growing up the drive."

Of course I'd like a velvet lawn, a lavender hedge and a bed of peach-coloured roses, but unless you get a free gardener with them, forget it.

Meanwhile, as I say, we never see the faces of our neighbours, but their backsides speak volumes. Undaunted, we wish them a cheery good evening and go on our way, smacking the hedges with a stick and sending clouds of dandelion clocks sailing over into their immaculate beds of coreopsis auriculata.

> "IF MEN HAD TO HAVE BABIES,
> THEY'D ONLY EVER HAVE ONE EACH"
> *Diana, Princess of Wales*

TO SAY I WAS IN TWO MINDS ABOUT THE PROSPECT would be altogether too simple. I was in several minds – roughly equal shares of delight and terror, anticipation and dread. "It's your hormones," I was assured. "You'll settle."

Of course I was an absolute curio at the ante-natal clinic. Downy-cheeked students were fetched from all quarters to inspect this "elderly *prima gravida*", as it said on my chart. They discussed delivery problems as if I were a parcel and tinkered with my innards like a car engine.

I bought a book of course – and read it. I didn't actually do any of the alarmingly energetic and healthful things it recommended. For me, knowing the theory has always been enough.

Out in the real world it was early May 1981 and the province was on the brink of political catastrophe. There was a palpable tension in the air, a mood of contained violence waiting to erupt and engulf us. Hunger strikers were dying daily. I read accounts of their deaths without emotion. After all, what was death to me who carried life? In an almost primitive way, I retreated into a mental and physical cocoon. Contented as a cow, I awaited the birth of this creature whose hard little heels were lodged under my ribs. This "it", whose gender I had not permitted myself to acknowledge as either male or female.

It was going to be a wonderful birth – a spinal injection, full consciousness and as dignified and decorous as a Mothercare catalogue. I had not bought so much as a vest. There was no pink or blue nursery prepared with fluffy toys or frilled Moses basket. All baby gifts were refused. "Wait," I said. And I did, for too long.

"No epidural injection for you," said the anaesthetist briskly. "Too late to be effective. You'll have to manage on your own." He, his trolley and my salvation trundled off down the corridor. "But I never read the chapter on natural childbirth!" I wailed after him. Too late. Too late.

In the next hour, large chunks of Fox's *Book of Martyrs* floated into my consciousness – the early Christians, their separate limbs tied to four horses sent speeding off in different directions; the Reformation martyrs cut down while still alive and disembowelled before their own eyes. I was suspended in a black roaring void. This new life, rushing to its birth was taking my life with it. "I'm dying," I thought, quite dispassionately. "I'm dying and I can't remember any prayers. No! In fact I'm dead and this is Hell, for all eternity."

A massive anger overtook me. A bitter rage against the conspiracy of silence among all my female friends; they conspired to portray this bloody and obscene nightmare as a fulfilling and sublime experience. I felt only a great sense of betrayal and I screamed in rage with what I assumed to be my last breath.

On page 16 of the old *Happy Venture* school readers, there is a picture of Brer Rabbit and the Tar Baby. The tar baby is a skinny black scarecrow-like creature on a stick, with splayed fingers, dangling legs and a highly indignant expression. "My God!" I thought as the doctor held it up to me, "This is what teaching does to you!"

One castor of the hospital trolley squeaked maddeningly as I was rolled back to the ward. Far away, in a day room, the bland burble of a television soap opera was interrupted by a newsflash. "Pope John Paul has been shot. He is gravely ill." "He can't be in any worse case than I am," I thought with some acerbity. "Oh, poor little baby, what a world to bring you into." I kissed the clotted cockscomb of dark hair.

Out of my private apocalypse had come a small purplish replica of my mother. I had left the care of one to care for another. I'd come full circle.

En route from the hospital, we stopped to buy a few things like a cot and a bath and a baby alarm. The Loving Spouse's face was grim as he wrestled them aboard the roof-rack. "I don't know why people spring these things on you at only nine months notice," he said.

I CAME LATE TO MOTHERHOOD, well-versed in the theory before embarking upon grim reality. I'd stood on the sidelines while my friends endured the trauma of childbirth, followed by prolonged periods of drudgery exacerbated by a small, sleepless, demanding creature utterly dependent in every particular. You could always tell a house with a baby in it. The eye-watering fumes of Parozone met you at the door mingled with the distinctive odour of Milton, both overlain by the pervasive reek of that destroying angel of all known bacteria, Dettol. There'd be banners of washing, damp things drying over radiators, dry things airing over clothes-racks and inevitably and unavoidably, in the corner of the kitchen, the lidded plastic pail that hid unspeakable things to be dealt with before bedtime. The burden of a baby was to have your lovely home transformed into a Magdalene laundry. I remember a neighbour's backyard line groaning with nappies, pegged out like Tibetan prayer-flags, rigid with frost on winter mornings.

Lord, what a business it was; the muslin nappy-liners, the terry squares, the jumbo-sized nappy pins and the crackling plastic pants which hardened and split within weeks. For gala occasions, these were embellished with ruched nylon frills, hen's bum-style. The irony was that none of this bulk could ensure a leak-proof result. Infants waddled about with a leg at each corner, their chubby thighs chafed and sore. It's a mercy they didn't all grow up bandy. A baby's a fragrant cuddlesome thing at one end, but at the other, a powerful self-contained, one-person methane plant. I knew one new father who recoiled and fled from his baby boy's first nappy and never could thereafter deal with the less salubrious aspects of his son's rearing.

The disadvantages of cloth nappies are legion. Getting a terry nappy on a baby is like trying to wrap a tin of Quality Street, which, as you attempt to get paper round it, rolls away. Sticking large pins into thick folds of fabric in the vicinity of a newborn's navel is not a job for the clumsy-handed who risk perforating the infant or skewering their own finger. Add to these impediments the fact that not all mothers are good washers. A lineful of nappies blowing in the breeze only pleases if they're dazzling white and fluffy, not if they're grey and scratchy. Every day you're forced to flag up your public unfitness as a mother.

I produced my only child at the beginning of the Eighties when bulk moved north to women's shoulder-pads and the neat, secure, self-sealing disposable nappy came into its own, to the same resounding acclaim that must've greeted the sliced pan. I bought them by the box-load, gleefully sure no lidded nappy-pail would ever darken my utility room door. "Using disposables?" The gossiping elders were dry-mouthed with disapproval. "Well, you must do what you think best dear," they'd add with a wry twist of the lip, implying you weren't much of a mother and disposables came under the heading at best, of sinful extravagance, at worst, of unnatural practices.

There was little talk then of their doing damage to the environment. The conservation debate had barely begun. Now, after more than twenty years of energetic argument on sustainable energy levels, we're told there's not a pin or sticky tab of difference between fabric nappies and disposables as far as environmental pollution is concerned. There must be many thousands of exhausted, prune-fingered mothers out there ready to kill dead things.

Our disposable baby was minded by her grandmother while we worked. Delivered each morning with a car-load of accessories including a large carton of disposable nappies, which, mysteriously, never seemed to dwindle, she was collected by her father in the evening. Until the day I arrived unexpectedly early from school. Driving in, I beheld Daughter Dear staggering down the garden, a miniature bow-legged John Wayne, backside encased in terry-towelling and plastic pants, like a Christmas pudding in a boiling cloth. Behind her on the line fluttered half a dozen Harrington's best terry squares, muslin liners and two pairs of hen's-bum knickers. Nanny Robinson dear, may you rest in peace. You did your bit to reduce global warming, but you wore yourself out for nothing.

THERE'S A BABYNEEDS SHOP near where I get my hair done. I was intrigued to see in its window something that looked like a small, heavily padded Centurion tank, equipped with the three wheels of a Robin Reliant. Beside its extortionate price tag was a notice that said, "Folds neatly away for your convenience." Everyone knows that anything with moving parts, from telescopic umbrellas to holiday tents, is governed by Sod's Law – "whatever can go wrong, will go wrong." It's a very long time since I've had any dealings with a pushchair, but I recall ours had a tendency, when you hit a patch of rough ground, to fold up with the baby still in it. Secretly I hankered after the big and classy Silver Cross or Pedigree pram, so beautifully sprung that, were it not for the restraining straps of the safety harness, the baby would be bounced out on its head. Indeed, as an early adolescent, I walked a variety of nephews and nieces in just such a carriage, my arms nearly wrenched out of their sockets to keep control of it. I remember having a fixation with the brake, a simple metal bar restraining one wheel. A particularly energetic infant occupant of the pram was quite capable of jump-starting it down the road to disaster. Years later, I saw the film *Battleship Potemkin* with its famous scene of a pram rolling and bouncing diagonally down a great flight of steps and I perspired anew at the memory of the steep slope at Brooke Park.

We bought a buggy complete with hood, apron, transparent weather protector, a metal rack underneath and shopping bag attachment. And a space for the baby! When fully laden with all her accoutrements, all I needed was a yellow jacket to be mistaken for the Corporation dustcart. Nothing daunted, off I set in a tight skirt and high heels over the uneven surface of St Columb's Park main thoroughfare. After about 500 yards I was walking like Dick Emery and the baby was grizzling and rubbing her eyes. That was the first, last and only time I ever took her anywhere. The buggy wasn't the only thing to fold up at the slightest provocation. Henceforth, her grandmother walked the roads with her to the mutual benefit of their health. And fresh and well they both looked on the strength of it.

MOST MEN AREN'T MUCH USE around very little children. They're handless with the helpless. They hang about on the fringes of rearing, waiting for the infant to be able to communicate properly and/or kick a ball. If forced to handle the child at all, they do so tensely, with the caution they might apply to the removal of a sizzling leg of lamb from a very hot oven, looking frantically about for somewhere safe to put it down quickly. Men are alarmed by the rag-doll limpness of the newborn and the way it kind of hangs in their hands, head and limbs lolling like a half-stone bag of flour and that's exactly why they heft it onto their shoulder where it invariably rewards them by vomiting down their back.

New Labour has introduced paternity leave for new dads. I don't suppose anybody thought to ask women whether the government's idea was a good one, or indeed if it was what women themselves wished. I suspect some of us think having a partner under your feet plus the new baby, amounts to looking after two children when you're not fit to cope with either. My heart goes out to today's young mothers who, it seems to me, give birth in almost indecent haste on an obstetrical conveyor belt and are immediately bundled home exhausted and ill, baby in one arm and a bag of National Health goodies in the other, with no guarantee of the rest, care and attention vital to both mother and child.

I was fortunate to have my daughter in what I consider to be the halcyon days of the maternity service when post-natal hospital care stretched to an unimaginable six or seven days. Battered and sore and feeling I'd never walk again, the warm informality of the maternity ward was balm to me. What a wealth of wisdom and compassion there was among the women there – experienced women who persuaded you to persevere with breast feeding when both you and the child were yelling for a bottle and comforted you when the baby blues set in. Friendships were forged; there was laughter and chocolate and the contentedness of women together adapting to the role they were created for.

And the best bit was, the men were shooed out the door by the ward sister after a baffled hour or so spent staring at the new arrival, vacuum-packed like a pork chop into its little Perspex crib at the foot of the bed. The importance of early paternal bonding had not yet been discovered. What passed for bonding in those days was the odd fatherly "coochie-coochie-coo" delivered with a tickling forefinger when passing the cot or pram; the supportive alarm system that shook you out of oblivion at 3am saying, "Waken up dear, the baby's crying"; the helpful and inexpert mixing of formula thick as semolina that wouldn't come out of the teat of the bottle and occasionally the nappy monitoring service, "Are you sure that child's alright? Nothing healthy could smell that bad."

Once the novelty of a new baby has worn off and it dawns on the parents this is, if not a life-sentence, then at least a twenty-year stretch, their mournful attention turns to their social life, now dwindled to faint memory. Friends? Oh yes, they remember friends and getting dressed up and going out. We solved the problem cheaply and to the satisfaction of all. There was a whole generation of children born and reared in the Eighties whose infancies were spent under a pile of coats in the spare room at parties. You brought a casserole, a bottle of wine and the baby. The guest bedroom became a parking-lot for carrycots and the occasional exhausted dad who'd been on floor duty the night before. Probably the chief difference between us and parents today is the degree of angst child-rearing engenders in the hearts and minds of perfectly capable people suddenly filled with self-doubt. A baby was assimilated into our lives with a minimum of fuss. We reared it on instinct and the accumulated wisdom of our mothers and grandmothers rather than experts and got on with the business of living. There were days when the grey vista of child dependence seemed endless, but it's gone in the blink of an eye; gone like snow off a ditch and the children with it.

HOT ON THE HEELS of my daughter Sarah's fourth birthday came polite enquiries from friends and neighbours about her starting school. "I suppose you have her name down?" they presumed. No, I hadn't. "I suppose you'll be going to Mummy's school?" they enquired of Sarah. No, she wouldn't. By late June and deadline time I'd come to the conclusion that I couldn't bear the thought of the child going to school at all – which is extremely odd for someone who has been teaching for twenty years, most of them in reception classes. And then it dawned on me that the harrowing part of the first day at school is not the wailing infants, but their mothers. The annual task of detaching them with difficulty from their children, talking them out of the door and being haunted for the rest of the morning by tear-stained maternal faces at the window, drives me potty. And this year I was cast in the part of emotional parent. I did not care for the reversal of roles one bit.

My psychological reluctance manifested itself in strange ways. The "kitting-out" of Sarah was left till the last possible moment. I rushed round the town buying her three of everything. "Isn't she big for her age?" marvelled all the shop assistants, automatically reaching for the larger sizes. And wasn't the bill for it all big for her age too! I signed cheques recklessly in mounting horror.

I took her home and put it all on her. There she stood like a little Confederate Army officer in her slightly-too-long grey pinafore and her slightly-too-long grey socks and her great big black shoes; a mouse-like, anonymous figure with my baby's head poking out the top. The Loving Spouse took one stricken look at her and disappeared upstairs for a long time. I put the uniform away till D-Day.

The night before (D-Day minus one), the uniform was ironed and hung up, the big black shoes polished and everyone ordered early to bed – for no better reason than it's what my mother would've done.

I lay for hours in the dark thinking, as every mother does, that it was only yesterday she was born, remembering all her pretty babyish ways and knowing everything would be changed irrevocably from tomorrow. A deep sigh from the right alerted me to the fact that Loving Spouse wasn't asleep either. "What are you thinking about?" I asked. "I'm wondering if she'll pass the Eleven Plus," he said.

The great morning came with all its attendant trauma of getting Sarah out to school and Sarah's mother out to a different school. Sarah couldn't wait. Debate waxed eloquent over the respective merits of biscuits or crisps for break. The Loving Spouse left for work, eventually, after returning three times to hug the daylights out of his little new schoolgirl. He was in a tizzy of anxiety about her ability to cope with life in the raw jungle of the reception class. "For heaven's sake go," I said. "You know if she meets any problems she'll talk her way out of them." "Just like her mother then," he muttered and went.

Sarah and I drove the short distance to her school. Out we got, Sarah skipped happily ahead while her mother lagged behind, calling, "Take your time." Inside, she hung up her coat, put her bag on the back of a chair, sat down with folded hands and asked, "When am I doing my writing?" The bemused class teacher looked at me. We engaged in a brief conversation. I checked my wristwatch. On the other side of the city 26 other mothers' children were waiting. I had to go. "Goodbye, Sarah," I called. She didn't turn her head. "Goodbye, Sarah; be good," I called again, lingering by the door. She was utterly engrossed in play. I hovered outside the window for a minute. She didn't look up. I drove all the way across the new bridge with the windscreen wipers flailing furiously on the only dry morning we'd had for weeks.

I'd regained my composure by the time she had to be collected. "Well, Sarah, what happened today?" I asked as she emerged, cardigan trailing, tie under her ear and socks concertinaed about her ankles. "A wee boy strangled me," she said in aggrieved tones. "Yes, but what did you do to him?" I countered with the infant teacher's conditioned response. "I hitted him," she said with great satisfaction. We drove out the road to Grandma who was waiting in a fever of anticipation to see how she'd got on on her first day. There was a long and thoughtful silence from Sarah in the back seat. Finally she leant over and asked, "Mummy, will I be a schoolgirl for ever and ever?"

"No, Sarah darling," I said. "It'll just seem like it."

HEALTH PROFESSIONALS ARE ALARMED at the increasing incidence of back trouble in the young. This, they say, is due to lack of physical exercise, serial slumping in front of the television, bad posture during long hours at the computer console, but mostly to schoolbags. A picture in the paper portrays a primary schoolchild (he looks about six) wearing a rucksack worthy of a round-the-world backpacker. It extends from the base of the ears to the backs of the knees and is obviously so heavy the poor kid can scarcely stand upright and indeed looks in imminent danger of turning turtle. Stand at the gate of any primary school and watch the little ones stagger through. Like miniature pedlar men, they are weighed down with stuff. Apart from the statutory satchel or rucksack, there's the lunch-box in one hand, the PE kitbag in the other, probably a bulky project folder, a musical instrument in its case and a bale of greenery for the nature table. Heads bowed, they struggle forward as if against strong wind. They're exhausted before they ever get through the classroom door.

And when they get there, what? Modernity decrees that the old-fashioned sit-up-and-beg school desk, with a lid and capacious storage space inside, is too formal and forbidding, so they've all been thrown out in favour of dinky little child-friendly tables and chairs and nowhere left to put anything but the floor. The result is that the average primary classroom looks like a transit-camp full of little refugees, each sitting in a circle of all their belongings. For the teacher moving round the classroom to give attention to individuals or groups, it is a never-ending army assault course undertaken in high heels.

The secondary schools' regime resembles a perpetual moonlight flit. Every 45 minutes or so, every pupil has to up sticks and move to a different classroom, taking everything (and I mean everything) with them. The incidence of pilfering and damage to personal property in some of these schools means that cloakrooms are virtually unused and every classroom chair is draped in its owner's coat. A student timetabled for six or seven subjects in a single day would need an airport trolley to trundle the weight of their textbooks around. Add to this equation the "cool" factor, that, however ergonomically well-designed the schoolbag he or she carries, the average teenager simply will not wear it in the approved manner. The "correct distribution of weight" principle, no matter how carefully instilled and re-iterated in health and personal development lessons, carries little weight and fewer kudos compared to the casual "hanging off the right shoulder" mode and slouching to the left to compensate. What are comfort and safety set against the laid-back look, and the possible long-term consequences to bone alignment are an unimaginable half a lifetime away? Besides, who wants to look like a studious, parent-pleasing nerd?

There were days that Daughter Dear could scarcely lift her schoolbag, let alone carry it. To her everlasting embarrassment, I stood up at a parents' evening and complained loudly, only to be informed by authority, with a fair degree of frost, that lockers could not be made secure and the to-ing and fro-ing necessary between classrooms and lockers would shave valuable minutes off the lessons. I didn't pursue the matter.

My sympathies for Daughter Dear were severely dented by the discovery that, rather than take on the tiresome task of repacking her schoolbag every night, she simply carried everything with her every day like a bag lady.

I bit back the recriminations as I guiltily recalled my own schooldays when I was no more sensible. Every schoolbag I ever had eventually burst under the tightly-packed weight of not-strictly-necessary textbooks. I remember, too, the harrowing shame of having to carry a traditional and very expensive leather satchel, bought by my indulgent parents when everybody else was sporting a modern brightly-coloured tartan duffle-bag. Eventually I achieved fashionable "in-crowd" status, painfully paid for with a shoulder rubbed red-raw by the duffle-bag cord and numbed and purple fingers when I gave the afflicted shoulder a rest.

Do parents ever think to check just what exactly it is their overburdened darlings are toting about day in, day out? As a teacher, the most frequently repeated phrase I ever heard from mothers was, "What note? I never got any note!" To the piping cry of "Miss! Miss! Somebody stole my dinner money!" the only response can be "Look for it properly. Turn out your schoolbag." Prepare for a revelation. A small landslide of rubbish slithers out on the table-top, only a quarter of it connected to school. Young children are like jackdaws. They hoard things: sweetie papers, comics, bits of elderly biscuit, a fossilised banana skin, homework task sheets (undone), funny-shaped stones, crayons, half-eaten rubbers, toy cars, Barbie clothes, swap-cards, broken jewellery, the previous term's lost reading book, the last three school circulars to parents – and the dinner money. Mind you, I wouldn't care to undertake the exercise with anybody over the age of twelve. You wouldn't know what you might find.

TIME SPENT WITH YOUR CHILDREN, say psychologists, is never wasted. It's "quality time" for you and the child. I beg to differ. It is 9.25 on a wet Wednesday night in a desolate car park and I have been waiting for a considerable time. (Come to think of it, I've been waiting on and off for 17 years.) Precipitation that is not quite sleet stars the windscreen. Light cast by the buildings' long windows shows rain gusting horizontal, pattering against the passenger side of the car like handfuls of wedding rice. I am cramped and frozen, dead from the knees down. I always mean to bring something to read, but the courtesy light is too dim and anyway I've no glasses with me. Ho hum. Turn the radio on. Radio Four. An earnest arts programme being earnest about the arts. On Radio One, Liam Gallagher, eyes closed, is bawling through his anorak. Ah! Here's a nice bit of light classical music but the reception's buzzy. I fiddle in the dark, surreptitiously push a few buttons despite the Loving Spouse's warning. "It took me ages tuning that radio properly. Don't touch anything, just switch it on and off." I cannot remember the permutations of buttons and wavebands. I lose everything, begin to press wildly and at random. He'll kill me! Better cover my tracks. Put a tape in. I go through the glove compartment. All the tapes out of their cases lying in dusty unprotected chaos are mine. All the neatly boxed ones are his. Where's me good Enya one with the "wah-wah" music I find so restful and therapeutic? Ah! That's it, crunching ominously under the heel of my left shoe. There's no sign of her yet.

Things I should be doing involve books to be marked, dishes to be done, soup to be made, not to mention dusting round and squaring up. How does anybody manage with more than one child? I suppose they don't sleep much. And what about the two sets of sheets and duvet covers that have resisted ironing for a fortnight? It's all waiting too. I comfort myself coldly with the fact that none of it will run away. But I might.

Twenty-to-ten. What's keeping her? This is the scenario familiar to aspirational parents everywhere. The cost of enhancing your offspring's cultural development is not just the fees for music lessons, ballet, drama and horse-riding, but the cost in man-hours, or woman hours I should say, since it's almost invariably mum sitting numb in the car park three nights a week.

I've often thought how I might improve the shining hour during these spells of compulsory inactivity, which form a measurable part of my schedule. I could learn a language perhaps, read *War and Peace* (all of it; not just the peace bits, which is cheating), or do those sitting-down aerobic exercises as recommended by health and beauty magazines, where you clench various groups of muscles in turn without anybody noticing. I saw a demonstration of that technique once on television. Well, actually, there wasn't much to see. The girl wore a leotard which twitched twice, and an immobile expression – that curious fixed look a hen has in the act of laying an egg. I wasn't impressed. Thinking about it, I think "thinking" is probably the easiest option since it requires no equipment and only a very little space. Ordinary thinking is perfectly serviceable for weekday waiting in car parks. Thoughts like: why does air freshener combine with a bad smell to make a bad smell worse? Or how come potatoes don't keep these days? And was the man who invented the safety pin not a greater and more useful genius than Mozart? I wouldn't go any deeper into the boggy ground of introspection if I were you, and steer clear of the quicksand of eastern philosophies while you're at it. I'm half-persuaded, you know, that transcendental meditation originated in an oriental car park with a guru waiting to pick up his wee one from dancing.

In other countries people pay good money to sit solitary in glass boxes tuning their minds in to themselves. "Therapy," they call it. You can get it for free here, in a car park near you. Your only requirement – a child who goes to evening classes.

THE PARENTAL EAR IS A MARVELLOUS ORGAN. It can distinguish between silence and suspicious silence. The parental ear can gauge the difference between the stillness of a sleeping child, lids translucent moons of innocence above flushed cheeks, and the feigned corpsing of a group of sub-teens piled together for a sleepover.

The parental ear can spontaneously differentiate between the busy silence of absorbed play and the unnatural absence of noise that means there's something going on. This palpable silence, weighty with significance, usually presages some sort of domestic or personal disaster. Every parent knows exactly what I mean. It is the moment after the three-year-old throws one shoe and her cardigan out the window of a moving car on the motorway. It is the moment after little Billy wedges three beads up his nose or swallows a coin of small denomination.

I experienced it first when I found four-year-old Daughter Dear sitting cross-legged and mute under the hall table having cut off all her front hair to the very bone with a pair of nail-scissors. It is this period of hiatus when the true enormity of what they've done dawns dimly upon the little darlings that I call the "silence of the lambs". And yes, it's always a horror story.

For example: We've always been extravagantly complimented by other parents on our daughter's sweet nature, social graces, general biddability and willingness to wear clothing chosen by a sad old fogey like her mother. However, pride comes before a fall.

"Where's the baby?" we asked each other one Sunday afternoon.

The baby is woman-big now but you get foolish when you've only got the one. Where is she? "I'm having a shower," came the ungracious and unlikely rejoinder from behind a firmly-locked bathroom door. "Funny time to have a shower, at 3pm on a Sunday afternoon," remarked the Loving Spouse. "You'll have yourself washed away," he addressed the unresponsive door.

A long time later we heard the door open. I peered into the bathroom. Condensation blinded the mirrors while the basin was smeared and streaked with dried blood; water stained a rusty red trickled in the base of the shower tray; a towel marbled with gore draped the bath. My heart lurched. The screaming violins of *Psycho* sounded in my head. Like any normal mother, I immediately thought the worst – a massive haemorrhage, or a suicide attempt at the very least.

There was one bloodied item in the wastepaper basket. "Chilli Pepper Red," the sachet said, "semi-permanent hair colour." Ah.

I knocked for admission to the temple of beauty. Sarah's towelling turban concealed all but a single vibrant lock. An interesting colour. "Oh Mum," said Sarah, biting her lip. "Your father will kill you."

It turned out that six of them all bought the same shade and were all putting it in that afternoon with a view to stunning the form-class on the morrow. The school will take a dim view of it, I know. I'm writing a note to her form teacher, trading on the fact that, as a school contemporary of mine, she'll remember the unfortunate incident with the peroxide in the science room in fourth year which nearly got both of us expelled.

The Loving Spouse is beside himself. "Still, I suppose it could've been a nose stud," he concluded gloomily. Indeed it might.

DAUGHTER DEAR HAS TAKEN A NOTION to redecorate her room. She favours a colour-scheme of lime-green and navy with wavy lines at dado height and stencilled furniture. In a house where the most vibrant colour is pale mushroom it will be a holy show, but I suppose we can always keep her door closed when people come.

Maybe it's me – a daughter of the design era of solid mahogany tables, magnolia paint and the three piece suite in uncut moquette. The most adventurous improvement in our domestic scenario was the modest rearrangement of the sideboard and the sofa and the daring introduction of a Bernard Buffet print framed in brushed aluminium circa 1967. Apart from that, the beige basket-weave wallpaper was replaced every third summer by an almost identical design – and Jimmy.

You wouldn't have described Jimmy as a professional, though he made his living at it. Small and extremely short-sighted, the lenses of his glasses, thick as beer-bottle bottoms, were further obscured by a million hardened specks of every colour he'd ever used in a 25-year career as painter and decorator. His vision was further impaired by a permanent plume of cigarette smoke from the endless Woodbine clamped to his lower lip as he worked. Despite the fact that Jimmy couldn't have identified his own mother at twenty paces, his joins were impeccable, his borders plumb-line straight. He worked extremely fast, cutting and pasting like greased lightning, the big black scissors fairly singing through the wallpaper and the stubby paste brush shooting thick gobbets of Polycell in a six-foot radius. Jimmy had a curious relationship with protective coverings. Though my mother shrouded everything three-deep in dust sheets, thirty minutes later Jimmy would be discovered pasting away on a polished surface, the dust sheets trampled underfoot. He was particularly fond of the top of the piano and once opened the lid to balance his cuppa tea on the keys so he wouldn't leave a heat-ring on the French polish. You could've tracked him through the house by his strange circular footprints, each boot heavy with a penumbra of pasty paper scraps.

Jimmy was an artist with a roller – a French impressionist. By the time he'd finished a ceiling, every stick of furniture beneath it was misted with colour in a delicate pointillist technique.

Cleaning up after Jimmy was akin to dealing with the aftermath of a large-scale natural disaster, time consuming, distressing and inevitable. But we knew Jimmy was past it when, after much pleading, I was at last allowed proper patterned wallpaper for my room. I chose a delicate design of drooping laburnum blossom, pendulous and graceful. Jimmy closeted himself for five hours, emerging only twice for tea and currant cookies. Through the door emanated a soulful sound which, though tuneful, did not qualify as song. It was Jimmy, fulfilled and happy, humming sonorously through his Woodbine. Alas, the smoke cleared to reveal four walls of yellow laburnum blossom scrambling determinedly upwards like runner beans. Jimmy had put it on upside down.

We got Bobby after that, a clean efficient non-smoker with 20/20 vision and a paste brush with hairs in it.

TRADITIONAL FAIRY STORIES are full of the legend of the changeling child. Long ago, it was said that the Little People would steal away a human infant and substitute a goblin baby, intractable and strange, to break the hearts of human parents. Well, don't look now, but I think fifteen years and two changes of address after the birth of our daughter, the fairies have finally caught up with us. They appear to have stolen away our sweet-natured, confiding and affectionate child and left us a replica of her. This alien being has taken up residence in our daughter's room, hitherto a pink and white shrine to little-girlhood with dolls, teddies and trinkets. The inexorable click of the door lock announces the beginning of a pogrom. In a ruthless exercise in ethnic cleansing, all tokens of infancy are banished in bin bag-loads to the loft.

Having disposed of the population of our daughter's kingdom, the changeling next turns her attention to the livestock, tearing all 212 pony pictures off the walls. A collage of thick-lipped, sex-crazed rock stars takes their place. The hermetically-sealed room becomes overnight an exotic hothouse of draperies, scented candles and gloom. It looks, well, decadent and a steady thrum of pop music makes the ornaments jump on the next-door mantelpiece.

Sometimes the changeling comes out of her room and looks at us distantly with barely-concealed impatience. Occasionally she betrays by a sphinx-like smile that it pleases her we should feed, clothe, transport and subsidise her. Regularly she flounces out in a perfumed whirl of smoky eyes, strawberry lips and haughty demeanour. Her social life is a closed book to us. The post-mortem is held over the next two days in interminable telephone conversations with others of her kind, conducted in a patois we barely understand.

Occasionally the changeling will honour us with her company for perhaps one course of a meal. Communication is minimal. She has picked up a few working phrases like "What?", "Yes", "No", and "I don't want anything more to eat", but mostly communicates with a single shrug of one eloquent shoulder or a remote and calculating stare.

The Loving Spouse is baffled, and hurt. He misses the romps, the jokes, the hugs. He misses Daddy's girl. He looks at the closed door in dismay. "What's she doing in there?" I can't be sure what she's doing, but I can make an educated guess. She's sitting for hours before a mirror despairing of her nose, her teeth, her skin, her eyes, her hair. She's standing for hours before a mirror yearning for longer legs, a smaller bum and a bigger bust. She's trying on every stitch she possesses just to reassure herself how ill-fitting, ugly and unsuitable it all is. She's weeping over the trite lyrics of pop songs and hysterical with loony laughter at the antics of second-rate comedians. She's testing the boundaries, trying out a new persona, re-inventing herself – one moment boisterous, arrogant and popular, the next friendless and crippled with self-doubt.

Meanwhile, outside her door we wait. She's in a foreign country to which our visa has expired, from which we are debarred by age and a language we no longer know or understand. But sometimes, in dead of night, we venture in illegally and look at the changeling sleeping peacefully in our Daughter Dear's bed. Often by a trick of the light, you'd swear you were looking at the childish, vulnerable and tender face of our own sweet baby. And sometimes the changeling stirs in its sleep and murmurs, "Love you Mum, love you Dad."

SOME FELLA'S ASKED OUR BABY out to the pictures. Her father will be distraught. He lives in daily dread of her falling in with anybody remotely like he used to be – and with good reason. I remember the way he used to be. It's taken me twenty years to get him the way he is now.

I'm equivocal about the whole thing. If I was any sort of mother I'm sure I should be more anxious but I suppose, like puberty, the Eleven Plus and piano exams Grade 5, it's another thing to be got through – another rational step on our daughter's road to independence and autonomy. Another step away from us.

In the middle of preparing dinner she appears over my shoulder. "Can I ask you something, Mum?" "Anything, darling!" I respond airily, chopping the vegetables for the stir-fry. "Sure you know you can talk to your old mum about anything." There is a lengthy silence. The vegetable knife suspends itself in mid-air. The cold hand of apprehension clutches my vitals. "Well, Mum, you know Jonathan?" "Vaguely, dear. Which one is he?" The old film begins to unreel in my head complete with soundtrack: "Who is this boy? Who are his people?" "He's the one with black hair. He's lovely. He's so sound, Mum. We get on really well." I drop the egg noodles into boiling water. "Where does he live? What school does he attend?" My mother's eyes hold mine. "You remember, Mum. We left him home one time." Ah yes, semi-detached with very healthy looking hanging baskets.

The onion rings and carrot sticks hit the hot oil with a resounding hiss. I stir busily, playing for time. "Well, y'know darling, it's different going out in a crowd. This is getting a bit particular don't you think? And you're very young." "Mu-u-u-m! I'm fifteen-and-a-half. I'm grown up. I know what I'm doing. Can I go, Mum? Can I?" "Sweetheart, I never got anywhere till I was 17." "Oh, for heaven's sake! That was in the dark ages. It's different now. Please say yes, Mum!" The bean sprouts turn glassy in the hot sauce. Thirty years dissolve as my mother's voice and mine say together, "You'll have to ask your father." There is a pregnant pause. "You ask him for me, Mum," she pleads. "No, Sarah, you're grown up now. Grown-ups ask for themselves." We pat the fruitless argument back and forth. Irritated, I think: Couldn't she have picked a long slow casserole day to introduce this topic. "No, Sarah, I will not speak to Daddy."

I carry the plates to the table. The egg noodles have congealed into a sticky yellow mass topped with slimy, exhausted-looking vegetables. The Loving Spouse peers down at his plate, puzzled. He lifts a forkful to his lips. "Darling," I say. "Sarah has something to ask you."

CAN ANYBODY TELL ME at what point do parents stop knowing everything and suddenly know nothing? At what point do one's children stop meekly accepting instructions in "how to do" and, irrespective of gender, suddenly turn into Harry Enfield's Kevin, complete with pitying stare at a parent's inability to cope with new technology. I'm well down the road towards idiot status by this stage, having signally failed to understand the workings of Walkmans (surely that should be Walkmen?), the video recorder, e-mail and most of all, the mobile phone.

Like many other women of my age, I got a mobile phone for purely functional reasons, because I'm frequently on the road in far-flung parts of the province and likely to get lost or stuck or held up by circumstances beyond my control. I know how to drive a car and recognise the little gauge that says it needs more diesel. I know where the wipers, lights and horn controls are located and have recently discovered (by a process of elimination) the windscreen washers. Anything else on the dashboard that flashes or bleeps in a warning class of a way sends me into instant panic because of course I've never read the car's handbook. Where would I get the time? I was mystified by the sinister little tune that plays every time I opened the driver's door till Daughter Dear informed me scathingly it's to tell me the driver's door is open. Doh! The DVD player we got for Christmas is an even deeper mystery.

It's my use of the mobile phone that puts Daughter Dear astray in the head. She watches me hold it well out in front of me so I can see the dialling panel clearly. I begin to poke at it with a rigid forefinger. "Look," she says, snatching it from my hand, "there's no need to stab it to death. Who're you ringing?" "Dad," I say. "Dad's work number is stored in its memory," she explains loudly and slowly as if to a foreigner. "It's simple." She begins kneading the number panel with the lightning twin thumbs of a Hong Kong masseuse. "There's the menu. Now just scroll up or down till it says 'Dad'." I try, but Dad keeps escaping off the top of the list into oblivion. I get the "gawd-you're-hopeless" look. Apparently, though, I'm not the worst. Her friend's mum claps the mobile to her ear in order to hear the caller, then holds it to her mouth like an ice-cream cone to respond.

"I'll show you how to leave a text message for Dad," she offers, all exaggerated patience. Again the flying fingers routine with an equally rapid running commentary. I'm lost within seconds. A sound like steam escaping from a pressure-cooker emerges from her pursed lips. She just can't grasp why I can't grasp it. In belated defence of myself, I observe, "I thought the whole point of a phone was to talk to people, not send them messages in gibberish."

But occasionally, just occasionally, my *amour propre* is restored and the tables are turned. Daughters reared to a life of clean pressed laundry left by the fairies need simple tuition in the art of ironing. "Look at the picture of the wee iron on the garment label. Count the number of dots on the wee iron. Turn the dial on the big iron to the same number of dots. If you iron a garment on two dots when the label says three dots, you'll be there till the grass grows round you. Basic rule, keep the iron moving otherwise you'll get an interesting pattern of brown triangles. Learn through experience; creases won't come out of anything that is too dry and press linen on the wrong side under a damp cloth. If there is a big X on the wee iron, it means do not use the big iron at all."

It may be necessary to adopt the same unvarnished simplicity in regard to men and culinary matters. "Listen up. Here is a supermarket quiche. It says on the box cook from frozen at 200°C for 20-25 mins but it's faster in a fan-assisted oven. Ours is a fan-assisted oven, so keep your eye on it." "How long does it take then?" he asks. "I don't know. You just sort of know when it's done." He turns away, baffled by feminine finer judgment that says if it looks ready, it probably is ready, except the bottom might need a minute or two extra to firm up the pastry.

Ah well, to each his own. We play to our individual strengths and learn not to sweat the small stuff. By the time you're the same age as the parents you thought were fools, you begin to realise how wise they were, but by that stage your own children are rolling their eyes in patient pity at you. Never mind. What goes around comes around. Give them twenty years and they'll be idiots too.

"TRAVEL IS GLAMOROUS ONLY IN RETROSPECT"
*Paul Theroux*


CONSIDER THE COLLECTIVE MINDSET of the day-tripper – that curious urge that invests several thousand people simultaneously with a fearsome unity of purpose that sends them rushing lemming-like to the sea. This is a poor analogy actually, since the "rushing" involves travelling very slowly nose to tail along congested roads, like Galapagos turtles heading for the beach to lay their eggs. Arriving at the sea, many of them (the trippers not the turtles) don't even leave their cars, but dispatch the browbeaten youngest for supplies, which they eat in cramped surroundings with the windows tightly wound up against the elements, the condensation of the carry-out obscuring the view from the inside, while the steady drumming downpour obscures the view from the outside. Having tossed their litter out the window, they drive home again under the impression they've been somewhere.

Let us examine closely the contents of one such vehicle as it throbs sulkily in an endless tailback. The car in front will do. The car in front is a Toyota. A two-year-old is waving out the rear window. The people in the car behind have made the initial mistake of waving back. Now they've tired of the game and stopped. The two-year-old begins to grizzle, whimper and tramp about over people's laps, treading on their tenderest parts with impunity prior to throwing a full-blown tantrum, having been prevented from dropping her shoes out the window. The thirteen-and-a-half-year-old slumped moodily in a corner oblivious to the din, is determinedly uninterested in everything. Deprived of video, computer games and a mooch round the shopping mall with his mates, he picks moodily at a pimple and responds to all conversational gambits with grunts of contempt. None of his friends would be got dead going anywhere with their parents.

"Oh look everybody – primroses!" Mum's bright tones belie her face full of tension and anxiety. At the back of her mind is the waiting pile of ironing, the greasy grill pan in the sink and the sure and certain knowledge that no matter where they eat or what they eat, an hour after they return somebody's going to ask, "Are you not making any tea?" She thinks longingly of the sun-lounger in the little back porch with a magazine and a cup of coffee, but Mother-in-law needs a wee run out. "Are you enjoying yourself, Gran?" she enquires with a half-turn of the head.

Gran is wedged in the back with the youngsters because her daughter-in-law's bad back necessitates a front seat. Damn all wrong with her if she'd leave off the high heels, thinks Gran. Look at the state of that young fella with his hair like a sheepdog and the knees out of his trousers, and his sister, a madam at sixteen with her black eyes and yon pelmet of a skirt. And that wee one wants a right good slap. Gran wonders what way they're being reared, where the next toilet is, and how she's going to tackle the coleslaw without her bottom set. At this moment she yearns for her little pensioner's bungalow where she could be watching Greer Garson in *Mrs Miniver* with a wee glass of sherry – but she wouldn't hurt her son by saying so.

She pats the back of his neck with a wrinkled hand. His grin is more like a grimace. His ankle's aching upon the accelerator as he trundles forward at 15 miles an hour. He could be watching the sport from a horizontal position with a newspaper over his face. "But I'd better take them somewhere," he'd thought. Now he's watching the engine overheat and coming dangerously close to boiling point himself. Gawd awmighty, even mowing the lawn would be better than this – or papering the spare room.

A souped-up Escort with massive spoiler and go-faster stripes drifts abreast in the neighbouring lane. It's crammed with boys with beer cans and back-to-front baseball caps. The harsh vibration of heavy metal music beats suddenly against the windows. They are loudly appreciative of the detailed physical charms of the sixteen-year-old daughter who folds up like an ironing board with embarrassment. For her father this is the last straw. "For two pins I'd get out and knock their heads together." "George, George, calm yourself," pleads Mum. With a final jeering catcall the yobboes pull away, leaving Gran tutting with disgust.

Up ahead the funeral procession of traffic gathers a temporary momentum. A flurry of windblown sleet stars the windscreen. The metronome beat of the wipers ticks away the long minutes of another fun-packed Spring Bank Holiday.

IT WAS DARWIN, wasn't it, who first propounded the theory that at one stage in our evolution we humans were marine-dwellers, cleaving the pearly waters of prehistoric oceans with webbed limbs, then sensibly losing our scales and fins and spending more and more time upright upon dry land?

This is not a concept I have any difficulty accepting, except in Northern Ireland's so-called summer, when half the human race seems hell-bent on returning to the element from whence it came, attired in skimpy bits of floral cotton, to jump up and down getting very wet in the name of entertainment. I refer of course to sea bathing, particularly, but not exclusively, in foreign climates.

The Irishman abroad is a byword for caution. He doesn't drink the water; he deplores the malodorous state of foreign sanitation; he eschews all suspect continental foods, going so far as to bring his own cornflakes; yet he, his wife and family, disport themselves with perfect equanimity in the semi-solid mass of floating effluent that is the nearly tideless Mediterranean Sea. For this he can be forgiven on the grounds of seeking respite from the broiling heat, but what's his excuse at home where only one day per decade is hot enough to justify taking your vest off in public?

Ponder if you will, the average Irish day by the sea in mid-August. People walking briskly upon a breezy beach are sensibly attired in draught-proof tracksuit bottoms, cosy fleece-lined jackets and stoutly-cushioned footwear. They may have a dog or a ball or a squad of similarly attired offspring or any permutation of the three. They are healthy, hearty people.

At this point I'd like you to note the fine observational detail of my fieldwork. On your behalf I have researched this topic thoroughly, by sitting in the car with all the windows fully wound up, a plentiful supply of newspapers, the radio and a bag of sucky sweets.

Watch our sample group of beach people now as they stride along the high-tide mark, eyes narrowed against the grit-laden wind that pastes their natty casuals to their sturdy limbs and lodges sand in the lace-holes of their designer trainers. I salute them through the car windscreen, noticing, as I do, how the combed and curled wavelets slap the sand and fan out into delicate foam-edged crescents like lace doyleys upon a plate.

Into view comes a limping male figure. Balding, and with a distinct paunch, it is naked save for a pair of very small bathing trunks, purchased perhaps in leaner, fitter days. The creature makes its barefoot, shivering way to the water's edge gingerly over shards of razor shell, glinting glass and the squelching cowpats of used disposable nappies. The icy sea-surge clamps its calves like leg irons. The figure flings up its arms and belly-flops unbeautifully into the brine, no doubt ingesting useful amounts of iodine and ozone. I know by the time I finish this article on the Russian economy, he'll be puffing past, purple faced and prune-fingered, body hair abristle, back to his beach base to balance upon one leg in a chill wind, removing sand from his most painfully intimate places. And sure as I know that eggs is eggs, he'll remark aloud to no one in particular, "Brrr! I enjoyed that."

I am immune to the siren call of the sea. I have no female affinity with its moon-governed tides. I think I'm the only person who ever put one foot in the Mediterranean in mid-July and discovered it was cold. Even as a child, a day at the beach was one of undiluted misery.

Coaxed into the water, I could never surrender myself to its natural buoyancy. I never experienced that vulnerable lightness of being, of young creatures in their natural element. Instead, standing waist-high in goose-fleshed terror, I felt the cold clutch of the swell, stealing my breath and lifting me off my feet. The treacherous shingle tumbled and slid, the shifting sand flowed out from under my insteps and my heels sank deep. I was mesmerised by the tide's magnetic and inexorable pull, out and away from the land. Time stopped. I watched like some silent film, projected upon a receding screen, the happy family tableau far up the beach. With leaden limbs I realised that the sinister sea was trying to take me away. The bright semaphore of a waving beach hat and a shout brought me to my senses. The spell broken, I stumbled yelling up the beach to be sandpapered with a hard towel and comforted with damp tomato sandwiches. Presently the others ran back to shriek and splash again. "Come on," they called, "the water's lovely." "No, it isn't," I said firmly to myself, and I have never taken up the invitation since.

IT'S THE ELEMENT OF COMPULSORY ENJOYMENT I think that nearly guarantees family holidays to be rated on a scale from disappointing to disastrous. To be far from home with few facilities and 24-hour enforced intimacy is the stuff of which prison riots are made. I'm surprised the government doesn't introduce legislation to outlaw family holidays, and as any marriage guidance counsellor will tell you, September sees their offices besieged by aggrieved individuals whose two weeks *en famille* have cost them an arm and a leg and the irretrievable breakdown of their relationship. From the minute you bring the luggage down from the top of the wardrobe you're in danger. The casual enquiry, "What d'you intend taking with you?" elicits the response, "You decide." It's only a matter of moments till you're standing, teeth sunk in the first bone of contention.

Nerves taut as bowstrings, two hours behind schedule and returning twice to check the locks, we drive away. Hooray! The holiday has begun. Hey-ho for the open road! Just beyond the city boundary I remember the basketful of salad stuff left in the utility room. I say nothing. As navigator on long journeys there are only two rules to be observed. One, never attempt to unfold a four-by-four road map while sitting in the front passenger seat in the process of circumnavigating a motorway roundabout at peak traffic time, and two, learn the names of the wee places on the way to the big places, since the big places only get mentioned every twenty miles or so. This will save you protracted sojourns in the less salubrious suburbs of major cities and spare you the bitter accusation that, in your case, third level education was a total waste of the taxpayers' money. Do not dismiss out of hand statements like, "Daddy, I saw a signpost for that place a few miles back." Sometimes the child is correct. Unfortunately this is often succeeded by the triumphant declaration, "See I was right, wasn't I, Daddy? And Mummy was wrong," repeated at frequent intervals over the next two hours.

Without doubt, one of the greatest holiday hazards to family relationships is eating out. It's international I think, the unerring instinct children have for loudly demanding the monkfish goujons at £8.50 when they could have the nourishing lasagne at £4.75. "I shall have," announces Sarah with relish, "warmed papaya slices in a sour/sweet glaze with pine nuts on a bed of lollo rosso." "You won't like it," says the Loving Spouse. "She might," I say on my second glass of wine. "Let her try it, it's all part of growing up, experimenting, finding herself." "She'll find herself locked in the bloody car with a fish supper if she doesn't behave herself," says her father.

Accommodation whilst on the move is now dealt with by a highly efficient book-ahead system whose only flaw is you're never sure what you're getting. It's the calculating eye of the booking agent which unnerves me as we present ourselves, hot, creased and grubby, and she doubtfully matches us up with something suitable. We feel it might be a tinkers' encampment. "Y'know, we should invest in a travel iron," muses the Loving Spouse, eyeing three impeccable Italian girls in crisply starched cotton.

"Travel iron?" I snarl. "Travel iron? Listen, I don't iron at home. I'm sure as hell not doing it here. What about inventing the travelling tumble-drier, smart ass?" I too have seen the Italian jobs.

The accommodation turns out to be spacious and gracious. No matter. In ten minutes it's draped with drying smalls like a Neapolitan slum. We climb gratefully into bed and position ourselves with plumped pillows for a chapter of holiday reading. The bed glides smoothly away from the fixed bedhead over the polished parquet while the pillows disappear down the ensuing chasm and our two skulls meet the headboard with a sudden and resounding crack.

Two weeks later, we put the key in our own front door. We inhale deeply the familiar smell of our own territory and something else – the basket of salad stuff now recycled to a stinking brown slime. "East, West, home's best," says Sarah, nuzzling her face into her own pillow.

IT IS HIGH SUMMER. The Derry natives, depending on their cultural conditioning, seek seasonal refuge in their traditional haunts of Donegal or the Antrim coast. As a family, we were never Bundoran or Portrush people. We went to County Down, because despite forty years' residence in Derry, for my parents that was home. Late July sees us on the platform of the long-gone GNR station at Foyle Road. Railways are romantic. All my life I lived by one, my days regulated by the clink of shunting goods-wagons in the chilly dawn and the soft susurration of steam, like a tired sigh, as the last train drew in at 11pm.

The metallic punctuation of the station timetable was better to me than any clock; the rhythmic ring of the wheel-tappers, the sporadic gunfire slam of a dozen carriage doors in quick succession, the shrill command of a whistle. Then the first long, slow, hollow C-H-U-F-F from deep in the engine's belly followed by a shuddering jolt and the curly blue and white letters of LONDONDERRY begin to slide past the window.

I'm twelve, travelling alone for the first time to my aunt's for the summer. For me, trains hold fascination and terror in roughly equal amounts. I'm petrified by the engine's great rear wheels whose diameter almost exceeds my height and their random habit of squishing great belches of steam about my bare knees. I stand in awe of the black-faced, glittering-eyed footplate men, their overalls shining stiffly with congealed grease and their air of casual bravery in the very maw of such an uncertain beast.

I live in mortal terror of falling down between the carriage steps and the edge of the platform or dropping my bag or my beloved teddy bear down there. As I set my crepe-soled Clarks sandal upon the footboard, I glance down at the rails dully gleaming and glimpse out of the corner of my eye the bold railway rats, their dun-coloured coats difficult to discern against the dusty sleepers, but their thin whip-like tails twitchily evident upon the sharp grey gravel.

In an agony of anticipation, I wait for my parents' decision on where I'm to sit. Although young, I have several well-developed theories regarding railway safety. Theory one, don't sit in the first carriage, you'll be killed in the head-on collision. Theory two, don't sit in the last carriage, you'll be killed by the runaway goods train crashing into you from behind. For a brief and glorious period I travel in the comfortable reassurance of a central coach, until I watch a railway-bridge sag and collapse, on a newsreel film, jettisoning the train's middle carriages into a raging torrent. Subsequently, the crossing of the River Bann becomes a nightmare.

The railway is a world hedged about by sanctions. These are engraved, embossed or enamelled and screwed to the walls of the carriage. You're allowed to do hardly anything – no spitting, no leaning out of windows, windows open no further than that point indicated by two brass arrows, do not attempt to alight while the train is in motion and definitely no using the toilet while the train is standing in the station. Any infringement of these regulations incurs the direst penalties. (The railways are very fond of the word "penalty".) And the direst of all is reserved for that tantalisingly situated object so temptingly within reach – the communication cord. To be used in EMERGENCY ONLY. Penalty for mis-use, FIVE POUNDS. I feel about the communication cord pretty much as Adam and Eve did about the tree of knowledge, but I also know, if you pull it, you get your name in the paper, your family is disgraced and probably an angel with a fiery sword is placed at the railway station booking-office to prevent your ever travelling again.

There isn't much else to do then but put my forbidden feet up on the prickly plush seats and watch my luggage overhead, bulging through the sagging wide-meshed net that lets smaller things fall through. The hedgerows foam with cow parsley rippling in the back-draught of our headlong passage. We flash by rural halts, their names picked out in whitewashed stones, beds of begonias standing to attention in regimental colours.

Almost as soon as I'm aboard I start worrying about getting off again. I eye the stout leather strap with metal eyelets that hauls the heavy sash window up or lets it down again with a slithering crash. I see myself struggling with this, fumbling futilely at the awkward brass door-handle while the train waits, crouched and hissing, ready to spring into life again and carry me far past my stop. This is as great a dread as the snarling dark of the tunnel, endured alone with a broken light-fitting. Worse than a closed carriage with no toilet facilities is the corridor train. A swaying, stumbling progress two or three carriages along, negotiating the concertina bit where the carriages join, which bucks and leaps as I bestride it, heart in mouth, waiting for the two pieces to part. Anxiously I tell off the station names like beads upon a rosary. I get my luggage down much too early. The backs of my legs are scourged by the bristling upholstery.

With a snarling contraction of muscle the train pulls into Portadown. I wrestle with the window strap. A kindly porter sees my white face at the window and throws open the carriage door. Stiff-legged with tension I descend to the platform. The engine spurts a final malicious hiss of steam in my direction. A smiling uncle steps forward to embrace me. "Aren't you the great girl, coming all this way yourself?" he says.

While my parents holiday in their home village, I'm conveyed a further five miles to the market town where my cousins live – all of us of an age to bicker away the summer days together and give our elders peace. I love coming here, up the fine Georgian main street to the top of the town, where stands a real castle, an empty mock-Gothic pile, complete with towers, crenellations and portcullis. Behind its high walls lies a huge demesne, acres of landscaped grounds gone to ruin and gardens run to seed. The tomboy cousin knows a way in and, at some detriment to our shins and toe-caps, we spend long illicit days there. We roam the sunny and the shady walks, plunge into cool damp undergrowth and lose ourselves in thickets of rainbow-stemmed bamboo. We find an oriental bridge across a boggy waste that once was a water-lilied pond and greedily plunder what's left of the fruit bushes – blackcurrants, loganberries, gooseberries translucent as amber lanterns. But the sharpest, sweetest taste sensation is the wild strawberries with their heart-shaped leaves, and nestled underneath, each no bigger than your little fingernail, the gleaming scarlet berries whose savour is all my childhood summers in one.

Sundays have magic of a different sort. We stroll the demesne legitimately with Uncle Walter, till, all by itself in a still, sunlit clearing, we come upon a Fairy Tree – not a native hawthorn, but some foreign species with dark foliage and gnarled roots standing proud of the ground, creating a veinous web of pockets and hidey-holes. Uncle Walter gives each of us a silver sixpence to insert edgewise into the deeply fissured bark and make a wish. Half solemn, half scared, we do so. He dispatches us to find placatory offerings to the fairies, a bird's feather, a quartz pebble, a speckled leaf, the list is as long as your arm. Dashing back with our booty, we find the glade deserted, the sixpences gone and, concealed in the tree-roots, lollipops and chocolate bars. Recalled by our noisy delight, Uncle Walter saunters through the grove, all astonishment at our good fortune. Though he owns both a greengrocer's and a sweetshop, I never make the connection with the bountiful largesse of the Little People.

My last visit to the demesne is at thirteen or fourteen. I'm too grown up for magic. They turned the castle into a potato-crisp factory. And very good crisps they are, but they don't do a wild strawberry flavour.

ADMIT IT NOW, most of us feel a vague unease when we stay in a four-star hotel. It can be as much an ordeal as a pleasure. From the moment we cross the threshold, we desperately want to look confident, even blasé. Heavens! We do this all the time! We realise we've made the first mistake when the under-manager gives us a pitying glance as we drag our shabby luggage to the reception desk ourselves, unaware of the hotel porter moving helpfully towards us. At the reception desk we're met with a supercilious, "Sir? Madam?" "We have a reservation," we say apologetically. His eyes price each item of our clothing. He looks sceptical. While he consults the computer, we resist the temptation to lean on the counter as if awaiting a fish supper. We try not to remark upon the exotic flower arrangements or the splendiferous décor. Then we blow it by saying, "Those lounge chairs are real leather."

"Would Sir like to sign?" We scrabble about for a cheap biro ignoring the proffered top-quality fountain pen. The porter is beckoned. We wince as he grasps the sweaty handles of our bags. Room 101. As we ascend in the plush, mirrored lift, one thought is uppermost – when to tip and how much? The terror of too little, the shame of too much. The porter knows, but you can never, ever ask him.

In a strange hotel room we become instantly incompetent. Windows refuse to open. Room service, summoned by phone, points out the simple release button marked "press" incorporated in the handle. We are mortified. We can't find the "off" switch for the bedside lamp without entangling a watchstrap in its fringed shade and pulling the whole thing over. Hangers resist being wrested from the wardrobe rail. We have to climb into the wardrobe to hang up our clothes. Next day, a chambermaid shows us how to detach the hanger from the hook in a simple upward movement. We're embarrassed.

Beds smell different and are totally inaccessible. It's like trying to get into an envelope. In the ensuite bathroom, the toilet flushes so forcefully, the cistern sings for the next 15 minutes or is so sluggish we crank the handle repeatedly till it jams in a downward position.

The contents of the bowl remain, revolving sulkily. We'll be talked about. The shower head is positioned immovably at seven feet. The chrome-plated controls belong on the flight-deck of Concorde. No matter how we twiddle, the water temperature remains freezing. We emerge from the icy deluge to discover the floor sopping wet. There is nothing to mop it up with save thick, expensive, pure white towels. What are the staff going to think?

Washed, brushed and only slightly creased, we descend to the swanky restaurant for dinner. Halfway across the dining floor, we realise we've committed another social gaffe. One must wait to be seated. We stop in the middle of an acre of gleaming parquet. What to do? Back-pedal subtly, hoping nobody has noticed? Remain marooned in the centre of the dining-room like parish charges, presuming the maitre d', whom we barged past, will come to us? Or boldly take up residence at a window table and risk the ignominy of relocation by the service door in full view of the other diners?

Once seated, there are the niceties to be observed. Catching the waiter's eye is the first. Of course, if the restaurant lives up to its reputation, it could be argued the waiter should materialise beside us in the manner of Bertie Wooster's Jeeves. But if he doesn't, how should he be summoned? Beginning at the discreet end of the scale, a raised eyebrow may work – if you're Roger Moore. From there, progress to a slight upward nod in his general direction. It may be enough to attract his attention. If not, place your elbow on the table (it's allowed in this situation only) and raise a slightly bent forefinger. If, after all of these moves he still hasn't taken you under his notice, then you're in trouble.

It is absolutely forbidden by the code of good manners to click your fingers, clap your hands, bang your cutlery on the table, wave your napkin aloft (unless you're Michael Winner), whistle or shout, "Oi, garçon!"

The menus are big as billboards and printed in Italian. The prices appear to be in euros but they're not. They really do want £19 for a bottle of house red. "We won't have a starter, thank you." It fools nobody. Of course, the rules of etiquette apply equally to the waiter.

A good waiter will not intimidate the customer into making a hasty choice. He will not sneer at your pronunciation of zabaglione. He will remember who ordered what and not arrive at the table enquiring loudly, "OK, who's having the lamb?"

And here I must offer a fruitful digression. Never order anything with its coat still on. It is impossible to eat without looking like a hog peering up from its trough. I once made the mistake of being persuaded into tackling a dish of piri-piri prawns. The waiter stepped across the floor bearing on high a small Vesuvius of very hot and bothered looking seafood, complete with armour, eyes and feelers. Wrestling matches have ended sooner. Each prawn was a miniature Fort Knox and the sauce in which they were cooked could've stripped paint. One hard-earned mouthful and the perspiration broke on me, my make-up slid down my face and I had to be physically prevented from drinking the contents of the finger-bowl. Fish has bones, olives have stones. How to dispose of the indigestible bits correctly, or at least gracefully? Apparently, masking the mouth discreetly with one's napkin camouflages the transfer to side plate, a technique unknown to someone I heard of who put his plum stones in his pockets. Exhausted, we seek our four-star bed and fight our way into it. We lie rigid as corpses in the alien dark, thinking of the price of it all.

GAWD, I HATE AIRPORTS! I loathe their echoing hugeness, their wonky-wheeled baggage trolleys with fascist tendencies; the milling directionless throngs of people anxiously scanning screens and the "bing-bong" muffled gibberish of public announcements that merely add to one's confusion. An airport is neither heaven nor hell, but a sort of limbo in which time is suspended and people behave altogether unlike themselves – a place in which we're all reduced to the status of imbecile – unnaturally docile, endlessly patient, resigned to being shunted about arbitrarily, starved of information and robbed blind by inflated prices for everything. In any other circumstances there'd be a riot.

The permanently-tired girls on the airline check-in desks are expressionless automatons. "Is this your case, Sir? Did you pack it yourself, Sir? Are you carrying any of these forbidden pointy things, Sir?" And all the while they are ceaselessly stapling, sticking and stamping documents in dead-eyed pre-programmed monotony.

We get the pre-menstrual one who makes up new rules as she goes along, "This must go separately, Sir." She indicates with a limp gesture our small (12 by 24 inches) telescopic luggage carrier which has travelled legitimately for years and crossed two continents, happily strapped to the side of one of our bags. We make the mistake of arguing. She is adamant. "No, it is not permitted in the cabin as hand luggage, Sir; it must be checked through the 'overweight, oversized or fragile items' desk, Sir, at the opposite end of the concourse." Note she addresses her remarks to the Loving Spouse. Overweight? Oversized? Fragile? Is she talking about me? We plod the distance and wait to be processed behind a double bass and a concert harp with our pathetic £12.99 piece of extending plastic and the beginnings of a migraine.

Worse than all else at an airport is a delay between connecting flights that is too short to book into an hotel overnight and too long to spend on a metal bench with the nearest cup of over-priced coffee 500 yards away round a corner and no one to mind your bags or keep your seat while you go for it. Airport food is one of the least subtle ploys of parting a captive fool from his money. They can charge you nearly a fiver for watery coffee and a ham sandwich, knowing you've no option but to pay up or go hungry. Like a bird in a cage, you can only escape by air – but not until morning.

Meantime the seasoned traveller, inured to hardship, has consumed his generous packet of sandwiches prepared at home, cannily marked out his territory and, pillowed on his rucksack, is slumbering at full length in a sleeping bag over three seats, leaving you the edge of a cast iron coffee table to lean against for the duration of the small hours.

We take turns to sit on the single end seat left vacant next to a pair of male feet in shabby trainers, while the other goes for a walk. In circumstances like these, the Loving Spouse drops instantly into cat-nap mode with his panama hat over his eyes. I'm a bundle of tension and fatigue, constantly shifting position as various bits of me go numb. Even my hair is sore. I'm just on the edge of a doze when, back from his safari, he looms up in front of me announcing, "Did you know you can buy a vacuum-cleaner in this airport?"

For the insomniac traveller, further "shopportunities" are provided by a plethora of duty-free goods as yet another means of relieving you of your cash. Let's get this straight. Duty-free shopping is a kind of contradiction in terms. Duty-free shops sell things nobody needs but feel duty-bound to purchase. What is the point of a reduction in price of an item if, when walking freely in the public street, you wouldn't buy it anyway? Nobody needs to lug a litre bottle of Amarullo cream liqueur halfway across Europe in a plastic bag nor will the quality of their life be significantly enhanced by the acquisition of a presentation coffret of five different Dior fragrances. The thing is, in this brightly-lit temple of commerce, the lost soul of the transit passenger wanders in a kind of retail trance, soothed by the music of pan pipes, scented by essential oils. In this lotus-eaters' paradise it seems perfectly reasonable to buy extortionately expensive silk scarves at 5.20am when what you're actually in need of is an emergency toothbrush, spare tights and disposable knickers.

Come the chill dawn, our flight is called and we hobble gratefully towards the security gate clutching our boarding cards. We are creased, crumpled, with cricks in our necks – he, unshaven; me with my eye shadow welded into wee railway lines. We stagger through the electronic arch and the bleeper goes bananas. Is it my watch or the neck-chain on my glasses? I surrender both. Nope. Then it must be the metal bits of my replacement hip joints. Surely they'll take my word for it or do they want to examine the scars? Parallel to this pantomime, the X-ray machine is studying our hand-baggage. "Wheep-wheep-wheep-wheep-wheep!" "Madam, there is a metal tube in your toilet bag." Shamefacedly, I turn out its grubby contents. At least the offending article has a bit of class. Yves St Laurent's Touche Eclat in its chic gilt case eliminates facial lines, erases wrinkles and makes dark shadows disappear, temporarily, at any rate. I hear myself explain all this to the stone-faced female security guard who looks like she could be doing with a couple of coats of it. Her expression remains impassive. It strikes me that, just at the moment, I'm no great advertisement for the product.

Punchy with fatigue, we tramp down miles of anonymous grey-carpeted corridors to the squeezy melodeon bit where they stick the steps onto the plane with corrugated cardboard and Sellotape. We stumble through into the wide white smile of the stewardess and two narrow seats in another metal tube. Now the real stress begins.

I AM 30,000 FEET ABOVE LIVERPOOL. The captain is encouraging us to look out. I do not wish to see Liverpool or anywhere else from this far up, thank you. Nice stewardesses with too much lipstick are clanking a comfort wagon along the narrow aisle dispensing hope, good cheer and immortality in miniature bottles. After the terror of the take-off when the plane raced along the runway on tiptoe, leapt suddenly into the air and my head went square with the G-force, I need a little something to settle me. I take another swig of the gin and tonic, which, at 9.55am, makes my complexion blaze.

There are 161 other people with me in this tin tube. They are talking, laughing, consuming with every appearance of relish, an airline savour snack. This is a shrink-wrapped wonder never encountered in any other catering context. Mine remains inviolate in its little recessed tray. The ten nerveless sausages, which served as fingers on mother earth, could not undo so much as a button at this altitude. None of these chomping, chortling fools seem to be aware that they're in imminent danger of becoming a statistic. I have thought of little else since I boarded this claustrophobic cylinder and belted myself into the narrow moulded-plastic niche that is to be my tomb. A musical "bing-bong" in the key of D heralds a public announcement. We have on board a Canadian award-winning fly-fishing team. A smatter of polite applause greets this intelligence. I can see the newspaper headlines, "Canadian fly-fishing team lost as shuttle falls out of clear blue sky for no apparent reason."

The current copy of *Vogue* magazine lies on my lap. In an effort to distract myself from my imminent demise, I read an article on the rejuvenating effects of facial exercise. Apparently you can knock ten years off yourself by making faces for forty minutes a day. I experiment with a few of them, thinking perhaps if I'm gonna be a goner I'll look younger when I'm laid out. The passenger on my immediate right catches me in mid-contortion and looks away quickly.

A sudden drop in altitude. I retrieve my stomach from above my head and the magazine from under my feet. The pilot (obviously in skittish mood) has chosen to descend in a series of graceful scallops that has my innards ricocheting off the cabin walls. Nobody else seems the least perturbed. A curious whirring sound joins the change in pitch of the engine note. That must be the wheels descending. I count carefully, one – two – it's like waiting for the other shoe to drop. Surely there should be three? Or is the tail section which I am occupying going to trail along the ground till the friction causes it to catch fire? Bits of suburbia magnify rapidly and, with a tooth-jarring jolt, we are down.

The hatch opens. Air! Light! Only a tight skirt and high heels restrain my urge to fall on my knees and kiss the tarmac. Endowed with immortality, I skip across the concrete to the baggage reclaim. Isn't God good and the world beautiful, I think as I wait for the carousel to deliver up my travel bag. And isn't God good indeed that I don't know at this moment that the return flight a few days hence will be a nightmare of delays, thunderstorms, turbulence and an unidentifiable hazard on the runway that turns out to be a dead cow? I grab my bag and exit into the London sunshine. On the horizon is a single cloud no bigger than a man's hand.

FLICKING THROUGH HOLIDAY ACCOMMODATION BROCHURES I see that the two chief selling points for any hotel or B&B are the ensuite bathroom and the full cooked breakfast. "Full English/Scottish/Welsh/Irish or Ulster Breakfast." It is itemised with geographical exactitude, though its constituents are identical. It's far from reassuring to realise that the whole of the tourist industry throughout the British Isles starts the day with a heart attack on a plate. Isn't it strange that most people go out to do a day's work on a cup of tea and half a slice of toast, but a morning's sightseeing in a strange city decrees taking aboard enough ballast for a full day's voyage. Were the average wife to serve up to the average husband on a daily basis nowadays the cholesterol time-bomb which is an Ulster Fry, she'd be had up for attempted manslaughter. But the catering trade is licensed to kill.

An allied oddity is the growing number of cafés, fast-food bars and restaurants who proudly proclaim in curly letters on a blackboard, "ALL DAY BREAKFAST – SERVED ALL DAY." A truly moveable feast. Some establishments go so far as to itemise in coloured chalk the constituents of their all-day breakfast, and it's sad to see the ethnic purity of the Ulster Fry corrupted by the substitution of such alien imports as baked beans and potato waffles in place of traditional soda farls and black pudding. Shame on them! But there you are. They wouldn't supply it if there was no call for it, and the steady stream of starving students, famished backpackers and long-distance lorry drivers justifies the day-long sizzle of the spitting pan, the blue smoke wreathing upwards, obscuring the Healthy Eating Certificate, while passers-by, noses twitching like Bisto kids, inhale the siren smell of hot fat.

Be honest. We're only partial converts to healthy eating, and backslide with great glee every opportunity we get! That's why whole families, who wouldn't eat three Weetabix between them at home, sit in shorts and T-shirts at 8am in hotel dining-rooms working their way stolidly through fruit juice and cereal and a full size fry-up and tea and toast and marmalade on the principle, "If you've paid for it, you might as well eat it," whether you want it or need it or enjoy it. Besides which, you'll be peckish by 11am.

Let us look closely at what they're consuming. The catering sausage is a peculiar animal, only distantly related to the one which might grace your plate at home. The catering sausage is a sleek beast, plump and varnished. Despite its attractive appearance, it is of uncertain pedigree, tasting of neither pork nor beef, but spicy pink flannel. Its companion, the rubber rasher, is rindless and fat-free, thus ensuring it to be flavour-free as well. The fried egg looks up at you with a single jaundiced eye and the squishy reddish glistening thing that implodes in your mouth like a water-bomb is a tinned tomato. Such is usually the sad reality. As the philosopher said, "The wonderful things are never as wonderful as you hope they'll be. The sea is less warm, the joke less funny, the taste is never as good as the smell." But occasionally the sublime fry-up lingers in the memory and we pursue its chimaera as King Arthur's knights did the Holy Grail. Savoury and tasty it may be but it leaves you with a thirst like a drunkard, a decidedly heavy feeling around the duodenum and a major processing job for the gastric juices. "Never again," we vow, white-lipped with bismuth tablets. But, like the habitual sinner, we're drawn inexorably to the kind of establishment where your arteries fur up just reading the menu.

Shall it be a "mini trucker" with just one each of sausage, bacon, egg, tomato, black pudding, white pudding, soda farl and potato bread? Or the mortal sin of the "Full Monty" on a plate the size of a wagon wheel? The smiling waitress is intent on killing you with kindness. "D'ye want chips with yer breakfast?" she asks.

> "A FLOW OF WORDS IS NO PROOF OF WISDOM
> – BUT THAT'S WHAT PAYS OFF THESE DAYS"
> *Anon.*

MY CHILDHOOD BRUSH WITH RADIO FAME in 1956 proved to be but a flash in the pan. Apart from a bit of acting at school and college, my public star waned sadly. A steady safe career in teaching beckoned. Creggan was a place with few facilities, an area where the birth rate rivalled Bombay's and unemployment was endemic. Till the day I went there as a twenty-year-old student teacher I'd never in my life been through Butcher Gate. The Bogside and Creggan were alien territory, the former a smoky warren of dingy Dickensian streets, the latter, raw, soulless new-build – a community in evolution towards identity.

Simply because I was asked, I wrote a series of articles for the newly established parish magazine – my first foray into print. I'd like to say they were perspicacious and worthy disquisitions challenging poverty and social injustice, but they were in fact, tongue-in-cheek features on fashion. Thereafter, I kept my head down and concentrated on becoming a good teacher. Consequently I never opened my mouth in public till I was twenty-seven and discovered the Colmcille Debating Society. A whole new chapter of my life opened up.

A long-established society, whose alumni included Paddy "Bogside" Doherty, Tom Frawley (Northern Ireland Ombudsman), Brendan Duddy (Policing Board), Joe Mahon (*Lesser Spotted Ulster*,

UTV), Ana Leddy (Head of RTÉ1 and Deputy Managing Director of RTÉ Radio), its fortunes were in the ascendant, its enrolment healthy, its audiences critically informed and the motions for debate both meaty and topical. Contrary to perceived opinion, it was neither exclusively Catholic nor middle class in its membership. As a weekly exercise in intellectual rigour and nervous terror I couldn't recommend it highly enough. The discipline of research, preparation and delivery focused the mind and schooled me in the art of writing for the ear, but best of all it was scary, challenging fun. The annual Baron von Munchausen (greatest liar) competition packed the Guildhall to its Victorian Gothic rafters. One of my proudest moments was winning with an Enid Blyton parody based on Derry City Football Club's financial embarrassment in the early Eighties and how they were rescued from ruin by the Nearly Famous Five and their dog Semtex ("though he didn't smell much, a little of him went a long way"). I'd never set foot in Brandywell Stadium in my life. Celebrity debates drew equally large audiences. Some visiting luminaries who patronisingly thought they were favouring us with their presence found themselves intellectually deconstructed.

I remained a member of the society for years, in one heady 18-month period becoming chairman, getting married, speaking in the Cambridge Union on my honeymoon (that's another story!) and having a baby. I owe a huge debt to the Colmcille Debating Society and the calibre of person I met there. Without it, and them, I'd never have written or spoken publicly. No subsequent fears ever exceeded that of defending the indefensible in front of an inimical house.

THE BEST PART OF A FORMAL DINNER or organised function is the bit after the pudding when you can lean back, loosen the waistband, metaphorically unbutton as it were, and listen to a really good after-dinner speech. So when people foregather for their annual bash they invite someone who ostensibly enjoys the perspiration-soaked experience of delivering a peroration to a largely indifferent but attentive audience. These persons are called public speakers and I am one of them, and no I don't enjoy it very much. In fact, every time I do it I resolve to never do it again, for it is a pastime beset with pitfalls. The man was right who said, "There is no such thing as a free lunch", nor a free dinner either. We public speakers sing for our supper. Despite rumour, the standard of cuisine is generally good, with some memorable exceptions. Not for nothing is it know as the "rubber chicken circuit".

Your neighbour at dinner is usually an officer of the society you're addressing, who's been delegated your minder. He encourages you warmly with such statements as "We had so-and-so last year – he was marvellous! People were weeping with laughter." They'll be weeping tonight alright too, you think grimly, moving the piece of gristle from the noisettes of lamb over to the other cheek.

Public eating before public speaking is a hazardous business. One is likely to rise to speak with spinach between the teeth, a gravy-spotted bosom and nervous flatulence caused by onions. But at least you've eaten. Degrees of hospitality can vary. I remember sitting on a hard chair in a chilly anteroom with only 125 portions of slowly-thawing lemon meringue pie and the caretaker for company. He paused long enough in his brushing-up to eye me speculatively and say, "Are you the turn?"

Over the fresh fruit salad you take a surreptitious look at the facilities – Hmmm, bad light and nowhere to rest your notes. Frequently there is a microphone, and a man who walks about officiously with it wedged against his top lip. "One two, one two, one two," he booms fluffily, adjusting buttons on a box to produce a high-pitched whine.

Audiences are always different, and ever the same. Now they're folding up small their After Eight envelopes and drawing patterns in the creepy brown sugar with a butter knife. Madam President tinkles her spoon for attention. With sinking heart I recognise the lady in cerise chiffon who's telling her friend, "I've heard her before y'know. I do hope she does the one about…" and has to be shushed. It's when Madam President is doing the preamble, the potted history, that you suffer the prolapse of the womb, and find the pit of your stomach down round your knees. Assailed by total doubt, you decide you've prepared a load of patronising, insulting and irrelevant rubbish which will alienate every person present. You should've listened when the Loving Spouse told you to put in more funny bits. You start looking wildly round for escape, but the doors are guarded by hard-faced waitresses with lethal linen teacloths. Unless you faint, or die, you have no option. On leaden legs you stand up and begin.

Exclusively female audiences price you from the feet up and can fix to within a fiver the cost of every stitch you're wearing, including your shoes, but they do exude supportive and sisterly warmth. A mixed audience feels and reacts quite differently. Men take you aside afterwards to advise you on how you might beef up your content – "they do a bit of this public speaking lark themselves, y'know" – and proceed to regale you with anecdotes of eye-popping obscenity which you promise faithfully to include in your next speech.

The next speech, two weeks hence. "How're you feeling?" asks the Loving Spouse as he drives me off to fulfil my engagement. "Terrible," I say, drying my damp palms down the sides of my second-best frock. "Why do I put myself through this?"

"Because you do so love the clapping," he says.

EVEN THE VIOLENT UNCERTAINTY of Derry's darkest days failed to extinguish the flame of the arts. Groups like the Theatre Club and the '71 Players continued to stage productions where the cast sometimes outnumbered the audience. Ah, the joys of amateur dramatics! All over the province rehearsals are in full swing for everything from *Boyd's Shop* to Beckett. Even as we speak, there are people out there not able to eat a bite at the imminent prospect of stepping onstage at 8pm in an ill-fitting wig and somebody else's shoes. Amnesiac with anxiety their one thought is "People are paying to see this!"

Apart from an unwise tendency to attempt *A Streetcar Named Desire* in Ballymena accents or *Blithe Spirit* in the refained tones of Bengor, amateur dramatic societies are fruitful fields for the amateur psychologist. All the stock characters are there. The leading lady, trembling on the menopausal edge of perhaps her last principal role, concealing her panic with patronising advice to up-and-coming novices, and investing her part with an ingénue's intensity. The leading lady's husband (playing a walk-on role) is none too happy with the fervour of the stage kiss bestowed nightly upon his spouse by the leading man, who is thinner, better looking and younger than himself. He lurks, glowering in the wings, counting the number of times it seems necessary to rehearse the scene, and does not include the young man in the drinks round later in the pub. Here's the dogged bit-part player whose every role, from duke to dustman, he plays entirely as himself. "I've been in every single production since the club was founded," he announces proudly. Everybody hates the producer, except the female juvenile lead, aged seventeen, who thinks he's Sir Peter Hall, a notion the producer does nothing to discourage. The producer wears a jumper with a logo on the breast and carries a heavily-annotated copy of the by-now illegible script. The players take as a personal affront any criticism, however mild, he casts upon their ability to deliver their lines, move from A to B or to convey emotion of any sort. Most of them privately feel they'd make a better hand of the production than he's doing, and in his darkest hours he's inclined to agree with them.

These all, of course, are mere marionettes. The true genius of amateur theatre lies backstage. Out of the limelight exist illustrious names, the names in the programme that nobody reads – set, lights, sound, wardrobe, prompter, stage-manager, names that can make or break a production and usually do. It is after all, as Noel Coward said, enough that actors should know their lines and not bump into the furniture. The stage-crew perform in a different nightmare, the recurring horrors of which are the phone which continues to ring long after the actor has picked up the receiver, the prison cell which yawns slowly open upon the crucial line, "And I'll never get out of here! Never! Never!"

Another staple embarrassment is the flimsily-built set door which slams with a hollow hardboard clap, and then sticks fast, necessitating the hero to exit sheepishly via the fireplace.

Costume drama brings its own hazards. I remember the frock-coated villain who stepped upon the hem of the heroine's gown, causing her bust to pop out of her bodice. His discomfiture was complete when he discovered the costume-hire company had sent him two left boots, reducing his macho swagger to a painful mince.

Nine or ten weeks of backstage back-stabbing, fluctuating allegiances and histrionic huffs and, at last, the first night is upon us. The onstage whiskey bottle is filled with brown, flat lemonade; the leading man is stapled into his trousers and the prompter is unique amongst the company in knowing the lines. The restless growl of a gathering audience begins out front. Feuds forgotten, in the fearful fellowship of drama, the cast are collectively reduced to a quaking mass of biddable idiots. The house lights die, the curtain rises; the magic of "theatah" is about to take over. Ah – the play's the thing!

WAS THERE A TIME BEFORE RADIO FOYLE? Ah yes, I dimly remember it. It was 25 years ago, the era when (allegedly) a map hung in the boardroom of BBC Belfast with everywhere beyond Glengormley marked Terra Incognita; a time when the northwest's input to Northern Ireland programming was a single weekly 57-minute slot entitled *What's West?* broadcast, I kid you not, from a bathroom in the Northern Counties Hotel in Waterloo Place. I always considered the title *What's West?* somewhat Freudian, in the light of the limp curiosity evinced by cosmopolitan Belfast about our simple parochial ways.

Suffice to say, I recall with great clarity being shepherded through "the morning after the bomb" debris by Valerie Buchanan to be interviewed by Ken McCormack and being struck for the first time by "broadcasters' bane" – instant paralysis of the vocal chords and total brain death – twin ailments that afflict me still in front of a microphone. I really only got my foot in the door after Radio Foyle relocated to a wonderful old house in Rock Road. The kitchen was presided over by Annie Nash (may she rest) who alternatively petted and scolded everyone and referred to the station manager as "wee Ian". The best programmes that never went on air were made in Annie's kitchen with big mugs of tea.

Technology was simpler then – the electronic equivalent of two cocoa tins and a bit of string. Celebrities and ordinary folk for interview were brought down the wooden backstairs, out through the boiler house, up the slimy stone steps skirting the big puddle and into the Portakabin where the presenter had to sit on the newsreader's lap to facilitate a smooth handover at 4.03.

It was a time vibrant with ideas and energy as the station strove to create its identity and a niche for itself in community consciousness, for that was the point of it all. Not for the purpose of music, news or aural wallpaper, nor yet a provincial parody of Radio Four, but a focus on quality speech-based programmes reflecting the interests of the community and its concerns, using local talent where possible.

BBC Foyle was born, weaned and reared in a climate of political turbulence. Listeners took an immediate and proprietorial interest in the output of the new station and weren't shy of informing you of its shortcomings when they met you on the street. "Tell that Don O'Doherty his music's rubbish!" Over all the years, the complaint has remained the same, only the presenter's name changes. "The music's rubbish!"

For a lengthy period the Protestant community held Radio Foyle at a distance. Producers were scrupulous in their efforts to create contributor balance, but frequently the invitation to participate was turned down by a courteous, but firm and unqualified "No". It was not long before ill-wishers implied political and religious bias and coined the scurrilous epithet "Vatican Radio" – an unpleasant perception which took long to dispel. More public service broadcasters than you could shake a stick at cut their milk teeth in Radio Foyle, where they learned to do everything, including make the tea, in a atmosphere that was generous, sharing and supportive.

Radio's an ephemeral medium. People only half-hear or half-listen, and once heard, they instantly forget. Occasionally someone will say, "Y'know that poem you wrote about the duck? I loved that." I have never written poetry, much less about a duck, but they insist they heard it. It's easier to smile and thank them for their kindness.

"Heard you a coupla weeks ago," says one. "It was great." "What was it about?" I ask. "Aw, I don't remember, but it was great." My contributions these days are chiefly scripted pieces but in the Eighties, apart from making series on topics as diverse as small businesses, aspects of writing and women's issues, I chaired a weekly round-table discussion on everything from psychokinesis to the Eleven Plus. To those who think, "I'd like to have a go at this presenting lark. It sounds a doddle," let me say I still have the dress that shrank while I was actually wearing it on air as a salutary reminder that the seemingly effortless takes the most talent.

A succession of producers always found room for me and commissions from Radio Ulster, Radios 2 and 4 and World Service followed. As Damon Runyon put it, "Bein' around scratch, some of it's bound to rub off." It was pure coincidence that I happened to be in Radio Foyle on other business the day Joe Mahon got sick and couldn't do his regular slot on *What's West?* Ian Kennedy opened his office door, saw me in the hall and said, "Can you write and deliver a six-minute radio piece on something topical?" Employing the same principle I've used for every offer ever since, I said, "Yes."

I wouldn't have missed the last 25 years for anything. I've made the most wonderfully erudite and entertaining friends. I've had the most surreal discussions edged with knife-sharp humour. I've felt part of the fabric of the community I live in and hope I've reflected some of their thinking. Above all, I've had the luxury and privilege of airtime to use as I will – so long as I don't involve the BBC in a court-case.

BY THE SAME KIND OF SERENDIPITOUS HAPPENSTANCE, the *Irish News* senior reporter in the north west rang me out of the blue to ask if I'd be willing to write a monthly article on some aspect of northwest life. As a family, we'd been regular readers of the *Irish News*. From childhood I'd loved the column called "Random Jottings", a quirky little collection of non-sequiturs. My monthly piece soon became a weekly one and I wish my father had survived to see it.

The launch of the *Derry News* brought the offer of a weekly tabloid page to fill and, with the introduction of twice-weekly publication, a second one – enough to ensure my almost permanent presence at the kitchen table with a dozen black biros and a ream of A4. Word processing? The term "cut and paste" to me means kitchen scissors and a Pritt stick. I don't do technology (but that's another story).

A hugely influential element in my writing life has been the Pushkin Trust, an organisation set up in memory of her ancestor, the Russian poet Alexander Pushkin, by the Duchess of Abercorn. Its mission – to develop in children north and south, creativity in all its forms, with a particular emphasis on writing. Over twenty years, the Pushkin model has been transforming the approach of both teachers and pupils in their search for the authentic voice of the writer within themselves. The Pushkin experience proved invaluable when, under the auspices of the Verbal Arts Centre and the Western Education and Library Board, I worked on a language development programme through the medium of story, poetry and creative writing in rural schools scattered throughout Counties Derry, Tyrone and Fermanagh. What a pleasure it was to drive through a picturesque landscape to the happy family atmosphere of a small school where the kettle was on for your arrival. What richness of dialect and vocabulary, imagination and spontaneity I found in still unspoiled country children and what commitment and dedication on the part of their teachers. It was, for me, a golden period in my teaching life, tough and energy-consuming, but every day brought its own reward.

I'm often asked by earnest careers teachers if I'd come and "do a little thirty-minute presentation to our pupils on how you broke into the media". I was in the right place at the right time, that's all, willing to tackle anything and had a brass neck.

Knowing nothing about a subject has never precluded my writing about it. "Observe and listen", that's what it boils down to. Of course, it helps if you've a passion for the English language, are widely read and of an argumentative disposition with a lively interest in all aspects of current affairs, but it's "bein' around scratch" that's probably most important. I write about the ordinary things that happen to me, my family and friends; what interests, intrigues or irritates us – the common currency of people's lives. I received a "fan letter" once from a man who wrote, "I was ready to dismiss you as just another retired lady teacher with her genteel *pensées* on pedestrian matters, but I grudgingly admit, some of it's quite amusing." It quite made my day.

## "I RECENTLY TURNED SIXTY. PRACTICALLY A THIRD OF MY LIFE IS OVER"
*Woody Allen*

IF YOU WERE HOPING there was at least one angst-free period of life – think again. Somewhere in life's chronology, between adolescence and senescence, is the newly discovered span of time called "middlescence", a neat portmanteau term to explain incidences of odd, uncharacteristic or unwise behaviour of people in their middle years.

As with puberty and senility, middlescence comes complete with its own symptoms, syndromes and psychological baggage. Of course middle age has frequently manifested many of the ills middle-aged flesh is heir to – "It's her time of life," conveyed in a Les Dawson wink and nudge; the theory of male menopause; the possibility that both sexes may undergo a mid-life crisis – all at one time or another dismissed as hysterical myths. Now they've put a name on the whole package and admitted it exists, we can settle down uncomfortably to suffer the lot.

Men are slower to exhibit symptoms than women, partly because middlescence begins in the male mind as a small seed of discontent, a tiny pebble in the comfortable shoe of living and can be, initially, ignored. But not for long. This is the period, he reasons, that he ought to be reaping the fruits of his early labours. He should be confident, content, coasting, with a bit of surplus cash at his disposal. Instead, the worm in the bud tells him this is as far on the promotion ladder he's going to get. He's been overtaken on the inside lane by sharp young thirty-somethings with even sharper suits. He's become "good old Bob, backbone of the business", put to mind some pipsqueak who'll eventually replace him in an exercise politely known as "mentoring".

At home things are – okay. Some days he feels the wife just puts up with him; to the kids he's nothing but a cash dispenser. Funny he never noticed before how lonely you can be in a house full of people. Even life-long friends have ceased to stimulate, chewing the eternal cud of the same topics every Friday night. Leisure pursuits? The twice-weekly tyranny of the garden and a wife who believes the house is the Forth Bridge – the minute he's finished painting one end of it, it's time to begin again at the other. His leisure clothes are a gardening cardigan and painting trousers, the highlight of his social life the monthly meeting of a fund-raising charity. He's in a rut and the sides of it are closing over his head.

The fruit of this inner turmoil manifest themselves in a variety of ways, all of them textbook examples of middlescent behaviour. He may take to tinting his grizzled bits with a toothbrush, changing his hairstyle or, if thin on top, opt for a convict-close crop which makes his head look like a dum-dum bullet. The purchase of a too-youthfully-styled casual jacket may follow. For a man faithful in thought, word and deed to the wife of his bosom, he begins to find the company of young empty-headed females dangerously fascinating. One fine day, suffering a severe mental aberration, he swaps the family saloon for a highly unsuitable low-slung sports car, thereby losing the run of himself altogether. Possibly worse than all these might be his decision to take premature retirement and "do something different". A laudable aim, as long as it's not education. He will adopt the entire student ethos and hang about the Union in denim and trainers being an antediluvian existentialist.

At the core of all this aberrant behaviour is the serious and central message of middlescence that has struck him like a thunderbolt. "Life is not a rehearsal." This is confirmed by the habit of the Grim Reaper of scything a few fifty-somethings from the fringes of the group. A couple of founderings in a wet cemetery at contemporaries' funerals fairly makes him ponder.

Women, naturally, prove not half so delinquent. Many of their middle-aged foolishnesses can be attributed to vanity, lack of fulfilment and fear of growing old. It's a struggle for a woman to shrug off the cloak of sexual invisibility that envelops her about forty. With the thoroughness for which she is renowned, she first of all goes blonde, embarks on two or three diets simultaneously, joins a gym or takes up that ridiculous power-walking that makes you look like Charlie Chaplin on speed. In her gloomier moments she tries to think of palatable alternatives to "Granny". She'll be one soon but sure as hell isn't going to be called one. Meantime she flirts with traffic wardens, attempts to enslave male shop assistants and spends money like water revamping her look. The nicest thing about middlescence, she believes, is its elasticity. You can postpone old age nearly indefinitely.

A middlescent friend of mine told me of an evening she spent in the company of a dishy and talented young poet. He singled her out for prolonged conversation. She basked in his attention. At the end of the evening he leaned over and kissed her on the cheek. "It's uncanny," he breathed, "you remind me so much of my mother."

THERE'S A GREAT DANGER if you stand about looking idle that somebody will think of something useful you could be doing. Never mind that your idleness is in fact legitimate and hard-won leisure that you've earned by maybe forty years or so of hard graft at the workface, it's a serious mistake to retire and allow people to spot you out on the skite and obviously enjoying yourself. People look upon retirees with a mixture of envy and exasperation. Of course they're all complimentary to your face, "I'm delighted for you! Aren't you looking well!" and then a kind of peevish resentment creeps into their consciousness – "irritable growl syndrome", I call it. They assess you as they would a horse. It's a wonder they don't pull down your jaw and examine your teeth. "Years of useful and productive life left in that one yet," you can hear them thinking, the inference being you're putting yourself prematurely out to pasture and they're subsidising it.

The Labour Government, in its happy-clappy short-term wisdom, positively encouraged early retirement to free up employment channels for the young and newly-qualified. With considerable alacrity, the fifty-plussers all rushed to the fairground exit, leaving a shortage of experienced personnel, people who actually knew what they were doing, and now we have an embarrassing skills shortfall. People over 55 are scarce as hen's teeth in major industries and services and there's no one left to mentor and nurse along the bright and brash young Turks who think they know what they're doing and knock the arrogant corners off them.

Meanwhile, a sizeable pool of youngish middle-aged talent and energy is perceived to be out golfing, dog-walking, doing a little genteel charity work and taking advantage of off-peak holiday fares to exotic places at the taxpayers' expense. Never mind that they've paid their pension dues for more than half a lifetime – more than they'll ever get back – they are seen to be unproductive and therefore a drain on the national exchequer.

It's obvious the government's beginning to think the same way as ordinary working punters. They're starting to make it harder to retire early and just to flag up the fact that the gravy train has finally run into the financial buffers, they're putting up spokesmen to utter gloomy prognostications. The consequence, they say, of a reduction in the size of the productive workforce, coupled with longer life expectancy, means that people in their twenties ought to buy in immediately to private pension schemes and be prepared to work until they are seventy-two if they want to have enough to live on in their old age, never mind any quality of life. What a frightful prospect.

I suppose when you think of it, the critics do have a point. A person retiring at 55 is likely to hang around for another thirty years as a non-contributor to the gross national product. Gawd! They'll be pushing us out of first-floor windows to get shot of us.

ACCORDING TO A WEEKEND MAGAZINE QUIZ, I am officially old. What probably confirms it is the sad, get-a-life fact that I took the time and trouble to answer the questions. In a series of multiple-choice responses, mine were consistently from category D, thus proving me (according to the compilers anyway) a cardie-wearing, politically hard-line misogynist, totally ignorant of any aspect of popular culture since about 1980. See if I care!

Why would I want to know about flash-in-the-pan group So Solid Crew when I got Mick Jagger's autograph on a flight to Belfast before the Stones were really famous? Forty years on, Jumpin' Jack Flash, now a scrawny sixty-plus, is still bopping away. Match that in 2042 Robbie Williams! Why do the young epitomise enjoyment as spending the evening drinking, sweating and shouting in semi-darkness? Been there, done that, had my head done in by the sound system and my eyes turned skelly by strobe lighting in Kelly's, Portrush, years ago, so it shouldn't be a matter of pitying wonder on your part, Junior, that I'd prefer a good dinner in a nice restaurant with stimulating conversation. It's called growing up and, furthermore, you realise it isn't social death to stay at home on a Saturday night because you're missing nothing.

Why does it not matter that I no longer recognise any of the buzz phrases – the elusive code of communication between the young. There's nothing more embarrassing to children than their elders aping their attitudes and slang in a pathetic attempt to be "with it". (There's one you haven't heard in a while!) Every parent over forty is familiar with the desperate plea, "Mum, Dad, promise you won't dance at the party disco? Please?" General opinion is that growing older hasn't a lot going for it, but you know, apart from the tendency of bits to wrinkle or migrate south, there are one or two bonuses – usually more leisure and more money, but most valuable of all, more time for oneself. For example, since I retired, I don't do Mondays.

It's a thoroughly good idea to have a "selfish" day. You can sit up in bed and read Jane Austen or old *Beano* annuals if you feel so inclined. You can drowse on the sofa with two cushions and watch fat Americans with bad teeth make fools of themselves on satellite TV. You might even turn out a drawer or two or reorganise your airing cupboard, though this smacks dangerously of purposefulness.

It's just a matter of conditioning your family into acceptance of arriving home at 5pm to find you still in your dressing-gown and no visible signs of dinner, because on the other six days of the week you're a cross between Mrs Beeton and Martha Stewart.

You can get away with murder when you're older. Making a fuss in shops doesn't take a flutter out of you now because the manager is so young. Ditto restaurants, and runs-in with errant plumbers and cowboy builders. *Vous êtes formidable*!

Older is stepping off the treadmill and onto the grassy path. Older is watching the young make all the same mistakes as you did – and letting them. Older is pleasing yourself and not giving a stuff. It's accepting with equanimity that, though the wrapping's getting a bit creased, the contents are as sound as ever.

I'll leave the final word to a ten-year-old schoolboy interviewed in the same magazine on the ageing issue: "There are good points to getting older," he said, "like you get to stay up late and drink alcohol." Enough said.

AS THE BIRTH RATE DECLINES and the graph of longevity rises, we're heading for a society with a significantly greater percentage of older people in it. For "older" read unproductive, non-contributing, infirm individuals, clogging up the Health Service and being a drain on the state's resources. The good news is old is officially postponed. In a rigorous exercise in moving the goalposts, fifty is made the new forty, marking the beginning of a glorious Indian summer of middle-age, while 66 is perceived as the onset of old age – an opinion unlikely to be shared by vibrant sexagenarians of my acquaintance.

We're obsessed by our own mortality. We spend the first quarter of our lives striving to appear older than we are and the rest of our allotted span, like Joan Collins, shaving off years to the point of public scepticism. In this era of rapid change we fear increasing age and consequent failure to keep up. It's necessary now to run faster and further simply to stay in the same place. Energy and adaptability are more valuable to an employer than experience and expertise. I visited a bush school once in Kwa-Zulu Natal, its desks eaten to honeycomb by white ants. There were few books, fewer pencils and a shortage of paper. The children were taught by sheer force of personality with the help of a battered blackboard and no small measure of ingenuity. I congratulated the principal on his good fortune in having three teachers, each with more than twenty years' experience. The headmaster, one of the new breed of South African educationalists obsessed with "learning-related outcomes", looked at me with an inscrutable expression and said dismissively, "It is hard to bend old wood."

The first shift that disturbs our equilibrium is when our children switch, almost overnight, from uncritical acceptance of our infallible erudition to knowing we know nothing at all. The second blow to our esteem, the briefness of our tenure at the pinnacle of our powers before self-doubt creeps in. Ageing is a state of mind which tempts us to start signing off rather than signing on. The brash young Turks come roaring up to overtake us on the inside lane and we feel like throwing in the towel.

HERE ARE SOME POINTERS to the inevitable to contemplate during the long insomniac night of the ageing soul.

1   Turning first to a magazine's medical page rather than the agony column and identifying with all the symptoms listed. It's but one small step to self-diagnosis via the internet and the sleeplessness of terror.

2   Boring everyone rigid with your new-found intolerance to wheat, dairy, fibre and refined sugar and keeping a blister pack of Rennies in every jacket pocket.

3   Facing a future without olives or marmalade because your grip has gone on screw-top containers and jam-jar lids. And needing a man to unstick sash windows.

4   Having to stop halfway up Shipquay Street and pretend to be looking in shop windows while you take a secret breather that feels like a heart-attack. It's only in going uphill, one realises how fast one is going downhill.

5   Does it strike you as alarming that the age-band you belong to doesn't appear at all on application forms?

6   Does it strike you as iniquitous that to type and make tea efficiently you must be under forty?

7   Do you realise with a jolt that you qualify for Saga holidays?

8   Do you know with dreadful certainty that you're not fit for a big night out in the middle of the working week?

9   Are you reconciled to being home before 2am from any function, because you recognise at a certain point in the evening that's as good as it's going to get?

DO YOU FIND YOURSELF:

- Looking at the Damart catalogue with interest and realising that purchasing thermals was the single most sensible thing you did last year?

- After an unfortunate incident involving a wrenched ankle, abandoning high-heeled mules for flat velour bedroom slippers?

- Avoiding red wine, blue cheese and shellfish, knowing you'll be awake all night?

- Going to the loo at 4.07 every morning?

- Leaving out your tablets, even if it's only vitamin supplements, so you won't forget to take them?

- Complaining in shops without going all wobbly with retrospective nerves afterwards?

HAVE YOU REFINED YOUR FRIENDS to the ones you really care about? Does your reading about the excesses of the disaffected young bring out the fascist in you?

Congratulations! Welcome to the Grey Area.

I forget who said there are no joys in growing older. The common apprehensions – having to write things down in order to remember them and then losing the piece of paper; going into a room and not recalling what you went in for – cause us mild distress.

The growing apprehension we feel about personal safety in the street or at home creates new and unwelcome feelings of isolation and vulnerability. Certainly the television advertising screened early afternoon when the preponderance of viewers are elderly or housebound, does nothing to cheer them, focused as it is on laxatives, walk-in baths and funeral plans.

Ageing is less a series of personal surrenders than society robbing you of opportunities. How quickly time telescopes between your parents advising you, "Wait till you're older…" and your children saying, "D'you not think you're a bit long in the tooth for that…?" How brief the interval between the dummy on a string and the reading glasses on a chain about your neck! The trick is to move from "enfant terrible" to "batty old bird" as swiftly as possible.

I'm with the guy who defined old age as "Fifteen years older than I am." Maybe half the fun of a Saga holiday is to go when you're fifty and be the "baby" of the tour, the bright young madcap? So long as we psychologically keep moving the goal posts, we retain positive attitudes and continued capacity to revel in a lifestyle untrammelled by duty. "No, I'm not available to look after the grandchildren. I'm doing an Open University degree." "Yes, Doris, I'll get on a bus to a place we've never been before just because it's Tuesday and the sun's shining."

Let's hear it for the fifty-plussers. Figures are in our favour. Statistically we are in the ascendant. We shall mow the opposition down with our shopping trolleys, trample them with our zip-up pom-pommed bootees and smother their cries in our beige acrylic cardigans. It's nature's immutable plan for all living things that the old give way to the young so the cycle of life continues smoothly. The trouble is, like German holidaymakers, we spread our proprietorial poolside bath towels long ago, but none of us is keen to relinquish our place in the sun. Nobody sees themselves as old, even when the man comes to install the safety rail in the bathroom or we discover the comfort of broad-fitting shoes with non-slip sole and the vicarious thrill of not going to things.

But in their hearts, younger than springtime, the truly ageless walk the paths of life with grace, avoiding the hills.

THE OLDER YOU GET, the more little things irritate you. I deplore pusillanimous political correctness that calls nothing by its proper name lest it offend or create feelings of marginalisation, exclusion, or loss of self-esteem. Notice how the over 65s are referred to now as "older people". "Older" is a comparative term. Older than what? Older than whom? I'm beginning to remind myself of the kind of people I love to hate: people who ring in to radio stations to complain about bad grammar; nitpicking pedants who write to papers under Latin *noms de plume*. I long to cry, "Get a life, you saddos!"

For a world where harsh reality bites ever more fiercely, we seem determined to shroud its terminology in ever thicker padding. Media and politicians between them have created a new language. Like toilet paper, it's designed to perform a dirty job daintily and shares some of that staple commodity's characteristics, being soft, strong and frequently incredibly long, a polyester patois delivered with an acrylic smile. Thus the police force becomes a service, borstals turn into training centres, secondary schools become colleges and examinations are graded alphabetically so nobody appears to ever fail anything. Indeed, "fail" has disappeared from education's vocabulary to be replaced by "deferred success". We're all trading upwards at least one social notch and the poor and feckless are well-nigh unrecognisable under the sobriquets "economically marginalised" and "socially disaffected". Unacceptable and inappropriate have replaced wicked and wrong.

I don't remember any marked sensitivity to the words elderly, pensioner or senior citizen, do you? Good serviceable terms that meant exactly what they said. And the "Darby and Joan Club" had a certain chintzy charm to it. It is, however, a sign of ageing that you get yourself in a lather about such things – when you secretly feel Tony Blair's too young to be in charge of anything important and

David Cameron's merely an eager schoolboy. It's a sign of ageing when you stop admiring that group of handsome boys in the street in all their youth and vigour and hug your handbag apprehensively to your chest as they pass. Older is when you lament the lack of manners, the drop in standards and begin to notice that the young have neither grace nor charm.

We're not the first generation to fear ageing, but we are the first to resist it for as long as possible. Our parents yielded with more grace to the inevitability of growing old.

Watch the old codgers in the shopping mall. They don't care, do they? Carefree and unselfconscious in a way not enjoyed since early childhood, she wears a pleated plastic rain hood and takes her teeth out in cafes. Like Boadicca in her chariot, she cuts a swathe of destruction through shoppers' ankles with a tartan shopper on wheels. He wears a gabardine coat belted high and cavalry twills in that odd oyster shade not sold to anyone under seventy. He has knitted gloves with plastic palms and says what he thinks audibly in buses. They are older on the outside than the inside and pray for the rest of us sliding to oblivion on an overstuffed cushion of weasel words.

DINING OUT WITH THE LADIES WHO LUNCH is at once therapeutic and inspirational. Conversation-wise, no turn is left unstoned. But by the pudding course (and despite cholesterol and carbohydrate phobics, dieters and Lent, we all chow down with gasps of orgasmic delight over the crème brulee) we settle to general topics. Business suits bolt their coffee and flee back to the task of making a living, leaving us to the luxury of a long afternoon. One of us poses the question, "Which generation is having the best time now?" Consensus is we are. We post-war baby-boomers are on a roll. But then we had it good from the start. In an era of relative political stability, we had a secure childhood in safe streets, free to roam and play. We came home to plain but wholesome fare and evenings filled with books, games, rationed radio listening and conversation. Our innocence was protected so we weren't forced to grow up before our time. We were obedient, well-disciplined and our few treats were appreciated. We knew intuitively not to ask for things our parents couldn't afford. The late 1940s Education Act opened the doors to further education, an opportunity of which we took grateful advantage, graduating mid-Sixties into a new meritocracy and the first rumblings of a social revolution. After that, in Northern Ireland it all went pear-shaped, but we'd had the privilege of an untainted childhood and a carefree adolescence – a basic human right denied to anyone born here post 1969.

We reared our own children in a new and inimical climate, doing our best to protect them from the poison of sectarianism and violence and the corrupt and corrupting values of a television age. Had we been totally successful, we mightn't be languishing today in a polarised political limbo, beset by insoluble social problems. Through it all we strove to preserve in schools and workplaces Christian decency, quality of life and a sense of normality in the midst of madness.

There's a new generation of movers and shakers now, most of them looking not old enough to be milk monitors. They're not a patch on us, of course, but we're inured to the fact that experience counts for nothing these days. It's not that they've usurped us exactly. We've chosen to move on, to the sunlit uplands of pleasing ourselves at least.

It's one of life's little ironies that when you have the energy and interest for leisure pursuits, you've neither the time nor the means to indulge in them. The young and hardy backpack the world on tuppence and a filled baguette, but not for us travel on a shoestring, concussing ourselves on a youth hostel's top bunk and enduring the purgatory of primitive sanitation. We want clean sheets and room service. We're the age-band on which tourism at home and abroad depends for its viability, not to mention its profit. The bottom would fall out of the ethnic crafts market if we weren't purchasing leather goods, indigenous pottery, folk art and hauling home hefty pieces of tribal carving that don't fit in the plane's overhead locker. Today the world trembles before the power of the grey pound. We have money, leisure and time and need nobody's permission to do our own thing.

I always considered Saga Holidays an unfortunately droopy name for over-fifties vacations. True, by the time we qualify for one, most of what we've got has sagged anyway and the cloak of sexual invisibility *vis-à-vis* male interest, already fallen on our hapless shoulders. Indisputable, too, that in order to enjoy yourself, you need to take the glucosamine tablets before you go, though when they break into Abba's "Dancing Queen", you discover you've no longer the knees for it. Still, better the baby on a Saga tour than the cardiganed menopausal matron on a coach-load of half-dressed twenty-somethings.

Such is our discourse as we scoff the free mints that accompany the lunch bill and divvy up, taking account of those who had a starter but no wine; wine, but no starter; and whose was the gin? The Ladies Who Lunch exit at 3.40pm in search of a little retail therapy. "Yes, thank you, the meal was lovely but there's no toilet-paper in the ladies' loo and your music is too loud." That's us. Baby-boomers with attitude!

EVERY AGE HAS ITS "ISM". We've just come through the era where chauvinism was successfully challenged by feminism. No sooner had we achieved a level playing field, rolled and ready for play, than the dandelions of a new "ism" began to push up their heads. Ageism. Like the conflict in Northern Ireland you're only aware of it when you're close to it and you wouldn't give a damn about it if you didn't think you'd be affected.

It's the natural order of things in human society that man grows, matures, moves in, takes over, moves on and eventually retires (gracefully or otherwise) to the sidelines to become a consultant sage or guru. Throughout history this happened at a measured and leisurely pace. You respectfully waited till your elders and betters went gaga or dropped off the twig and then it was your turn. Like Edward VII or Prince Charles, you might have to tarry till you were nearly past your sell-by-date in order to exert a little authority and gain a little respect.

Now people are getting pushy. Upstarts of thirty or thereabouts are seeking their place in the sun and shouldering their seniors aside. In their suits and overweening confidence they walk the walk, talk the talk, put on the Jumpin' Jack Flash act and consider themselves God's gift to business industry or whatever. Once in, they bounce about energetically talking up the new technology and talking down traditional skills and attitudes in negative terms like "hidebound, inflexible, limited, reactionary" until gradually, everybody round them over forty begins to feel a total dork, their confidence eroded and the seed of doubt planted in their minds that they've outlived their professional usefulness. After that it's only a matter of time before the collecting tin for the leaving present is being shaken in the faces of their colleagues.

The saddest aspect of this brash can-do culture is the new contempt for experience. These young Turks need nothing from us. To them, energy's worth more than experience, inspiration more than application. Experience is a beige cardigan with leather elbow patches hanging incongruously among the natty designer jackets on the office coat-rack. Occasionally you get the odd middle-aged saddo leaving off his tie, adopting a mullet hairstyle and pushing his jacket sleeves up in an attempt to be part of the zeitgeist, selectively deaf to the derogatory remarks of the young bloods around him.

How relieved I am not to be starting a career in this uncertain climate, but able to look back at it through the telescope of experience and cringe at my arrogant certainty that I knew it all. The truth is, I learned to teach, not at training college, but on the job, fostered, minded and saved from my wildest excesses by more experienced teachers.

For the tips, shortcuts and expertise they so generously shared, I am eternally grateful. They were not recorded in any textbook, but part of the natural legacy of good practice and common sense that is passed on from practitioner to neophyte, so that the wheel need not be reinvented in every discipline in every generation.

These role models (for that's what they were) formed the solid bedrock upon which the firm foundations of education were laid.

Learning could afford the colour and noise of the enthusiastic young teacher while it knew the consistent, persistent and sterling efforts of the experienced were securing the future for our children. Now education wants teachers young and cheap and there's practically nobody left as a model of good practice. I suspect it's the same in other professions.

We live in sudden times. I frequently wonder, were we thrown on the scrapheap tomorrow, how we'd draw up a list of marketable skills that would fit us for meaningful alternative employment. This is merely an exercise in ad-hoc-ery you understand. Please feel free to add your own suggestions.

EXPERIENCED PEOPLE CAN:

- parse a sentence;
- write with a fountain pen;
- do long tots when the supermarket tills crash;
- know the Latin roots of English words;
- sew up a hem with proper stitches;
- remember all the lyrics from famous film musicals;
- cook a real gravy dinner using only fresh ingredients.

EXPERIENCED PEOPLE KNOW:

- the difference between a sense of perspective and a sense of proportion;
- can distinguish a dilemma from a crisis and realise in nine days time it won't amount to a hill of beans;
- that what goes around comes around;
- to just stay still and twice in your life you'll be right.

IT MIGHT GET YOU A JOB as a part-time cook-cum-psychiatrist-cum-game show-contestant. But it does amount to a more or less rounded human being.

Lift up your hearts! Age cannot wither us nor custom stale our infinite variety. Besides which, as a more Machiavellian sentiment puts it, "Age and treachery will always overcome youth and skill."